MORE Taste of Home
TEST KITCHEN
FAVORITES

TASTE OF HOME BOOKS • RDA ENTHUSIAST BRANDS, LLC • MILWAUKEE, WI

Taste *of* Home

© 2022 RDA Enthusiast Brands, LLC.
1610 N. 2nd St., Suite 102, Milwaukee WI 53212-3906

Visit us at *tasteofhome.com* for other Taste of Home books and products.

International Standard Book Number:
978-1-62145-860-9

Component Number:
119700118H

Executive Editor: Mark Hagen
Senior Art Director: Raeann Thompson
Senior Editor: Julie Schnittka
Assistant Editor: Sammi DiVito
Senior Designer: Jazmin Delgado
Deputy Editor, Copy Desk: Dulcie Shoener
Copy Editor: Sara Strauss

Cover Photography: *Taste of Home* Photo Studio

Pictured on front cover:
Chorizo Tacos, p. 8
Holiday Pretzel Salad, p. 165
Chicken Parmesan Burgers, p. 103
Breakfast BLT Waffles, p. 48
Cranberry Bog Bars, p. 195

Pictured on title page:
Apple Pie Cupcakes
with Cinnamon Buttercream, p. 205

Pictured on back cover:
Hearty Muffuletta, p. 91
Four-Cheese Stuffed Shells, p. 145
Apple Spice Cake with
Brown Sugar Frosting, p. 202
Focaccia, p. 10

Printed in China
1 3 5 7 9 10 8 6 4 2

More ways to connect with us:

Brimming with the Best

Every now and again, I like to poll different Test Kitchen team members by asking them, "What's your favorite *Taste of Home* recipe?" The question is almost always met with a look toward the ceiling, a head tilt and a response like, "Do I have to pick just *one*?"

Since we work in a professional test kitchen and photo studio where we're surrounded by tantalizing dishes day in and day out five days a week, it's almost impossible to single out only one favorite recipe. There are simply too many that we've come to love over the years. Deciding on a single best *Taste of Home* recipe is almost like trying to answer which child you favor the most. (Can't do it!) But a list of *multiple* favorite recipes? Now that's a breeze to put together!

DISHING WITH

Sarah Farmer
Taste of Home
Executive Culinary Director

And that's just what we did in this new cookbook! We collected batches of standout recipes from everyone on the Test Kitchen team. Whether the dish was reviewed by our testers or was beautified by our food stylists, these are the tasty gems that we first came across at work, ogled over and quickly adopted as personal faves. Now we prepare them time and time again in our own home kitchens.

Four-Cheese Chicken Fettuccine (page 110) from Rochelle Brownlee made the list. Some reviewers say this contest-winning specialty is even better than the version found at a popular Italian American chain restaurant. And it's no surprise nominations came in for the chocolaty, delicious (and oh-so-easy-to-make) Texas Sheet Cake from Susan Ormond (page 215). I've heard Sarah Tramonte, our Associate Culinary Producer, and others rave about this dessert for many years.

In this book, you'll find a good number of top picks from James Schend, our culinary team's Deputy Editor who's pictured next to me on the cover. Besides being so fun to work with, he's a professionally trained culinary leader who knows the ins and outs of great recipes. James and his team of food editors, Peggy and Rashanda, are skilled at curating readers' recipes and other food content for all *Taste of Home* magazines and cookbooks. They also know what it takes to make exceptional original recipes from scratch—and you'll find many of their inspiring and tasty creations in here, too! (Turn to the Staff Recipes chapter on page 6.)

Some delectable bites we all adore, and others are simply personal favorites for one reason or another (like my love for the Chimichurri Monkey Bread on page 73). But one thing all of us on the Test Kitchen team have in common is our shared passion for food and cooking—and making others feel happy with home-cooked delights that warm the heart.

Be inspired by what you find in this cookbook and give these recipes a spin. Maybe some will become your favorites, too!

Happy cooking,

Sarah Farmer

CATHERINE · TURAN · ALICIA · MAGGIE

PEGGY

SUZANNE

JAMES

SARAH F.

SHANNON

JOSH

RASHANDA · MARK · SARAH T. · ELLEN

What "Test Kitchen Approved" Means

Our Test Kitchen staff (pictured on this page) puts every *Taste of Home* recipe through a rigorous approval process. It all starts with home cooks (like you!) who share recipes that have been tested in their own kitchens and approved by family and friends.

1. THE FOOD EDITORS SORT OUT THE BEST

Our food editors (James, Peggy and Rashanda) review recipes, looking for fresh ideas and new spins on classics (or for dishes that just sound irresistible). They also consider if a recipe uses everyday ingredients and is simple enough for home cooks.

2. PREP COOKS ASSEMBLE THE INGREDIENTS

In our Prep Kitchen, Catherine and Mark get the food ready for our recipe testers (and later for our food stylists).

3. EXPERT COOKS TEST EACH RECIPE

Test cooks (Alicia and Maggie) prepare each recipe, ensuring that the amounts, equipment, temperature and method are accurate, and making adjustments if needed.

4. TASTE TESTERS WEIGH IN

Taste testers evaluate the prepared recipes according to many factors, such as flavor, texture, appearance, overall appeal and level of difficulty.

5. RECIPES ARE EDITED FOR PRECISION AND EASE

Our recipe editors once again review the recipe's directions for clarity and conciseness.

6. THE PHOTO AND VIDEO TEAMS TAKE OVER

In the Photo Studio, food stylists (Shannon, Josh and Sarah F.) and Associate Culinary Producer, Sarah T., work closely with art directors, photographers, and set and prop stylists on dishes, linens, surfaces and more.

Throughout the whole process, Ellen, our Culinary Assistant, and dishwashers Turan and Suzanne help keep the ship afloat!

PAGE 139

CONTENTS

FAVORITE...

VERTICAL CARROT CAKE,
PAGE 21

Staff Recipes

Get ready to indulge in mouthwatering recipes created by our *Taste of Home* staff, and approved and loved by our Test Kitchen!

THE BEST PECAN PIE

CHORIZO TACOS
—James Schend, Deputy Culinary Editor

Prep: 10 min. • **Cook:** 25 min.
Makes: 16 servings

- 2 tsp. canola oil
- 1 small onion, chopped
- 1 poblano pepper, seeded and chopped
- 1 lb. fresh chorizo, casings removed
- 16 mini flour tortillas
  Optional: Fresh cilantro, sliced radishes, sliced jalapeno, lime wedges and salsa

In a large skillet, heat oil over medium-high heat. Add onion and poblano; cook and stir until tender, 5-7 minutes. Add the chorizo; cook, breaking into small crumbles, until fully cooked and starting to char and crisp, 12-15 minutes. Drain. Serve filling on warm tortillas. If desired, serve with toppings.
1 taco: 176 cal., 11g fat (4g sat. fat), 25mg chol., 447mg sod., 9g carb. (0 sugars, 1g fiber), 8g pro.

DISHING WITH

James Schend
Deputy Culinary Editor

If you're looking for a quick bite or snack, street tacos are the perfect thing. They cook really quickly, everyone loves them and you can customize them to your personal tastes.

THE BEST PECAN PIE
I was on a quest to create the ultimate version of pecan pie. I think this might be it!
—James Schend, Deputy Culinary Editor

Prep: 15 min. • **Bake:** 55 min. + cooling
Makes: 8 servings

- Dough for single-crust pie
- ½ cup butter
- 2½ cups coarsely chopped pecans
- ¾ cup packed brown sugar
- ¾ cup maple syrup
- ½ tsp. salt
- 3 large eggs, beaten
- 2 Tbsp. whiskey or bourbon, optional
- 2 tsp. vanilla extract
  Optional: Whipped cream and ground cinnamon

1. Preheat oven to 350°. On a lightly floured surface, roll dough to a ⅛-in.-thick circle; transfer to a 9-in. pie plate. Trim crust to ½ in. beyond rim of plate; flute the edge. Refrigerate while preparing filling.
2. In a Dutch oven or large saucepan, melt butter over medium heat. Add pecans; cook, stirring constantly, until very fragrant and pecans start to brown, 4-5 minutes. Remove pecans with a slotted spoon, reserving butter in pan. Stir in brown sugar, maple syrup and salt; bring to a boil. Reduce heat; simmer 2 minutes. Remove from the heat. In a bowl, whisk a small amount of the hot mixture into eggs; return all to the pan, whisking constantly. Stir whiskey, if desired, and vanilla into brown sugar mixture; stir in pecans. Pour into crust.
3. Bake until a knife inserted in the center comes out clean, 55-60 minutes. Cover the edges with foil during the last 30 minutes to prevent overbrowning if necessary. Cool on a wire rack. If desired, top with whipped cream and cinnamon. Refrigerate leftovers.
Dough for Single-Crust Pie: Combine 1¼ cups all-purpose flour and ¼ tsp. salt; cut in ½ cup cold butter until crumbly. Gradually add 3-5 Tbsp. ice water, tossing with a fork until the dough holds together when pressed. Shape into a disk; wrap and refrigerate 1 hour.
1 piece: 695 cal., 49g fat (17g sat. fat), 130mg chol., 430mg sod., 60g carb. (40g sugars, 4g fiber), 8g pro.

CHORIZO TACOS

FOCACCIA

Focaccia is one of my favorite breads, and it is one of the least labor-intensive since there isn't any kneading. I have been adjusting the quantities over the years and am happy where this recipe stands. The dough is wet, which is perfect for a tender, chewy bread with a very distinct salt bite.
—James Schend, Deputy Culinary Editor

- -

Prep: 30 min. + rising • **Bake:** 20 min.
Makes: 1 loaf (24 pieces)

- 1 pkg. (¼ oz.) active dry yeast
- 1¼ cups warm water (110° to 115°), divided
- 1 Tbsp. honey
- 3 cups all-purpose flour
- ¼ cup plus 3 Tbsp. olive oil, divided
- ¾ tsp. kosher salt
- 1 tsp. flaky sea salt, optional

1. In a large bowl, dissolve yeast in ½ cup warm water and honey; let stand 5 minutes. Add the flour, ¼ cup oil, kosher salt and remaining ¾ cup water; mix until smooth (dough will be wet). Scrape sides of the bowl clean; cover and let rise in a warm place until doubled, about 45 minutes.
2. Preheat oven to 425°. Brush a 13x9-in. baking dish or 12-in. cast-iron skillet with 1 Tbsp. oil. Gently scrape the dough directly into pan. With oiled hands, gently spread the dough. If the dough springs back, wait 10 minutes and stretch again. With your fingers, make indentations in the dough. Drizzle with remaining 2 Tbsp. oil; let rise until doubled in size, 30-40 minutes.
3. If desired, sprinkle with sea salt. Bake until golden brown, 20-25 minutes. Cut into squares; serve warm.
1 piece: 95 cal., 4g fat (1g sat. fat), 0 chol., 61mg sod., 13g carb. (1g sugars, 1g fiber), 2g pro.

FOCACCIA

PUMPKIN SPICE SANGRIA

This pumpkin sangria is made of sweet white wine, spices, and fresh pears and apples. Using canned pumpkin makes it easy to assemble.
—James Schend, Deputy Culinary Editor

- -

Prep: 25 min. + chilling
Makes: 12 servings

- 3   cinnamon sticks (3 in.)
- 10   whole allspice
- 10   whole cloves
- 3   cups water
- 1   can (15 oz.) pumpkin
- ¼   cup lemon juice
- 1   bottle (750 ml) sweet white wine
- 1   cup apple brandy or plain brandy
- 1   large apple, thinly sliced
- 1   large pear, thinly sliced

1. Place cinnamon, allspice and cloves on a double thickness of cheesecloth; bring up corners of the cloth and tie with string to form a bag.
2. Place water, pumpkin, lemon juice and spice bag in a large saucepan. Bring to a boil. Remove from the heat; cover and steep for 5 minutes. Transfer to a pitcher; stir in wine, brandy and fruit. Cover and refrigerate at least 3 hours. Discard spice bag. Stir just before serving.
¾ cup: 126 cal., 0 fat (0 sat. fat), 0 chol., 5mg sod., 10g carb. (5g sugars, 2g fiber), 1g pro.

PEPPERMINT BARK TRIFLE

We're always looking for showstopping desserts, especially during the holidays. This one is very impressive but couldn't be easier to make. No one will ever know it's made with a store-bought angel food cake.
—James Schend, Deputy Culinary Editor

- -

Prep: 20 min. + chilling • **Makes:** 12 servings

- 2   pkg. (8 oz. each) cream cheese, softened
- ½   cup sugar
- 3   Tbsp. 2% milk
- 1   tsp. peppermint extract
- 3   cups heavy whipping cream, whipped
- 1   prepared angel food cake (8 to 10 oz.), cut into 1-in. cubes
- 3   Tbsp. crushed peppermint candies
- 1½   lbs. chocolate peppermint bark

1. In a bowl, beat cream cheese, sugar, milk and extract until smooth. Fold in whipped cream; set aside.
2. Place a third of cake in a 3- or 4-qt. trifle dish or serving bowl. Top with a third of each of the cream cheese mixture, crushed peppermint and peppermint bark. Repeat layers twice; garnish with additional bark. Cover and refrigerate at least 4 hours.
1 cup: 426 cal., 35g fat (22g sat. fat), 106mg chol., 279mg sod., 25g carb. (13g sugars, 0 fiber), 5g pro.

TEST KITCHEN TIP
Place peppermint candies in a resealable bag and use a rolling pin to crush them.

PEPPERMINT BARK TRIFLE

GRILLED CHEESE &
PEPPERONI SANDWICH

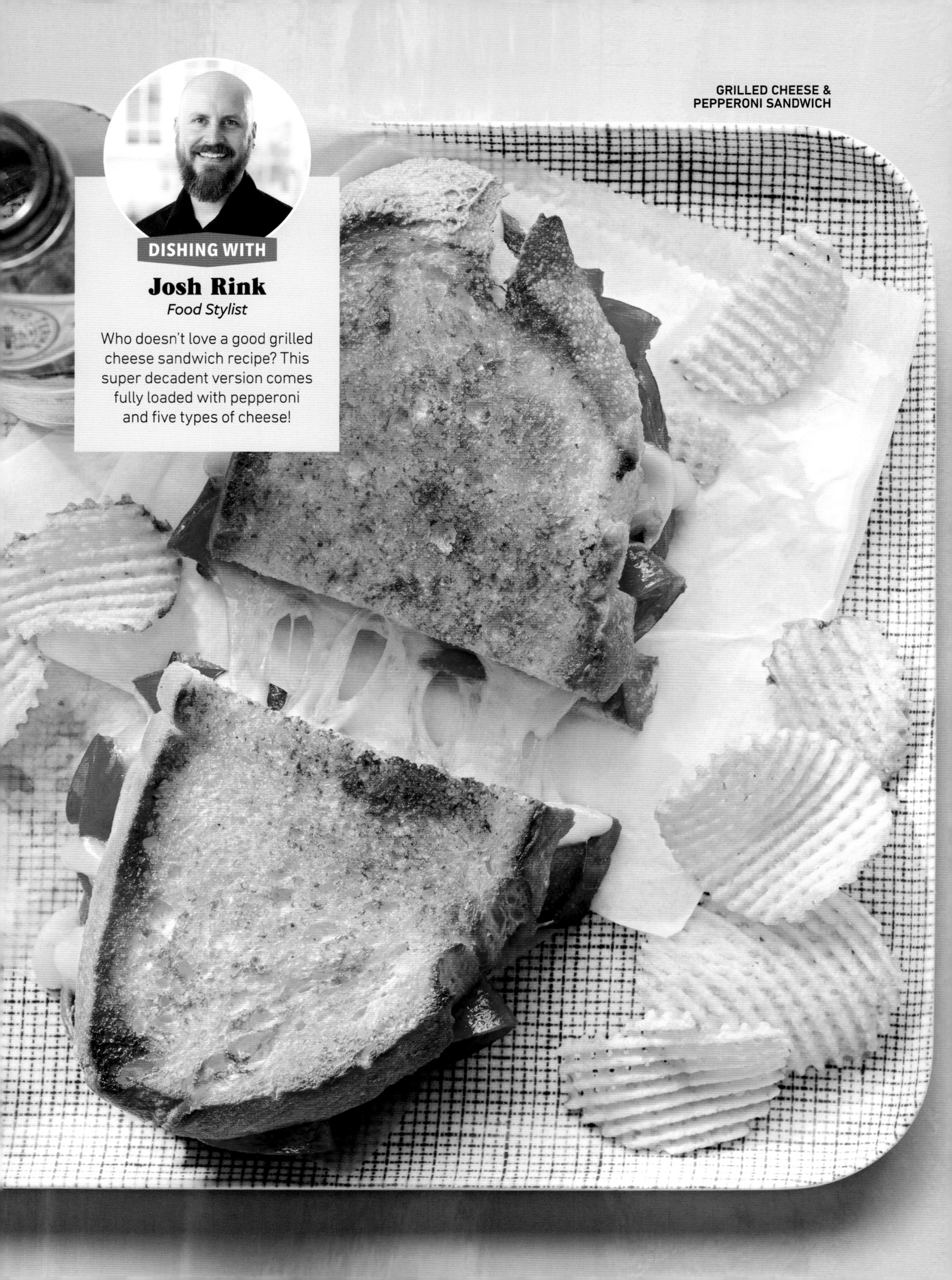

DISHING WITH

Josh Rink

Food Stylist

Who doesn't love a good grilled cheese sandwich recipe? This super decadent version comes fully loaded with pepperoni and five types of cheese!

GRILLED CHEESE & PEPPERONI SANDWICH

—Josh Rink, Food Stylist

Takes: 25 min. • **Makes:** 4 servings

- 6 Tbsp. butter, softened, divided
- 8 slices sourdough bread
- ½ cup shredded sharp white cheddar cheese
- ½ cup shredded Monterey Jack cheese
- ½ cup shredded Gruyere cheese
- 3 Tbsp. mayonnaise
- 3 Tbsp. finely shredded Manchego or Parmesan cheese
- ⅛ tsp. onion powder
- 24 slices pepperoni
- 4 oz. Brie cheese, rind removed and sliced

1. Spread 3 Tbsp. butter on 1 side of bread slices. Place the bread, butter side down, in a large cast-iron skillet or electric griddle over medium-low heat for 2-3 minutes or until golden brown; remove. In a small bowl, combine the cheddar, Monterey Jack and Gruyere. In another bowl, mix together the remaining 3 Tbsp. butter, mayonnaise, Manchego cheese and onion powder.

2. Top toasted side of 4 bread slices with pepperoni; add sliced Brie. Sprinkle cheddar cheese mixture evenly over Brie. Top with remaining bread slices, toasted side facing inward. Spread butter-mayonnaise mixture on the outsides of each sandwich. Place in same skillet; cook 5-6 minutes on each side or until golden brown and cheese is melted. Serve immediately.

1 sandwich: 719 cal., 55g fat (29g sat. fat), 134mg chol., 1207mg sod., 30g carb. (3g sugars, 1g fiber), 27g pro.

BRAISED CORNED BEEF

You'll need a bit of time to prepare this braised corned beef, but the end results make all that time worth it. Cook this for your St. Patrick's Day celebration or for an extra-special meal.

—Josh Rink, Food Stylist

Prep: 20 min. + cooling + brining
Cook: 5 hours + resting • **Makes:** 10 servings

FOR BRINE
- 2 qt. plus 2 cups water, divided
- 1 cup kosher salt
- ¾ cup packed brown sugar
- 2 Tbsp. curing salt, such as Prauge powder
- 2 Tbsp. whole peppercorns
- 1 Tbsp. mustard seed
- 1 tsp. ground ginger
- 10 whole allspice
- 10 whole cloves
- 10 whole juniper berries
- 2 bay leaves
- 2 cinnamon sticks (2-3 in.)
- 2 whole star anise
- 2 lbs. ice cubes
- 1 fresh beef brisket (4 to 5 lbs.), trimmed

FOR BRAISING
- 3 large carrots, peeled and cut into thirds
- 3 celery ribs, cut into thirds
- 2 large onions, skins removed and quartered

1. To make brine, place 2 qt. water plus the next 12 ingredients in a large 6-8 qt. stockpot; bring to a boil. Reduce heat and simmer, stirring occasionally, until sugar and salts have dissolved, 4-5 minutes. Remove from heat; add ice and stir until ice has melted. Place brine in the refrigerator and allow to cool completely. In a large bowl or shallow dish, add brisket and pour brine over beef. Cover, removing as much air as possible, ensuring brisket is completely submerged. Transfer to refrigerator; allow to rest for 10 days, agitating bowl occasionally to redistribute spices and liquid.

2. After 10 days, remove brisket from brine; rinse brisket thoroughly and discard brine. To braise the brisket, preheat oven to 300°. Place the carrots, celery and onion in large roasting pan; pour remaining 2 cups water into pan until water level is ½ in. high. Place the brisket over the vegetables and cover with aluminum foil; transfer to oven. Cook, covered, until very tender, 5-6 hours.

3. Remove brisket from pan, discarding the vegetables and cooking juices; tent beef with foil and allow to rest for 10 minutes before serving. Or, to slice for Reuben sandwiches, wrap corned beef well after cooling for 10 minutes; place in refrigerator and allow to cool completely overnight. Slice thinly against grain.

4 oz. cooked beef: 194 cal., 7g fat (2g sat. fat), 64mg chol., 938mg sod., 1g carb. (1g sugars, 0 fiber), 31g pro.

BRAISED CORNED BEEF

GREEK CHICKEN PASTA

This hearty main dish has fantastic Mediterranean flavor.
—Susan Stetzel, *Taste of Home* Community Cooks Coordinator

- -

Takes: 25 min. • **Makes:** 5 servings

    2   cups uncooked penne pasta
    ¼   cup butter, cubed
    1   large onion, chopped
    ¼   cup all-purpose flour
    1   can (14½ oz.) reduced-sodium
        chicken broth
    3   cups shredded rotisserie chicken
    1   jar (7½ oz.) marinated quartered
        artichoke hearts, drained
    1   cup (4 oz.) crumbled feta cheese
    ½   cup chopped oil-packed
        sun-dried tomatoes
    ⅓   cup sliced pitted Greek olives
    2   Tbsp. minced fresh parsley

1. Cook the penne pasta according to package directions.
2. Meanwhile, in a large ovenproof skillet, melt butter over medium-high heat. Add onion; cook and stir until tender. Stir in flour until blended; gradually add broth. Bring to a boil; cook and stir for 2 minutes or until thickened. Stir in chicken, artichoke hearts, cheese, tomatoes and olives.
3. Drain pasta; stir into the pan. Broil 3-4 in. from the heat for 5-7 minutes or until bubbly and golden brown. Sprinkle with parsley.
1⅓ cups: 556 cal., 30g fat (12g sat. fat), 111mg chol., 916mg sod., 36g carb. (3g sugars, 3g fiber), 35g pro.

CIDER-GLAZED PORK TENDERLOIN

This is a super easy recipe full of sweet fall flavor. The maple syrup really shines through in every bite.
—Susan Stetzel, *Taste of Home* Community Cooks Coordinator

- -

Takes: 30 min. • **Makes:** 4 servings

    1   pork tenderloin (1 lb.)
    ¼   tsp. salt
    ½   tsp. pepper, divided
    1   Tbsp. olive oil
    ¾   cup apple cider or juice
    ¼   cup maple syrup
    2   Tbsp. cider vinegar

1. Preheat oven to 425°. Cut tenderloin in half to fit skillet; sprinkle with salt and ¼ tsp. pepper. In a large skillet, heat the oil over medium-high heat; brown pork on all sides. Transfer to a 15x10x1-in. pan. Roast until a thermometer reads 145°, 12-15 minutes.
2. Meanwhile, in the same skillet, bring cider, syrup, vinegar and remaining pepper to a boil, stirring to loosen browned bits from the pan. Cook, uncovered, until the mixture is reduced to a glaze consistency, about 5 minutes.
3. Remove the pork from oven; let stand 5 minutes before slicing. Serve with glaze.
3 oz. cooked pork with 1 Tbsp. glaze: 239 cal., 7g fat (2g sat. fat), 64mg chol., 200mg sod., 19g carb. (17g sugars, 0 fiber), 23g pro. **Diabetic exchanges:** 3 lean meat, 1 starch, 1 fat.

CIDER-GLAZED PORK TENDERLOIN

BUFFALO CHICKEN CHILI

VEGAN RANCH DRESSING
—Peggy Woodward, Senior Food Editor

Prep: 10 min. + chilling • **Makes:** 1¼ cups

1   cup vegan mayonnaise
¼   to ½ cup unsweetened
    almond milk or soy milk
3   Tbsp. minced fresh parsley
    or 1 Tbsp. dried parsley flakes
1   Tbsp. minced chives
2   tsp. cider vinegar
1   garlic clove, minced
¾   tsp. onion powder
½   tsp. dill weed
¼   tsp. salt
¼   tsp. pepper
¼   tsp. paprika
    Additional minced chives, optional

In a bowl, whisk first 11 ingredients. Cover;
refrigerate at least 1 hour before serving.
If desired, garnish with additional chives.
2 Tbsp.: 74 cal., 8g fat (1g sat. fat), 0 chol.,
96mg sod., 0 carb. (0 sugars, 0 fiber), 0 pro.

DISHING WITH

Peggy Woodward
Senior Food Editor

There are so many ways to
serve ranch dressing! Use this
vegan version for dipping, on
salads or in recipes that call for
regular ranch dressing. Fresh
herbs really brighten the flavor,
but dried herbs can be used, too.

BUFFALO CHICKEN CHILI
This Buffalo chicken chili is rich in the best
way. The cream cheese, blue cheese and
tangy hot sauce join forces for a dinner
recipe everyone will love.
—Peggy Woodward, Senior Food Editor

Prep: 10 min. • **Cook:** 5½ hours
Makes: 6 servings

1   can (15½ oz.) navy beans,
    rinsed and drained
1   can (14½ oz.) chicken broth
1   can (14½ oz.) fire-roasted
    diced tomatoes
1   can (8 oz.) tomato sauce
½   cup Buffalo wing sauce
½   tsp. onion powder
½   tsp. garlic powder

1   lb. boneless skinless
    chicken breast halves
1   pkg. (8 oz.) cream cheese,
    cubed and softened
    Optional toppings: Crumbled
    blue cheese, chopped celery
    and chopped green onions

1. In a 4- or 5-qt. slow cooker, combine
the first 7 ingredients. Add chicken. Cover
and cook on low 5-6 hours or until chicken
is tender.
2. Remove the chicken; shred with 2 forks.
Return to slow cooker. Stir in cream cheese.
Cover and cook on low until the cheese is
melted, about 30 minutes. Stir until blended.
Serve with toppings as desired.
1¼ cups: 337 cal., 16g fat (8g sat. fat),
80mg chol., 1586mg sod., 25g carb.
(5g sugars, 5g fiber), 25g pro.

MEDITERRANEAN
KOFTA MEATBALLS

BIRTHDAY CAKE FUDGE
—Rashanda Cobbins, Food Editor

- -

Prep: 10 min. + chilling • **Makes:** 64 pieces

- 1 can (14 oz.) sweetened condensed milk
- 1½ cups white baking chips
- 3 Tbsp. butter
- ⅛ tsp. salt
- 1½ cups unprepared Funfetti cake mix
- 3 Tbsp. sprinkles

1. Line an 8-in. square pan with foil or parchment; grease foil lightly. In a large heavy saucepan, cook and stir milk, baking chips, butter and salt over low heat until smooth. Remove from heat; stir in cake mix until dissolved. Spread into prepared pan; top with the sprinkles. Refrigerate, covered, until firm, about 2 hours.
2. Using foil, lift fudge out of pan. Remove foil; cut fudge into 1-in. squares. Store in an airtight container in the refrigerator.
1 piece: 59 cal., 2g fat (2g sat. fat), 4mg chol., 47mg sod., 9g carb. (7g sugars, 0 fiber), 1g pro.

DISHING WITH

Rashanda Cobbins
Food Editor

This decadent treat is the perfect thing to make your birthday special. Or prepare it ahead and package it as a surprise gift for a friend.

MEDITERRANEAN KOFTA MEATBALLS

For a new take on meatballs, try this quick version of kofta—flavorful Mediterranean meatballs full of spices and herbs. Shape the meat mixture around soaked wooden skewers and grill for a more authentic twist.
—Rashanda Cobbins, Food Editor

- -

Takes: 25 min.
Makes: 4 servings

- 1 small onion, chopped
- ½ cup packed fresh parsley sprigs
- ¼ cup fresh mint leaves
- 1 Tbsp. minced fresh oregano
- 2 garlic cloves
- 1 tsp. lemon-pepper seasoning
- ½ tsp. salt
- ½ tsp. paprika
- ¼ tsp. ground cumin
- 1 lb. ground lamb
- 1 Tbsp. canola oil
  Hot cooked couscous

- 1 cup plain Greek yogurt
- 2 plum tomatoes, cut into wedges
- 3 Tbsp. minced red onion
  Fresh mint leaves
- 2 lemons, cut into wedges

Place onion, parsley, mint, oregano and garlic in bowl of food processor. Pulse until minced. In a large bowl, combine the herb mixture, lemon pepper, salt, paprika and cumin. Add lamb; mix lightly but thoroughly. With wet hands, shape into 16 balls. In a large skillet, heat oil over medium heat. Brown meatballs in batches; drain. Remove and keep warm. Serve meatballs over cooked couscous. Top with yogurt, tomato wedges and red onion. Garnish with mint leaves and lemon wedges.
4 meatballs with ¼ cup yogurt and ½ tomato: 339 cal., 24g fat (10g sat. fat), 90mg chol., 482mg sod., 8g carb. (4g sugars, 2g fiber), 22g pro.

BIRTHDAY CAKE FUDGE

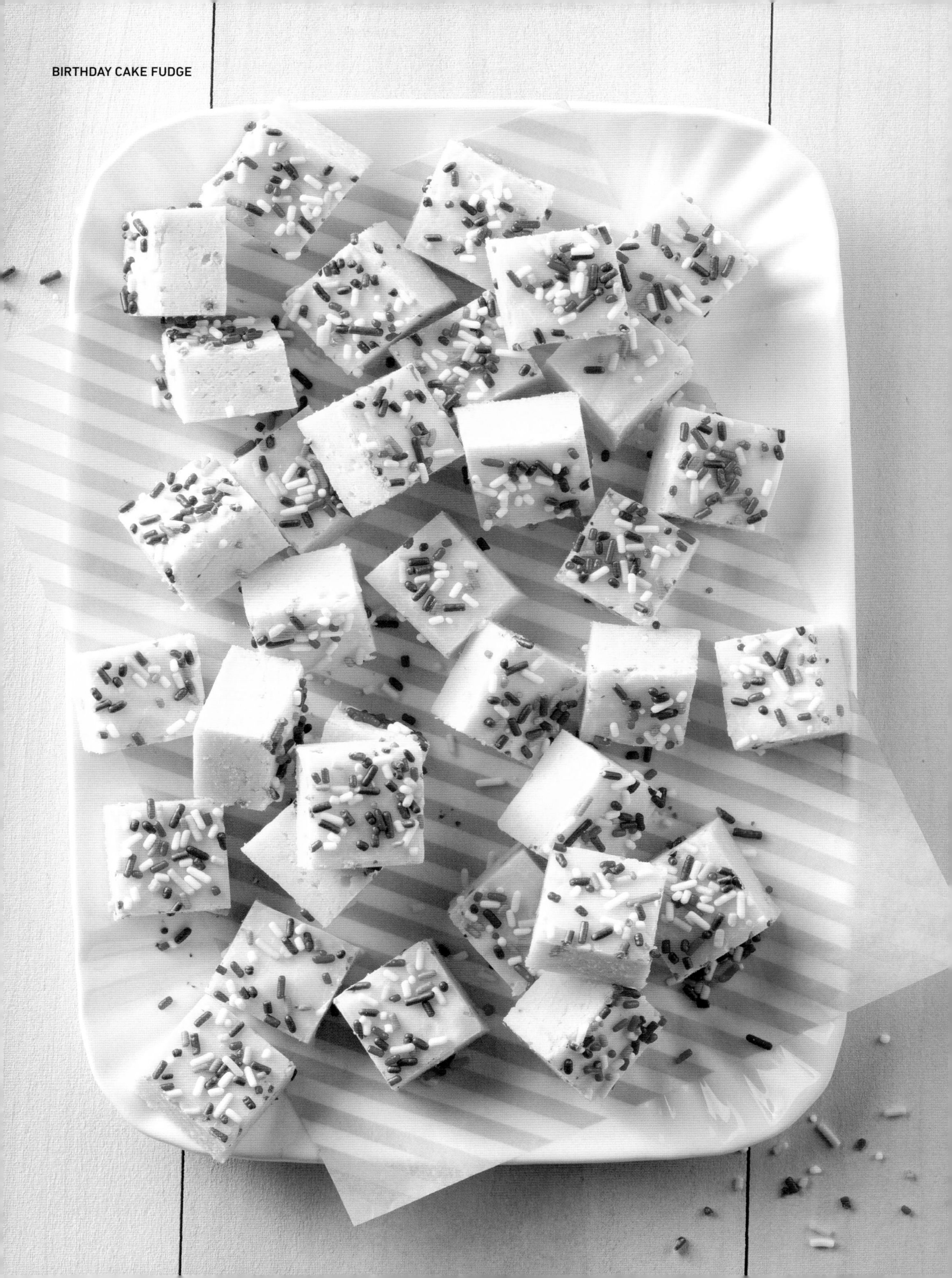

SMOKY TEMPEH BACON

Even meat eaters will love this! The meatless bacon made with tempeh gets its smoky flavor from liquid smoke and smoked paprika, and then it is crisped in a hot skillet. Eat it alone or use it on a sandwich or salad.
—Rashanda Cobbins, Food Editor

- -

Prep: 5 min. + chilling • **Cook:** 15 min.
Makes: 6 servings

  3 Tbsp. liquid smoke
  1 Tbsp. maple syrup
  2 tsp. smoked paprika
  ½ tsp. ground cumin
  1 pkg. (8 oz.) tempeh, thinly sliced
  2 Tbsp. canola oil

1. Whisk together liquid smoke, maple syrup, paprika and cumin in an 8-in. square baking dish; add sliced tempeh. Gently toss to coat. Cover and refrigerate at least 1 hour.
2. Heat oil in large saucepan over medium heat. In batches, cook the tempeh until golden brown, 2-3 minutes per side. Serve immediately.
1 serving: 125 cal., 9g fat (1g sat. fat), 0 chol., 5mg sod., 6g carb. (2g sugars, 0 fiber), 8g pro.

DID YOU KNOW?
Tempeh is a vegetarian meat substitute that's made of fermented soybeans.

**SMOKY
TEMPEH BACON**

TOFU CHICKEN NUGGETS

These plant-based nuggets can be made ahead to use throughout the week.
—Rashanda Cobbins, Food Editor

Prep: 15 min. • **Cook:** 40 min.
Makes: 10 servings

1	pkg. (14 oz.) soft tofu, patted dry
2¾	cups vital wheat gluten, divided
1½	tsp. poultry seasoning
½	tsp. salt
½	tsp. garlic powder
½	tsp. white pepper
1¼	cups water, divided
¼	cup vegan egg substitute (powdered)
	Oil for frying

1. Combine tofu, 1½ cups wheat gluten, poultry seasoning, salt, garlic powder and pepper in large bowl just until combined. Add ¼ cup water, a little at a time, until dough forms a ball. On a surface lightly dusted with vital wheat gluten, roll dough into a circle about a ½ in. thick. Gently cut or tear dough into 50 pieces.

2. In a large saucepan, place steamer basket over 1 in. water. In batches, place dough pieces in basket. Bring water to a boil. Reduce heat to maintain a low boil; steam, covered, until pieces look puffed and firm, 10-15 minutes. Remove and keep warm.

3. Place the remaining 1¼ cups wheat gluten in a shallow bowl. In a separate shallow bowl, mix the egg substitute with remaining 1 cup water; let stand for 5 minutes to thicken. Dip the pieces in the egg mixture, then in wheat gluten. In a Dutch oven, heat oil to 375°. Fry pieces in batches 2-3 minutes on each side or until golden brown; drain on paper towels. Serve immediately.

5 pieces: 268 cal., 11g fat (1g sat. fat), 0 chol., 56mg sod., 14g carb. (0 sugars, 0 fiber), 26g pro.

LAZY CAKE

This cake will fix that sweet tooth craving! The no-bake treat is made with cookie pieces stirred with hazelnut spread. Then chill it for a super simple dessert.
—Rashanda Cobbins, Food Editor

Prep: 10 min. + chilling • **Makes:** 6 servings

⅓	cup heavy whipping cream
⅓	cup Nutella
2	Tbsp. butter
1	Tbsp. baking cocoa
20	Marie biscuits or Maria cookies

1. Line a 6-in. round cake pan with aluminum foil; spray with cooking spray and set aside. Place first 4 ingredients in a large bowl. Microwave on high for 1 minute; stir until smooth and blended. Stir in cookies; mix gently until combined.

2. Press cookie mixture into prepared pan; cover. Refrigerate overnight. Slice to serve.

1 piece: 289 cal., 19g fat (8g sat. fat), 25mg chol., 136mg sod., 30g carb. (19g sugars, 1g fiber), 3g pro.

TOFU CHICKEN NUGGETS

DISHING WITH

Mark Neufang
Culinary Assistant

This vertical spin on a cherished classic is packed with spices and sure to impress. The brown butter cream cheese frosting truly takes the cake over the top!

VERTICAL CARROT CAKE

VERTICAL CARROT CAKE

—Mark Neufang, Culinary Assistant

Prep: 1½ hours + chilling
Bake: 20 min. + cooling • **Makes:** 16 servings

CARROT CAKE
- ½ cup plus 1 Tbsp. all-purpose flour
- ½ tsp. ground ginger
- ½ tsp. ground cinnamon
- ¼ tsp. ground nutmeg
- ¼ tsp. salt
- ⅛ tsp. ground cloves
- 1 cup pecan halves, toasted
- ½ lb. carrots, peeled and finely grated
- 1 Tbsp. minced fresh gingerroot
- ½ tsp. grated orange zest
- 8 large eggs, separated, room temperature
- ⅔ cup plus 2 Tbsp. sugar, divided

BROWNED BUTTER
CREAM CHEESE FROSTING
- 1½ cups unsalted butter, cubed and divided
- 4 large egg whites
- 1 cup sugar
- Dash salt
- 1 tsp. vanilla extract
- 2 pkg. (8 oz. each) cream cheese, softened

1. Preheat oven to 350°. Line 2 greased 15x10x1-in. baking pans with parchment; grease paper. Set aside. Sift flour, ground ginger, cinnamon, nutmeg, salt and cloves together twice. Place the pecans in a food processor; pulse until finely ground. Transfer pecans to a bowl; toss with carrots, fresh ginger and zest.

2. In a large bowl, beat the egg yolks until slightly thickened. Gradually add ⅔ cup sugar, beating on high speed until thick and lemon-colored. Fold in flour mixture, then carrot mixture.

3. Place egg whites in another large bowl. With clean beaters, beat the egg whites on medium until soft peaks form. Gradually add remaining sugar, 1 Tbsp. at a time, beating on high after each addition until sugar is dissolved. Continue beating until stiff glossy peaks form. Fold a fourth of the whites into the batter, then fold in the remaining whites. Transfer to prepared pans, spreading evenly.

4. Bake until golden brown and tops spring back when lightly touched, 18-22 minutes. Cool 5 minutes. Invert cakes onto tea towels dusted with confectioners' sugar. Gently peel off paper; trim ends. Roll up cakes in towels jelly-roll style, starting with a short side. Cool completely on a wire rack.

5. For frosting, place 1 cup butter in a small heavy saucepan; melt over medium heat. Heat until golden brown, 5-7 minutes, stirring constantly. Remove from the heat. Cool until thick and creamy, but not hard, stirring occasionally.

6. Meanwhile, in a heatproof bowl of stand mixer, whisk the egg whites, 1 cup sugar and salt until blended. Place over simmering water in a large saucepan over medium heat. Whisking constantly, heat mixture until a thermometer reads 160°, 8-10 minutes. Remove from heat. With whisk attachment of stand mixer, beat on high speed until cooled to 90°, about 7 minutes. Using the paddle attachment, gradually beat in the remaining ½ cup butter, a few tablespoons at a time, on medium speed until smooth. Beat in vanilla and cooled browned butter until smooth; transfer to another bowl. Add cream cheese to mixer bowl, beat until smooth. Gradually add buttercream back to bowl; beat until combined.

7. Unroll cakes; cut each into two 15x5-in. strips. Spread 1 cup frosting on each strip to within ½ in. of edges. Refrigerate until frosting is firm, at least 20 minutes.

8. To assemble cake, tightly roll up 1 strip jelly-roll style, starting with a short side, lifting slightly as you roll. Carefully align seam of roll with short side of another strip. Continue to roll, jelly-roll style, adding the remaining strips; seal seam. Carefully stand rolled cake on its end on a serving platter. Spread remaining frosting over the top and sides of cake. Refrigerate at least 2 hours or overnight. Let stand at room temperature 15 minutes before slicing.

1 piece: 445 cal., 34g fat (18g sat. fat), 167mg chol., 193mg sod., 30g carb. (25g sugars, 1g fiber), 7g pro.

BROCCOLI VEGGIE PASTA PRIMAVERA

Chock-full of veggies, this simple, colorful pasta makes a filling dinner. In smaller servings, it works equally well as a side dish.
—Stephanie Marchese, Executive Director, Visual Production

Takes: 25 min. • **Makes:** 4 servings

- 8 oz. uncooked linguine
- 1 cup thinly sliced fresh broccoli
- 1 medium carrot, thinly sliced
- ½ cup sliced green onions
- ¼ cup butter, cubed
- 1½ cups sliced fresh mushrooms
- 1 garlic clove, minced
- 1 tsp. dried basil
- ½ tsp. salt
- ¼ tsp. pepper
- 6 oz. fresh or frozen snow peas (about 2 cups), thawed
- ¼ cup dry white wine or chicken broth
- ¼ cup shredded Parmesan cheese

1. Cook the linguine according to the package directions.

2. Meanwhile, in a large skillet, cook the broccoli, carrot and onions in butter for 3 minutes. Add mushrooms, garlic, basil, salt and pepper; cook 1 minute longer. Add snow peas and wine. Cover and cook for 2 minutes or until peas are crisp-tender.

3. Drain linguine; add to skillet and toss to coat. Sprinkle with cheese.

1 cup: 376 cal., 14g fat (8g sat. fat), 34mg chol., 514mg sod., 49g carb. (6g sugars, 5g fiber), 13g pro.

BENEDICTINE DIP,
PAGE 26

Appetizers & Beverages

These snacks and sippers are the ones our staffers rely on most when they want to get the party started!

ANTIPASTO
PLATTER

ANTIPASTO PLATTER

We entertain often, and antipasto is one of our favorite crowd-pleasers. Guests love having their choice of so many tasty nibbles, including pepperoni and cubes of provolone.
—Teri Lindquist, Gurnee, IL

- -

Prep: 10 min. + chilling
Makes: 16 servings (4 qt.)

- 1 jar (24 oz.) pepperoncini, drained
- 1 can (15 oz.) garbanzo beans or chickpeas, rinsed and drained
- 2 cups halved fresh mushrooms
- 2 cups halved cherry tomatoes
- ½ lb. provolone cheese, cubed
- 1 can (6 oz.) pitted ripe olives, drained
- 1 pkg. (3½ oz.) sliced pepperoni
- 1 bottle (8 oz.) Italian vinaigrette dressing
   Lettuce leaves

1. In a large bowl, combine pepperoncini, beans, mushrooms, tomatoes, cheese, olives and pepperoni. Pour vinaigrette over mixture; toss to coat.
2. Refrigerate at least 30 minutes or overnight. Arrange on a lettuce-lined platter. Serve with toothpicks.
1 cup: 178 cal., 13g fat (4g sat. fat), 15mg chol., 852mg sod., 8g carb. (2g sugars, 2g fiber), 6g pro.

TEST KITCHEN TIP
This appetizer is best when made ahead because the flavors get richer as it sits.

PINEAPPLE APPETIZER MEATBALLS

I blend a can of crushed pineapple into my meatballs to create a taste-tempting treat. Best of all, the sweet and tangy glaze that coats these bite-sized snacks is a snap to prepare.
—Karen Mellinger Baker, Dover, OH

Takes: 30 min. • **Makes:** 2 dozen

- 1 can (8 oz.) crushed pineapple
- 1 large egg
- ¼ cup dry bread crumbs
- ⅛ tsp. pepper
- ½ lb. bulk pork sausage
- ½ lb. ground beef

GLAZE

- ¼ cup packed brown sugar
- ¼ cup ketchup
- ¼ cup white vinegar
- ¼ cup water
- 2 Tbsp. Dijon-mayonnaise blend

1. Drain pineapple, reserving juice. Place pineapple and 2 Tbsp. juice in a large bowl (set remaining juice aside for glaze). Add the egg, bread crumbs and pepper to pineapple. Crumble the sausage and beef over mixture and mix lightly but thoroughly. Shape into 1-in. balls.

2. Place the meatballs on a greased rack in a shallow baking pan. Bake, uncovered, at 450° for 12-15 minutes or until a thermometer reads 160°.

3. Meanwhile, in a large skillet, combine glaze ingredients and reserved pineapple juice. Add meatballs. Bring to a boil over medium heat. Reduce heat; cook and stir for 5-10 minutes or until heated through.

1 meatball: 66 cal., 3g fat (1g sat. fat), 19mg chol., 136mg sod., 5g carb. (4g sugars, 0 fiber), 3g pro.

MINI GRILLED CHEESE

If you're looking for a fantastic make-ahead snack, try these. They're nice to have in the freezer for lunch with soup or a salad. My family loves to nibble on them anytime.
—Anita Curtis, Camarillo, CA

Takes: 30 min. • **Makes:** 8 dozen

- 1 cup butter, softened
- 2 jars (5 oz. each) sharp American cheese spread, softened
- 1 large egg
- 1 can (4 oz.) chopped green chiles, drained
- ¼ cup salsa
- 2 cups shredded cheddar cheese
- 2 loaves (1½ lbs. each) thinly sliced sandwich bread, crusts removed

1. Preheat oven to 350°. Cream the butter, cheese spread and egg until smooth. Stir in chiles, salsa and cheddar cheese. Spread about 1 Tbsp. cheese mixture on each slice of 1 loaf of bread.

2. Top with remaining bread; spread with more cheese mixture. Cut each sandwich into 4 squares or triangles; place on a baking sheet lined with parchment. Bake until cheese is melted, 10-15 minutes.

1 piece: 77 cal., 4g fat (2g sat. fat), 10mg chol., 168mg sod., 7g carb. (1g sugars, 0 fiber), 2g pro.

PINEAPPLE
APPETIZER MEATBALLS

BENEDICTINE DIP

COWBOY BEEF DIP

In a foods class, a group of us developed this recipe to enter in the North Dakota State Beef Bash Competition. Our dip won the contest, and now my family requests this for all our special gatherings!
—Jessica Klym, Dunn Center, ND

- -

Prep: 20 min. • **Cook:** 25 min.
Makes: 12 servings (3 cups)

- 1   lb. ground beef
- 4   Tbsp. chopped onion, divided
- 3   Tbsp. chopped sweet
      red pepper, divided
- 2   Tbsp. chopped green
      pepper, divided
- 1   can (10¾ oz.) condensed nacho
      cheese soup, undiluted
- ½   cup salsa
- 4   Tbsp. sliced ripe olives, divided
- 4   Tbsp. sliced pimiento-
      stuffed olives, divided
- 2   Tbsp. chopped green chiles
- 1   tsp. chopped seeded
      jalapeno pepper
- ¼   tsp. dried oregano
- ¼   tsp. pepper
- ¼   cup shredded cheddar cheese
- 2   Tbsp. sour cream
- 2   to 3 tsp. minced fresh parsley
      Tortilla chips

1. In a large skillet, cook the beef, 3 Tbsp. onion, 2 Tbsp. red pepper and 1 Tbsp. green pepper over medium heat until meat is no longer pink, breaking it into crumbles; drain. Stir in the soup, salsa, 3 Tbsp. ripe olives, 3 Tbsp. pimiento-stuffed olives, chiles, jalapeno, oregano and pepper. Bring to a boil. Reduce heat; simmer, uncovered, for 5 minutes.
2. Transfer to a serving dish. Top with the cheese, sour cream and parsley; sprinkle with the remaining onion, peppers and olives. Serve with tortilla chips.
Note: Wear disposable gloves when cutting hot peppers; the oils can burn skin. Avoid touching your face.
¼ cup: 116 cal., 7g fat (3g sat. fat), 26mg chol., 336mg sod., 4g carb. (1g sugars, 1g fiber), 8g pro.

BENEDICTINE DIP

Benedictine is a creamy spread studded with chopped cucumbers. It was named in honor of Jennie Carter Benedict, a chef and restaurateur from Louisville, Kentucky, who created the condiment at the turn of the 20th century. Originally used for cucumber sandwiches, Benedictine is now commonly enjoyed as a cold dip for chips or as a spread on crackers.
—*Taste of Home* Test Kitchen

- -

Takes: 15 min. • **Makes:** 1¾ cups

- 4   oz. cream cheese, softened
- 1   log (4 oz.) fresh goat cheese
- 2   Tbsp. minced fresh parsley
- 1   Tbsp. mayonnaise
- ¼   tsp. salt
- ⅛   tsp. cayenne pepper
- ⅛   tsp. pepper
- 1   drop green food coloring, optional
- ¾   cup finely chopped peeled
      cucumber, patted dry
- ¼   cup finely chopped green onions
      Assorted crackers

In a small bowl, combine cheeses, parsley, mayonnaise, salt, cayenne, pepper and food coloring if desired; beat until smooth. Stir in the cucumber and onion. Chill until serving. Serve with crackers.
2 Tbsp.: 51 cal., 5g fat (3g sat. fat), 15mg chol., 105mg sod., 1g carb. (0 sugars, 0 fiber), 2g pro.

TEST KITCHEN TIP

When peeling cucumbers or other vegetables, be sure to go slow and always peel away from yourself to avoid any accidental cuts.

COWBOY
BEEF DIP

BACON-WRAPPED
STUFFED JALAPENOS

BACON-WRAPPED STUFFED JALAPENOS

Sunday is grill-out day for my husband, Cliff, and these zesty peppers are one of his specialties. We usually feature them at our annual Daytona 500 party. They disappear from the appetizer tray!
—Therese Pollard, Hurst, TX

- -

Prep: 1 hour • **Grill:** 40 min. • **Makes:** 2 dozen

- 24 medium jalapeno peppers
- 1 lb. uncooked chorizo or bulk spicy pork sausage
- 2 cups shredded cheddar cheese
- 12 bacon strips, cut in half

1. Make a lengthwise cut in each jalapeno, about ⅛ in. deep; remove seeds. Combine the sausage and cheese; stuff into jalapenos. Wrap each with a piece of bacon; secure with toothpicks.

2. Grill the jalapenos, covered, over indirect medium heat for 35-40 minutes or until a thermometer reads 160°, turning once. Grill, covered, over direct heat for 1-2 minutes or until bacon is crisp.

Note: Wear disposable gloves when cutting hot peppers; the oils can burn skin. Avoid touching your face.

1 stuffed jalapeno: 132 cal., 10g fat (4g sat. fat), 30mg chol., 365mg sod., 1g carb. (1g sugars, 0 fiber), 8g pro.

ASK SARAH

HOW CAN I SOOTHE MY SKIN AFTER A BURN FROM JALAPENOS?

Place your hands in hot, soapy water and gently scrub with a clean kitchen brush until the pain subsides.

CLASSIC HUMMUS

CLASSIC HUMMUS

We love hummus, and this version is really amazing. If you have an electric pressure cooker, this is an easy, tasty reason to pull it out! We pair hummus with fresh veggies for a meal or snack.
—Monica and David Eichler, Lawrence, KS

- -

Prep: 20 min. + soaking
Cook: 15 min. + chilling • **Makes:** 2½ cups

- 1 cup dried garbanzo beans or chickpeas
- 1 medium onion, quartered
- 1 bay leaf
- 4 cups water
- ¼ cup minced fresh parsley
- ¼ cup lemon juice
- ¼ cup tahini
- 4 to 6 garlic cloves, minced
- 1 tsp. ground cumin
- ¾ tsp. salt
- ⅛ tsp. cayenne pepper
- ¼ cup olive oil
  Assorted fresh vegetables

1. Rinse and sort beans; soak according to package directions. Drain and rinse the beans, discarding liquid. Transfer to a 6-qt. electric pressure cooker; add onion, bay leaf and water.

2. Lock the lid; close pressure-release valve. Adjust to pressure-cook on high for 12 minutes. Let pressure release naturally. Drain mixture, reserving ½ cup cooking liquid. Discard onion and bay leaf.

3. Place beans, parsley, lemon juice, tahini, garlic, cumin, salt and cayenne in a food processor; cover and process until smooth. While processing, gradually add the oil to mixture in a steady stream. Add enough reserved cooking liquid to achieve the desired consistency.

4. Cover and refrigerate for at least 1 hour. Serve with vegetables.

¼ cup: 139 cal., 10g fat (1g sat. fat), 0 chol., 190mg sod., 14g carb. (1g sugars, 6g fiber), 5g pro. **Diabetic exchanges:** 1½ fat, 1 starch.

PUMPKIN PIE LATTE

Enjoy this espresso drink during the holidays or all year round! With just the right amount of spice, it tastes like the popular version found at gourmet coffee shops.
—*Taste of Home* Test Kitchen

Takes: 15 min. • **Makes:** 2 servings

- 2 cups whole milk
- 2 Tbsp. canned pumpkin
- 2 Tbsp. sugar
- 2 Tbsp. vanilla extract
- ½ tsp. pumpkin pie spice
- ½ cup hot brewed espresso
  Optional: Whipped cream, pumpkin pie spice and ground nutmeg

1. In a small saucepan, combine the milk, pumpkin and sugar. Cook and stir over medium heat until steaming. Remove from the heat; stir in vanilla and pie spice. Transfer to a blender; cover and process for 15 seconds or until foamy.

2. Pour into 2 mugs; add espresso. Garnish with whipped cream and spices if desired.

1¼ cups: 234 cal., 8g fat (5g sat. fat), 33mg chol., 122mg sod., 26g carb. (24g sugars, 1g fiber), 8g pro.

AUSSIE SAUSAGE ROLLS

I was born and raised in Australia but moved to the U.S. when I married my husband. When I long for a taste of my homeland, I bake up a batch of these cute little sausage rolls and share them with my neighbors or co-workers.
—Melissa Landon, Port Charlotte, FL

Prep: 30 min. • **Bake:** 20 min.
Makes: 3 dozen

- 1 medium onion, finely chopped
- 2 Tbsp. minced fresh chives or 2 tsp. dried chives
- 2 tsp. minced fresh basil or ½ tsp. dried basil
- 2 garlic cloves, minced
- ½ tsp. salt
- ¼ tsp. pepper
- 1 tsp. paprika, divided
- 1¼ lbs. bulk pork sausage
- 1 pkg. (17.3 oz.) frozen puff pastry, thawed

1. Preheat oven to 350°. Combine first 6 ingredients and ¾ tsp. paprika. Add sausage; mix lightly but thoroughly.

2. On a lightly floured surface, roll each pastry sheet into an 11x10½-in. rectangle. Cut lengthwise into 3 strips. Spread ½ cup sausage mixture lengthwise down the center of each strip. Fold over sides, pinching edges to seal. Cut each log into 6 pieces.

3. Place on a rack in a 15x10x1-in. pan, seam side down. Sprinkle with remaining ¼ tsp. paprika. Bake until golden brown and the sausage is no longer pink, 20-25 minutes.

1 appetizer: 116 cal., 8g fat (2g sat. fat), 11mg chol., 198mg sod., 8g carb. (0 sugars, 1g fiber), 3g pro.

AUSSIE SAUSAGE ROLLS

ROASTED RED PEPPER TRIANGLES

SESAME CHICKEN BITES

These bites have been a party favorite at our house for many years. You can make the sauce the night before to make day-of prep even easier.
—Kathy Green, Layton, NJ

- -

Takes: 30 min.
Makes: about 2½ dozen (¾ cup sauce)

SAUCE
  ¾ cup mayonnaise
  4 tsp. honey
  1½ tsp. Dijon mustard
CHICKEN
  ½ cup dry bread crumbs
  ¼ cup sesame seeds
  2 tsp. minced fresh parsley
  ½ cup mayonnaise
  1 tsp. onion powder
  1 tsp. ground mustard
  ¼ tsp. pepper
  1 lb. boneless skinless chicken breasts, cut into 1-in. cubes
  2 to 4 Tbsp. canola oil

1. In a small bowl, mix sauce ingredients. Refrigerate until serving.
2. In a shallow bowl, mix bread crumbs, sesame seeds and parsley. In a separate shallow bowl, mix the mayonnaise and seasonings. Dip chicken in mayonnaise mixture, then in crumb mixture, patting to help coating adhere to all sides.
3. In a large cast-iron or other heavy skillet, heat 2 Tbsp. oil over medium-high heat. Add chicken in batches; cook until chicken is no longer pink, turning occasionally and adding additional oil as needed. Serve with sauce.
1 chicken bite with about 1 tsp. sauce: 102 cal., 9g fat (1g sat. fat), 9mg chol., 73mg sod., 2g carb. (1g sugars, 0 fiber), 4g pro.

ROASTED RED PEPPER TRIANGLES

I sandwich full-flavored meats, cheeses and roasted red peppers between layers of flaky crescent dough for this sensational treat. We like to have marinara sauce on hand for dipping.
—Amy Bell, Arlington, TN

- -

Prep: 35 min. • **Bake:** 50 min.
Makes: 2 dozen

  2 tubes (8 oz. each) refrigerated crescent rolls
  1½ cups finely diced fully cooked ham
  1 cup shredded Swiss cheese
  1 pkg. (3 oz.) sliced pepperoni, chopped
  8 slices provolone cheese
  1 jar (12 oz.) roasted sweet red peppers, drained and cut into strips
  4 large eggs
  ¼ cup grated Parmesan cheese
  1 Tbsp. Italian salad dressing mix

1. Preheat oven to 350°. Unroll 1 tube of crescent dough into 1 long rectangle; press onto bottom and ¾ in. up sides of a greased 13x9-in. baking dish. Seal seams and perforations. Top with half of the ham; layer with Swiss cheese, pepperoni, provolone cheese and remaining ham. Top with the red peppers.
2. In a small bowl, whisk eggs, Parmesan cheese and salad dressing mix; reserve ¼ cup. Pour the remaining egg mixture over peppers.
3. On a lightly floured surface, roll out remaining crescent dough into a 13x9-in. rectangle; seal seams and perforations. Place over filling; pinch edges to seal.
4. Bake, covered, for 30 minutes. Uncover; brush with reserved egg mixture. Bake until crust is golden brown, 20-25 minutes longer. Cool on a wire rack for 5 minutes. Cut into triangles. Serve warm.
1 piece: 165 cal., 10g fat (4g sat. fat), 50mg chol., 485mg sod., 8g carb. (2g sugars, 0 fiber), 8g pro.

PARTY CHEESE BREAD

GRUYERE & CARAMELIZED ONION TARTS

Garlic and onion is a match made in heaven, in my opinion. So I love creating new recipes to showcase the pair. Gruyere cheese adds fantastic flavor to this eye-catching starter.
—Lisa Speer, Palm Beach, FL

Prep: 45 min. • **Bake:** 15 min.
Makes: 2 dozen

- 1   large sweet onion, thinly sliced
- 2   Tbsp. olive oil
- 1   Tbsp. butter
- 3   garlic cloves, minced
- ¼   tsp. salt
- ¼   tsp. pepper
- 1   pkg. (17.3 oz.) frozen puff pastry, thawed
- 1   cup shredded Gruyere or Swiss cheese
- ¼   cup grated Parmesan cheese
- 2   Tbsp. minced fresh thyme

1. In a large skillet, saute onion in oil and butter until softened. Reduce the heat to medium-low; cook, uncovered, for 40 minutes or until deep golden brown, stirring occasionally. Add garlic; cook 1 minute longer. Stir in salt and pepper.
2. Unfold each puff pastry sheet onto an ungreased baking sheet. Using a knife, score decorative lines around the edges of each sheet. Spread onion mixture to within ½ in. of edges. Sprinkle with the cheeses and thyme.
3. Bake at 400° for 12-15 minutes or until golden brown. Cut each tart into 12 pieces. If desired, top with additional fresh thyme and Parmesan cheese. Serve warm.
1 piece: 142 cal., 9g fat (3g sat. fat), 7mg chol., 125mg sod., 13g carb. (1g sugars, 2g fiber), 3g pro.

PARTY CHEESE BREAD

You can't go wrong with this recipe. The cheesy, buttery loaf looks fantastic and is so simple to make—people just flock to it. The taste is positively sinful, and it's better with pasta than the usual garlic bread.
—Karen Grant, Tulare, CA

Prep: 25 min. • **Bake:** 30 min.
Makes: 16 servings

- 1   round loaf sourdough bread (1 lb.)
- 1   lb. Monterey Jack cheese, sliced
- ½   cup butter, melted
- 2   Tbsp. lemon juice
- 2   Tbsp. Dijon mustard
- 1½ tsp. garlic powder
- ½   tsp. onion powder
- ½   tsp. celery salt
    Minced fresh chives, optional

1. Preheat oven to 350°. Cut bread into 1-in. slices to within ½ in. of bottom of loaf. Repeat cuts in opposite direction. Insert cheese in cuts.
2. Mix all remaining ingredients except chives; drizzle over bread. Wrap in foil; place on a baking sheet.
3. Bake 20 minutes. Unwrap; bake until cheese is melted, about 10 minutes. If desired, sprinkle with chives.
1 serving: 237 cal., 15g fat (9g sat. fat), 41mg chol., 468mg sod., 15g carb. (2g sugars, 1g fiber), 10g pro.

TEST KITCHEN TIP
A sharp serrated knife works best when cutting this bread so you don't end up tearing it.

GRUYERE &
CARAMELIZED
ONION TARTS

PUMPKIN QUESO

I like serving this dip with veggie chips like sweet potato or kale, but it's also great with good old tortilla chips. It can be made with vegetable stock and gluten-free flour if you have dietary restrictions.
—Darla Andrews, Boerne, TX

- -

Takes: 25 min. • **Makes:** 3½ cups

3	Tbsp. butter
3	Tbsp. all-purpose flour
1½	cups chicken stock
½	cup heavy whipping cream
3	cups shredded extra sharp cheddar cheese
½	cup canned pumpkin
2	tsp. ground cumin
½	tsp. garlic powder
¼	tsp. salt
¼	tsp. pepper
	Tortilla chips
	Optional: Pumpkin seeds and minced cilantro

In a large saucepan, melt the butter over medium heat. Stir in flour until smooth; gradually whisk in stock and cream. Bring to a boil, stirring constantly; cook and stir until thickened, 4-5 minutes. Stir in cheese, pumpkin and seasonings until cheese is melted. Serve with tortilla chips and, if desired, sprinkle with pumpkin seeds and cilantro.

2 Tbsp.: 81 cal., 7g fat (4g sat. fat), 20mg chol., 139mg sod., 2g carb. (0 sugars, 0 fiber), 3g pro.

"The layers of flavor that pumpkin, cumin and chicken stock provide give this queso recipe a depth that you won't soon forget."

—LAUREN PAHMEIER, ASSOCIATE EDITOR

PUMPKIN QUESO

POMEGRANATE GINGER SPRITZER

Conveniently, a pitcher of this non-alcoholic beverage can be made a day before guests arrive. Add club soda just before serving.
—*Taste of Home* Test Kitchen

Prep: 10 min. + chilling • **Makes:** 7 cups.

- ½ cup sliced fresh gingerroot
- 1 medium lime, sliced
- 3 cups pomegranate juice
- ¾ cup orange juice
- 3 cups chilled club soda
  Optional: Lime wedges, pomegranate seeds and ice

1. Place ginger and lime slices in a pitcher; stir in the pomegranate and orange juices. Refrigerate overnight.

2. Just before serving, strain and discard ginger and lime. Stir club soda into juice mixture. Garnish as desired.

1 cup: 80 cal., 0 fat (0 sat. fat), 0 chol., 35mg sod., 20g carb. (17g sugars, 0 fiber), 1g pro.

MARINATED OLIVE & CHEESE RING

We love to make Italian meals into a fun celebration, and an antipasto always kicks off the party. This one is almost too pretty to eat, especially when it's sprinkled with pimientos, fresh basil and parsley.
—Patricia Harmon, Baden, PA

Prep: 25 min. + chilling • **Makes:** 16 servings

- 1 pkg. (8 oz.) cream cheese, cold
- 1 pkg. (10 oz.) sharp white cheddar cheese, cut into ¼-in. slices
- ⅓ cup pimiento-stuffed olives
- ⅓ cup pitted Greek olives
- ¼ cup balsamic vinegar
- ¼ cup olive oil
- 1 Tbsp. minced fresh parsley
- 1 Tbsp. minced fresh basil or 1 tsp. dried basil
- 2 garlic cloves, minced
- 1 jar (2 oz.) pimiento strips, drained and chopped
  Toasted French bread baguette slices

1. Cut cream cheese lengthwise in half; cut each half into ¼-in. slices. On a serving plate, arrange cheeses upright in a ring, alternating cheddar and cream cheese slices. Place the olives in center.

2. In a small bowl, whisk vinegar, oil, parsley, basil and garlic until blended; drizzle over the cheeses and olives. Sprinkle with pimientos. Refrigerate, covered, at least 8 hours or overnight. Serve with baguette slices.

1 serving: 168 cal., 16g fat (7g sat. fat), 34mg chol., 260mg sod., 2g carb. (1g sugars, 0 fiber), 6g pro.

TEST KITCHEN TIP

This stylish appetizer is super adaptable. Any cheeses will work in place of the cream cheese and sharp cheddar. Just keep the overall weight the same. For more variety, fold thin slices of deli cuts such as pepperoni and salami in half and tuck them between the cheese slices.

MARINATED OLIVE & CHEESE RING

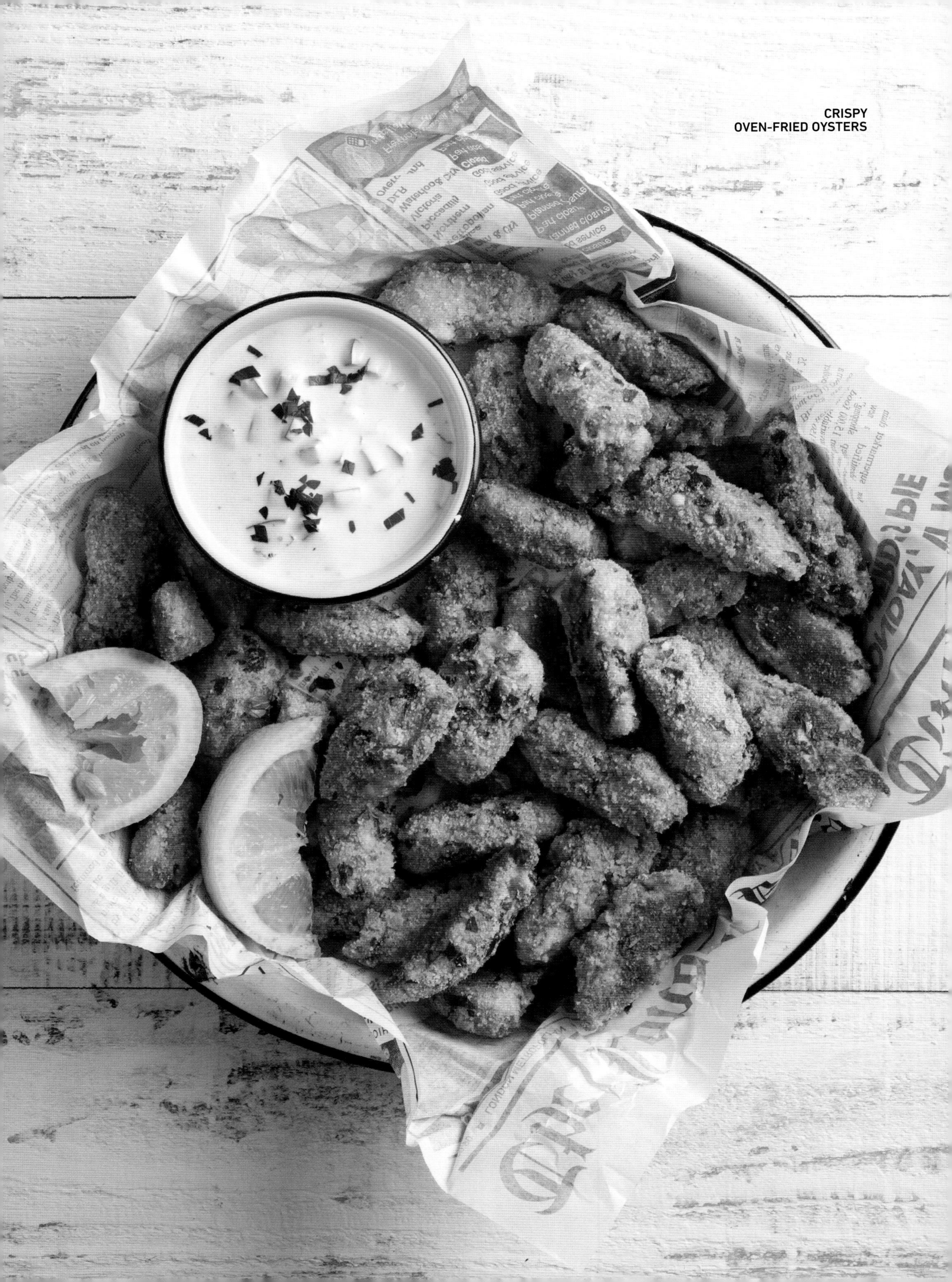

CRISPY
OVEN-FRIED OYSTERS

CRISPY OVEN-FRIED OYSTERS

These flavorful breaded and baked oysters, served with a zippy jalapeno mayonnaise, are just divine. I entered this recipe in a seafood contest and took first place in the hors d'oeuvres category.
—Marie Rizzio, Interlochen, MI

Takes: 30 min. • **Makes:** about 2½ dozen (about ⅔ cup jalapeno mayonnaise)

- ¾ cup all-purpose flour
- ⅛ tsp. salt
- ⅛ tsp. pepper
- 2 large eggs
- 1 cup dry bread crumbs
- ⅔ cup grated Romano cheese
- ¼ cup minced fresh parsley
- ½ tsp. garlic salt
- 1 pint shucked oysters or 2 cans (8 oz. each) whole oysters, drained
- 2 Tbsp. olive oil

JALAPENO MAYONNAISE
- ¼ cup mayonnaise
- ¼ cup sour cream
- 2 medium jalapeno peppers, seeded and finely chopped
- 2 Tbsp. 2% milk
- 1 tsp. lemon juice
- ¼ tsp. grated lemon zest
- ⅛ tsp. salt
- ⅛ tsp. pepper

1. Preheat oven to 400°. In a shallow bowl, combine flour, salt and pepper. In another shallow bowl, whisk eggs. In a third bowl, combine bread crumbs, cheese, parsley and garlic salt.
2. Coat oysters with flour mixture, then dip in eggs and coat with crumb mixture. Place in a greased 15x10x1-in. baking pan; drizzle with oil.
3. Bake until golden brown, 12-15 minutes. Meanwhile, in a bowl, whisk mayonnaise ingredients. Serve with oysters.
Note: Wear disposable gloves when cutting hot peppers; the oils can burn skin. Avoid touching your face.
1 oyster with about 1 tsp. jalapeno mayonnaise: 75 cal., 4g fat (1g sat. fat), 25mg chol., 146mg sod., 6g carb. (0 sugars, 0 fiber), 3g pro.

CRANBERRY FIZZ

CRANBERRY FIZZ

With just five basic ingredients, this wonderfully tangy punch couldn't be much simpler to stir together.
—Suzette Jury, Keene, CA

Prep: 5 min. + chilling • **Makes:** 2 qt.

- 1 bottle (32 oz.) cranberry juice
- 1 cup orange juice
- 1 cup ruby red grapefruit juice
- ½ cup sugar
- 2 cups ginger ale, chilled
  Optional: Orange slices and fresh or frozen cranberries

In a pitcher, combine cranberry, orange and grapefruit juices and sugar. Refrigerate, covered, until chilled. Just before serving, stir in ginger ale. To serve, pour mixture over ice.
1 cup: 154 cal., 0 fat (0 sat. fat), 0 chol., 7mg sod., 40g carb. (36g sugars, 0 fiber), 1g pro.

HOT GINGER COFFEE

This warm winter drink is wonderful after shoveling, skiing or sledding! You can also try the crystallized ginger in baked goods or over ice cream.
—Audrey Thibodeau, Gilbert, AZ

Takes: 25 min. • **Makes:** 6 servings

- 6 Tbsp. ground coffee (not instant)
- 1 Tbsp. grated orange zest
- 1 Tbsp. chopped crystallized ginger
- ½ tsp. ground cinnamon
- 6 cups cold water
  Optional: Whipped cream, cinnamon sticks and additional orange zest

1. Combine coffee, orange zest, ginger and cinnamon. Place in a coffee filter and brew with cold water according to the manufacturer's directions.
2. Pour into mugs; if desired, garnish with whipped cream, cinnamon sticks and orange zest.
1 cup: 22 cal., 0 fat (0 sat. fat), 0 chol., 3mg sod., 5g carb. (2g sugars, 0 fiber), 1g pro.

SPINACH-ARTICHOKE STUFFED MUSHROOMS

Guests will think you worked all day on these rich, creamy stuffed mushrooms, but they go together so easily. The flavorful artichoke filling makes this party appetizer something special.
—Amy Gaisford, Salt Lake City, UT

Prep: 20 min. • **Bake:** 20 min.
Makes: about 2½ dozen

- 3 oz. cream cheese, softened
- ½ cup mayonnaise
- ½ cup sour cream
- ¾ tsp. garlic salt
- 1 can (14 oz.) water-packed artichoke hearts, rinsed, drained and chopped
- 1 pkg. (10 oz.) frozen chopped spinach, thawed and squeezed dry
- ⅓ cup shredded part-skim mozzarella cheese
- 3 Tbsp. shredded Parmesan cheese
- 30 to 35 large fresh mushrooms, stems removed
   Additional shredded Parmesan cheese

1. Preheat oven to 400°. Mix the first 4 ingredients. Stir in artichoke hearts, spinach, mozzarella cheese and 3 Tbsp. Parmesan cheese.
2. Place mushrooms on foil-lined baking sheets, stem side up. Spoon about 1 Tbsp. filling into each. If desired, top with the additional Parmesan cheese. Bake until mushrooms are tender, 16-20 minutes.
1 stuffed mushroom: 51 cal., 4g fat (1g sat. fat), 4mg chol., 116mg sod., 2g carb. (0 sugars, 0 fiber), 2g pro.

SPINACH-ARTICHOKE STUFFED MUSHROOMS

TACO MEATBALL RING

While it looks complicated, this attractive meatball-filled ring is very easy to assemble. My family loves tacos, and we find that the crescent roll dough is a nice change from the usual tortilla shells or chips.
—Brenda Johnson, Davison, MI

Prep: 30 min. • **Bake:** 15 min.
Makes: 16 servings

- 2 cups shredded cheddar cheese, divided
- 2 Tbsp. water
- 2 to 4 Tbsp. taco seasoning
- ½ lb. ground beef
- 2 tubes (8 oz. each) refrigerated crescent rolls
- ½ medium head iceberg lettuce, shredded
- 1 medium tomato, chopped
- 4 green onions, sliced
- ½ cup sliced ripe olives
- 2 jalapeno peppers, sliced
  Optional: Sour cream and salsa

1. In a large bowl, combine 1 cup cheese, water and taco seasoning. Crumble the beef over the mixture and mix lightly but thoroughly. Shape into 16 balls.
2. Place the meatballs on a greased rack in a shallow baking pan. Bake, uncovered, at 400° until meat is longer pink, about 12 minutes. Drain the eatballs on paper towels. Reduce heat to 375°.
3. Arrange crescent rolls on a greased 15-in. pizza pan, forming a ring with pointed ends facing the outer edge of the pan and wide ends overlapping.
4. Place a meatball on each roll; fold point over meatball and tuck under wide end of roll (meatball will be visible). Repeat. Bake until rolls are golden brown, 15-20 minutes.
5. Transfer to a serving platter. Fill center of the ring with lettuce, tomato, onions, olives, jalapenos, remaining cheese, and sour cream and salsa if desired.
Note: Wear disposable gloves when cutting hot peppers; the oils can burn skin. Avoid touching your face.
1 piece: 203 cal., 12g fat (5g sat. fat), 24mg chol., 457mg sod., 14g carb. (3g sugars, 1g fiber), 8g pro.

TACO MEATBALL RING

TEST KITCHEN TIP
Lining your pizza pan with parchment or nonstick foil (and leaving a little extra hanging over the side) will help ensure a seamless transfer from pan to platter.

MINI CORN DOGS

TURTLE CHIPS

Salty-sweet, crunchy-chewy—so many sensations in one delectable bite. This is the absolute easiest recipe to make! Everyone will be reaching for this goodie.
—Leigh Ann Stewart, Hopkinsville, KY

Takes: 25 min. • **Makes:** 16 servings

  1 **pkg. (11 oz.) ridged potato chips**
  1 **pkg. (14 oz.) caramels**
 ⅓ **cup heavy whipping cream**
  1 **pkg. (11½ oz.) milk chocolate chips**
  2 **Tbsp. shortening**
  1 **cup finely chopped pecans**

1. Arrange whole potato chips in a single layer on a large platter. In a large saucepan, combine caramels and cream. Cook and stir over medium-low heat until caramels are melted. Drizzle over chips.
2. In a microwave, melt the chocolate and shortening; stir until smooth. Drizzle over caramel mixture on potato chips; sprinkle with pecans. Serve immediately.
½ cup: 396 cal., 24g fat (7g sat. fat), 13mg chol., 223mg sod., 43g carb. (27g sugars, 2g fiber), 5g pro.

> "My daughter loves chips and trying different variations. These are the perfect sweet-and-salty treat. And she has so much fun making them."
>
> —RAEANN THOMPSON, SENIOR ART DIRECTOR

MINI CORN DOGS

Bring a county fair favorite into your home with these bite-sized corn dogs! Kids and the young of heart love them.
—Geralyn Harrington, Floral Park, NY

Takes: 30 min. • **Makes:** 2 dozen

1⅔ **cups all-purpose flour**
 ⅓ **cup cornmeal**
  3 **tsp. baking powder**
  1 **tsp. salt**
  3 **Tbsp. cold butter**
  1 **Tbsp. shortening**
  1 **large egg, room temperature**
 ¾ **cup 2% milk**
24 **miniature hot dogs**
HONEY MUSTARD SAUCE
 ⅓ **cup honey**
 ⅓ **cup prepared mustard**
  1 **Tbsp. molasses**

1. In a bowl, combine the first 4 ingredients. Cut in butter and shortening until mixture resembles coarse crumbs. Beat egg and milk. Stir into dry ingredients until a soft dough forms; dough will be sticky.
2. Turn onto a generously floured surface; knead 6-8 times or until smooth, adding additional flour as needed. Roll out to ¼-in. thickness. Cut with a 2¼-in. biscuit cutter. Fold each dough circle over a hot dog and press the edges to seal. Place on greased baking sheets.
3. Bake at 450° for 10-12 minutes or until golden brown. In a bowl, combine sauce ingredients. Serve with corn dogs.
1 corn dog: 109 cal., 5g fat (2g sat. fat), 18mg chol., 306mg sod., 14g carb. (5g sugars, 0 fiber), 3g pro.

TURTLE CHIPS

SHRIMP TARTLETS

Mini tart shells are filled with a tasty cream cheese mixture, then topped with seafood sauce and shrimp for this picture-perfect, tasty appetizer. You could also serve several as a fast, light meal.
—Gina Hutchison, Smithville, MO

- -

Takes: 20 min. • **Makes:** 2½ dozen

  1 pkg. (8 oz.) cream cheese, softened
1½ tsp. Worcestershire sauce
  1 to 2 tsp. grated onion
  1 tsp. garlic salt
  ⅛ tsp. lemon juice
  2 pkg. (1.9 oz. each) frozen miniature phyllo tart shells
  ½ cup seafood cocktail sauce
 30 peeled and deveined cooked shrimp (31-40 per lb.), tails removed
     Optional: Minced fresh parsley and lemon wedges

1. Beat the first 5 ingredients until blended. Place tart shells on a serving plate. Fill with cream cheese mixture; top with cocktail sauce and shrimp.
2. Refrigerate until serving. If desired, sprinkle with parsley and serve with lemon wedges.
1 tartlet: 61 cal., 4g fat (2g sat. fat), 23mg chol., 143mg sod., 4g carb. (1g sugars, 0 fiber), 3g pro.

HONEY-BARBECUE CHICKEN WINGS

The slightly sweet barbecue flavor of the sauce provides mass appeal—and the need to keep eating more wings!
—*Taste of Home* Test Kitchen

- -

Prep: 20 min. • **Cook:** 10 min./batch
Makes: 2 dozen

2½ lbs. chicken wings
  ½ cup reduced-sodium soy sauce
  ½ cup barbecue sauce
  ½ cup honey
  1 cup all-purpose flour
  2 tsp. salt
  2 tsp. paprika
  ¼ tsp. pepper
     Oil for deep-fat frying

1. Cut wings into 3 sections; discard wing tip sections. In a small saucepan, combine the soy sauce, barbecue sauce and honey. Bring to a boil; cook until liquid is reduced to about 1 cup.
2. Meanwhile, in a large bowl, combine the flour, salt, paprika and pepper. Add wings, a few at a time, and toss to coat.
3. In an electric skillet or deep fryer, heat oil to 375°. Fry wings, a few at a time, until no longer pink, 3-4 minutes on each side. Drain on paper towels. Transfer wings to a large bowl; add sauce and toss to coat. Serve immediately.
Note: Uncooked chicken wing sections (wingettes) may be substituted for whole chicken wings.
1 piece: 129 cal., 8g fat (1g sat. fat), 15mg chol., 419mg sod., 8g carb. (7g sugars, 0 fiber), 6g pro.

TACO TATER SKINS

I wanted to make a version of these with ingredients most people have on hand. We make a meal out of these skins, but they're also great for parties as appetizers.
—Phyllis Douglas, Fairview, MI

- -

Prep: 20 min. + cooling • **Bake:** 65 min.
Makes: 2 dozen

  6 large baking potatoes (about 13 oz. each)
  ½ cup butter, melted
  2 Tbsp. taco seasoning
  1 cup shredded cheddar cheese
 15 bacon strips, cooked and crumbled
  3 green onions, chopped
     Optional: Salsa and sour cream

1. Preheat oven to 375°. Scrub the potatoes; pierce several times with a fork. Place on a baking sheet; bake until tender, 60-70 minutes. Cool slightly. Reduce oven setting to 350°.
2. Cut potatoes lengthwise into quarters; remove pulp, leaving a ¼-in. shell (save pulp for another use). Mix melted butter and seasoning; brush over both sides of the potato skins. Place on greased baking sheets, skin side down. Sprinkle with the cheese, bacon and green onions.
3. Bake until cheese is melted, 5-10 minutes. If desired, serve with salsa and sour cream.
1 piece: 153 cal., 7g fat (4g sat. fat), 20mg chol., 227mg sod., 17g carb. (1g sugars, 2g fiber), 5g pro.

BLACK FOREST HAM PINWHEELS

Dried cherries are the sweet surprise alongside savory ingredients in these delightfully different spirals. I roll up the tortillas and pop them in the fridge well before party time, and then I just slice and serve.
—Kate Dampier, Quail Valley, CA

- -

Prep: 20 min. + chilling
Makes: about 3½ dozen

- 1 pkg. (8 oz.) cream cheese, softened
- 4 tsp. minced fresh dill
- 1 Tbsp. lemon juice
- 2 tsp. Dijon mustard
  Dash each salt and pepper
- ½ cup dried cherries, chopped
- ¼ cup chopped green onions
- 5 flour tortillas (10 in.),
  room temperature
- ½ lb. sliced deli Black Forest ham
- ½ lb. sliced Swiss cheese

1. In a small bowl, beat cream cheese, dill, lemon juice, mustard, salt and pepper until blended. Stir in cherries and onions. Spread over each tortilla; layer with ham and cheese.
2. Roll up tightly; securely wrap in waxed paper. Refrigerate at least 2 hours. Cut into ½-in. slices.
1 piece: 78 cal., 4g fat (2g sat. fat), 13mg chol., 151mg sod., 6g carb. (2g sugars, 0 fiber), 4g pro.

HOT ALMOND & CREAM DRINK

Just a few sips of this drink, with its rich almond flavor, will warm you up quickly. It's a favorite each year at our Christmas party.
—Kaye Kirsch, Bailey, CO

- -

Takes: 20 min. • **Makes:** 4 cups mix

- 1 cup butter, cubed
- 1 cup sugar
- 1 cup packed brown sugar
- 2 cups vanilla ice cream, softened
- 2 tsp. almond extract
  Ground nutmeg

1. In a small saucepan over low heat, cook and stir butter and sugars for 12-15 minutes or until butter is melted. Pour into a large bowl; add ice cream and extract. Beat on medium speed for 1-2 minutes or until smooth, scraping the bowl often.
2. To make 1 serving: Spoon ¼ cup mix into a mug; add ¾ cup boiling water and stir well. Sprinkle with the nutmeg. Serve immediately.
1 cup: 236 cal., 13g fat (8g sat. fat), 38mg chol., 134mg sod., 30g carb. (28g sugars, 0 fiber), 1g pro.

"This recipe is unbelievably delicious. I made it on a whim for a girls' night and was so pleased with how it turned out."

—ANNAMARIE HIGLEY, ASSOCIATE EDITOR

DEVILED EGGS WITH BACON

These yummy deviled eggs went over so well at our summer cookouts, I started making them for holiday dinners as well. Everyone likes the flavorful addition of crumbled bacon.
—Barbara Reid, Mounds, OK

- -

Takes: 30 min. • **Makes:** 2 dozen

- 12 hard-boiled large eggs
- ⅓ cup mayonnaise
- 3 bacon strips, cooked and crumbled
- 3 Tbsp. finely chopped red onion
- 3 Tbsp. sweet pickle relish
- ¼ tsp. smoked paprika

Cut eggs in half lengthwise. Remove yolks; set whites aside. In a small bowl, mash yolks. Add mayonnaise, bacon, onion and relish; mix well. Stuff into egg whites. Refrigerate until serving. Sprinkle with paprika.
1 stuffed egg half: 68 cal., 5g fat (1g sat. fat), 108mg chol., 82mg sod., 1g carb. (1g sugars, 0 fiber), 3g pro.

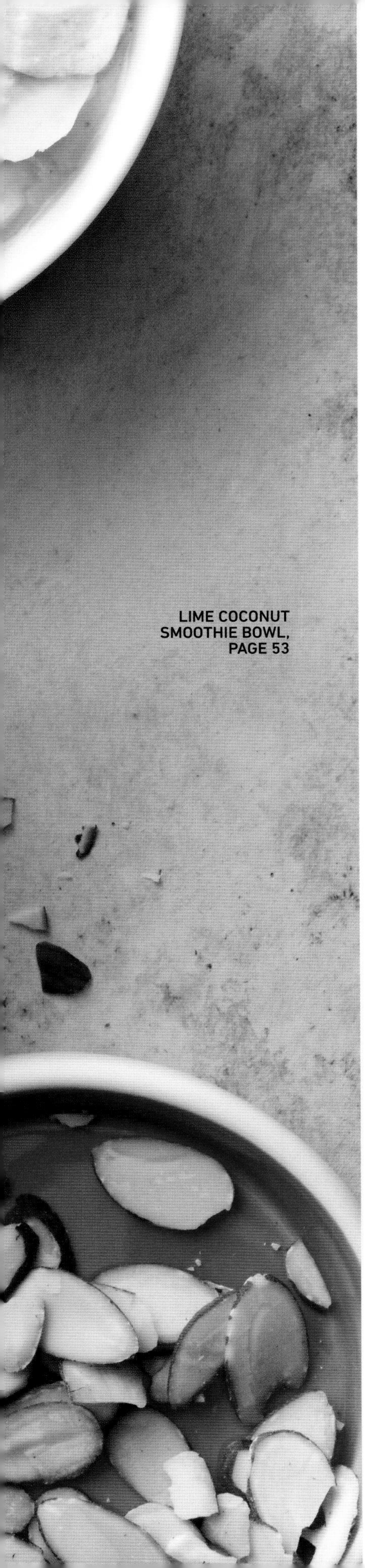

LIME COCONUT SMOOTHIE BOWL, PAGE 53

FAVORITE

Breakfasts

Early-morning eating doesn't get any better than this rise-and-shine selection of pancakes, waffles, bakes, breads and more.

HOME FRIES

FLUFFY WAFFLES

A friend shared the recipe for these light and tasty waffles. The cinnamon cream syrup is a nice change from maple syrup, and it keeps quite well in the fridge. Our two children also like it on toast.
—Amy Gilles, Ellsworth, WI

Prep: 25 min. • **Cook:** 20 min.
Makes: 10 waffles (6½ in.) and 1⅔ cups syrup

- 2   cups all-purpose flour
- 1   Tbsp. sugar
- 2   tsp. baking powder
- ½   tsp. salt
- 3   large eggs, separated
- 2   cups milk
- ¼   cup canola oil

CINNAMON CREAM SYRUP
- 1   cup sugar
- ½   cup light corn syrup
- ¼   cup water
- 1   can (5 oz.) evaporated milk
- 1   tsp. vanilla extract
- ½   tsp. ground cinnamon
      Mixed fresh berries, optional

1. In a bowl, combine flour, sugar, baking powder and salt. Combine the egg yolks, milk and oil; stir into dry ingredients just until moistened. In a small bowl, beat egg whites until stiff peaks form; fold into batter. Bake in a preheated waffle iron according to manufacturer's directions.
2. Meanwhile, for syrup, combine sugar, corn syrup and water in a saucepan. Bring to a boil over medium heat; cook and stir for 2 minutes or until thickened. Remove from the heat; stir in the milk, vanilla and cinnamon. Serve with waffles. If desired, serve with fresh berries.
Freeze option: Cool waffles on wire racks. Freeze between layers of waxed paper in a freezer container. Reheat waffles in a toaster on medium setting. Or, microwave each waffle on high for 30-60 seconds or until heated through.
1 waffle with 2½ Tbsp. syrup: 424 cal., 12g fat (4g sat. fat), 94mg chol., 344mg sod., 71g carb. (41g sugars, 1g fiber), 9g pro.

HOME FRIES

When I was little, my dad and I would get up early on Sundays and make these for the family. The rest of the gang would be awakened by the tempting aroma.
—Teresa Koide, Manchester, CT

Prep: 25 min. • **Cook:** 15 min./batch.
Makes: 8 servings

- 1   lb. bacon, chopped
- 8   medium potatoes (about 3 lbs.), peeled and cut into ½-in. pieces
- 1   large onion, chopped
- 1   tsp. salt
- ½   tsp. pepper

1. In a large skillet, cook chopped bacon over medium-low heat until crisp. Remove bacon from pan with a slotted spoon and drain on paper towels. Remove bacon drippings from pan and reserve.

2. Working in batches, add ¼ cup bacon drippings, potatoes, onion, salt and pepper to the pan; toss to coat. Cook and stir over medium-low heat until potatoes are golden brown and tender, 15-20 minutes, adding more drippings as needed. Stir in cooked bacon; serve immediately.
1 cup: 349 cal., 21g fat (8g sat. fat), 33mg chol., 681mg sod., 31g carb. (3g sugars, 2g fiber), 10g pro.

TEST KITCHEN TIP
To speed up the cooking time, microwave the potatoes for a few minutes before adding to the pan.

FLUFFY WAFFLES

BREAKFAST BLT WAFFLES

BREAKFAST BLT WAFFLES

I'm not a big fan of sweets for breakfast, but I love a crisp waffle. My son and I tried these BLT waffles, and they were a huge success! We used gluten-free, dairy-free waffles with fantastic results.
—Courtney Stultz, Weir, KS

- -

Prep: 10 min. • **Cook:** 25 min.
Makes: 4 servings

8 bacon strips
4 cups chopped fresh kale
4 large eggs
4 frozen waffles
1 large tomato, sliced
½ cup shredded cheddar cheese
   Optional: Chipotle mayonnaise and minced fresh parsley

1. In a large nonstick skillet, cook bacon over medium heat until crisp. Remove to paper towels to drain. Discard drippings, reserving 2 Tbsp. Cook and stir the kale in 1 Tbsp. drippings in same pan over medium heat until tender, 6-8 minutes. Remove and keep warm. Add remaining 1 Tbsp. drippings to pan. Break the eggs, 1 at a time, into pan; reduce heat to low. Cook until whites are set and yolks begin to thicken, turning once if desired.
2. Meanwhile, prepare waffles according to package directions. Top each waffle with kale, tomato slices, 1 egg, 2 Tbsp. cheese and 2 bacon strips. If desired, serve with chipotle mayonnaise and parsley.
1 serving: 382 cal., 26g fat (9g sat. fat), 228mg chol., 695mg sod., 19g carb. (3g sugars, 2g fiber), 18g pro.

ASK SARAH

HOW DO I REMOVE THE STEM FROM KALE?
Fold the kale leaf in half and cut off the stem where it meets the leaves.

OATMEAL BREAKFAST BARS

These soft and chewy treats have a hint of orange marmalade, so they're a fun change of pace from typical granola bars. They are so easy to put together and super delicious, you will likely find yourself making them all the time.
—Barbara Nowakowski,
North Tonawanda, NY

- -

Takes: 25 min. • **Makes:** 2½ dozen

4	cups quick-cooking oats
1	cup packed brown sugar
1	tsp. salt
1½	cups chopped walnuts
1	cup sweetened shredded coconut
¾	cup butter, melted
¾	cup orange marmalade

In a large bowl, combine oats, brown sugar and salt. Stir in remaining ingredients. Press into a greased 15x10x1-in. baking pan. Bake at 425° for 15-17 minutes or until golden brown. Cool on a wire rack. Cut into 30 bars.

1 bar: 182 cal., 10g fat (4g sat. fat), 12mg chol., 141mg sod., 22g carb. (13g sugars, 1g fiber), 3g pro.

TEST KITCHEN TIP

These oatmeal bars stay fresh for about a week when stored in an airtight container.

GRAPEFRUIT ALASKA

Easily impress your guests with this quick dessert. It takes just 30 minutes to prepare, and you'll receive rave reviews.
—Peg Atzen, Hackensack, MN

- -

Takes: 30 min. • **Makes:** 8 servings

4	large grapefruit
2	tsp. rum extract
½	cup heavy whipping cream, whipped
3	large egg whites, room temperature
1	tsp. cornstarch
¼	tsp. cream of tartar
¼	cup sugar
8	maraschino cherries

1. Preheat oven to 350°. Halve grapefruits and section; remove membranes. Return grapefruit sections to grapefruit halves. Drizzle ¼ tsp. rum extract over each. Top each with 1 rounded Tbsp. of whipped cream. Place on an ungreased foil-lined baking sheet.
2. In a large bowl, beat the egg whites, cornstarch and cream of tartar on medium speed until soft peaks form. Gradually beat in sugar, 1 Tbsp. at a time, on high until stiff glossy peaks form and the sugar is dissolved. Mound ½ cup on top of each grapefruit half; spread meringue to edges to seal. Bake until meringue is browned, 15 minutes. Top each with a cherry. Serve immediately.
½ grapefruit: 152 cal., 6g fat (3g sat. fat), 20mg chol., 26mg sod., 24g carb. (21g sugars, 2g fiber), 3g pro.

OATMEAL
BREAKFAST BARS

CRUNCHY GRANOA

CRUNCHY GRANOLA

This crisp, lightly sweet mixture is great just eaten out of hand or as an ice cream topping.
—Lorna Jacobsen, Arrowwood, AB

- -

Prep: 15 min. • **Bake:** 30 min. + cooling
Makes: 8 cups

- ⅔ cup honey
- ½ cup canola oil
- ⅓ cup packed brown sugar
- 2 tsp. vanilla extract
- 4 cups old-fashioned oats
- 1 cup sliced almonds
- 1 cup sweetened shredded coconut
- ½ cup sesame seeds
- ½ cup salted sunflower kernels
- 2 cups raisins

1. Preheat oven to 300°. In a small saucepan, combine honey, oil and brown sugar; cook and stir over medium heat until the sugar is dissolved. Remove from heat; stir in vanilla.
2. In a bowl, combine the oats, almonds, coconut, sesame seeds and sunflower kernels. Add honey mixture, stirring until evenly coated. Spread onto 2 greased 15x10x1-in. baking pans.
3. Bake 20 minutes, stirring frequently. Stir in raisins. Bake until lightly toasted, about 10 minutes longer. Cool in pans on wire racks, stirring occasionally. Store in an airtight container.
½ cup: 366 cal., 18g fat (3g sat. fat), 0 chol., 51mg sod., 50g carb. (30g sugars, 5g fiber), 6g pro.

TEST KITCHEN TIP

For perfect granola clusters, stir occasionally when baking, and slowly fold over the granola to keep it in bigger chunks.

OPEN-FACED FRICO EGG SANDWICH

OPEN-FACED FRICO EGG SANDWICH

The layer of melted and crisped cheese—the frico—is what makes this creamy sandwich unique. If you like spicy aioli, add two large cloves of garlic.
—Julie Solis, Congers, NY

- -

Takes: 30 min. • **Makes:** 4 servings

- ¼ cup mayonnaise
- 1 Tbsp. olive oil
- 1 garlic clove, minced
- ⅛ tsp. salt
  Dash pepper
- ½ cup shredded Parmesan cheese
- 4 large eggs
- 4 slices Italian bread (1 in. thick), lightly toasted
- ½ cup sandwich giardiniera, drained and finely chopped
- 4 thin slices tomato
  Minced fresh parsley

1. For aioli, in a small bowl, combine the mayonnaise, olive oil, garlic, salt and pepper.
2. Sprinkle Parmesan into a large nonstick skillet; heat over medium heat. Cook just until melted, about 2 minutes. Break the eggs, 1 at a time, into a custard cup or saucer, then gently slide into pan over Parmesan. Immediately reduce heat to low. To prepare eggs sunny-side up, cover pan and cook until yolks thicken but are not hard, 4-5 minutes.
3. Spread the aioli over toasted bread. Top with giardiniera, tomato and egg. Sprinkle with parsley.
1 sandwich: 408 cal., 23g fat (5g sat. fat), 194mg chol., 1188mg sod., 33g carb. (3g sugars, 2g fiber), 16g pro.

PEAR QUINOA BREAKFAST BAKE

In an effort to eat healthier, I've been trying to incorporate more whole grains into our diet. My husband and I enjoy quinoa, so I created this breakfast bake for our Sunday brunch. The quinoa is a nice change of pace from oatmeal.
—Sue Gronholz, Beaver Dam, WI

- -

Prep: 15 min. • **Bake:** 55 min. + standing
Makes: 2 servings

- 1   cup water
- ¼   cup quinoa, rinsed
- ¼   cup mashed peeled ripe pear
- 1   Tbsp. honey
- ¼   tsp. ground cinnamon
- ¼   tsp. vanilla extract
      Dash ground ginger
      Dash ground nutmeg

TOPPING
- ¼   cup sliced almonds
- 1   Tbsp. brown sugar
- 1   Tbsp. butter, softened
      Plain Greek yogurt, optional

1. Preheat oven to 350°. In a small bowl, combine the first 8 ingredients; transfer to a greased 3-cup baking dish. Cover and bake for 50 minutes. In another small bowl, combine almonds, brown sugar and butter; sprinkle over quinoa mixture.
2. Bake, uncovered, until lightly browned, 5-10 minutes longer. Let stand 10 minutes before serving. If desired, serve with yogurt.
1 serving: 267 cal., 13g fat (4g sat. fat), 15mg chol., 49mg sod., 35g carb. (18g sugars, 4g fiber), 6g pro. **Diabetic exchanges:** 2½ fat, 2 starch.

BLUEBERRY SOUR CREAM PANCAKES

When our family of 10 goes out blueberry picking, we have a bounty of berries in no time. We especially enjoy them in these tender pancakes topped with a homemade sauce made of—you guessed it—more blueberries.
—Paula Hadley, Somerville, LA

- -

Prep: 20 min. • **Cook:** 5min./batch
Makes: about 20 pancakes (3½ cups topping)

- ½   cup sugar
- 2   Tbsp. cornstarch
- 1   cup cold water
- 4   cups fresh or frozen blueberries

PANCAKES
- 2   cups all-purpose flour
- ¼   cup sugar
- 4   tsp. baking powder
- ½   tsp. salt
- 2   large eggs, room temperature, lightly beaten
- 1½ cups 2% milk
- 1   cup sour cream
- ⅓   cup butter, melted
- 1   cup fresh or frozen blueberries

1. In a large saucepan, combine sugar and cornstarch. Stir in water until smooth. Add blueberries. Bring to a boil over medium heat; cook and stir for 2 minutes or until thickened. Remove from the heat; cover and keep warm.
2. For pancakes, in a large bowl, combine the flour, sugar, baking powder and salt. Combine the eggs, milk, sour cream and butter. Stir into dry ingredients just until moistened. Fold in blueberries.
3. Pour batter by ¼ cupfuls onto a greased hot griddle. Turn when bubbles form on top; cook until the second side is golden brown. Serve with blueberry topping.
Note: If using frozen blueberries, use without thawing to avoid discoloring the batter.
2 pancakes with ⅓ cup topping: 332 cal., 13g fat (8g sat. fat), 79mg chol., 387mg sod., 48g carb. (26g sugars, 3g fiber), 6g pro.

BLUEBERRY SOUR CREAM PANCAKES

PROSCIUTTO, APPLE & CHEESE STRATA

LIME COCONUT SMOOTHIE BOWL

This bowl is the most refreshing thing! One taste, and I know you'll agree.
—Madeline Butler, Denver, CO

Takes: 15 min. • **Makes:** 2 servings

- 1 medium banana, peeled and frozen
- 1 cup fresh baby spinach
- ½ cup ice cubes
- ½ cup cubed fresh pineapple
- ½ cup chopped peeled mango or frozen mango chunks
- ½ cup plain Greek yogurt
- ¼ cup sweetened shredded coconut
- 3 Tbsp. honey
- 2 tsp. grated lime zest
- 1 tsp. lime juice
- ½ tsp. vanilla extract
- 1 Tbsp. spreadable cream cheese, optional
  Optional: Lime wedges, sliced banana, sliced almonds, granola, dark chocolate chips and additional shredded coconut

Place the first 11 ingredients in a blender; if desired, add cream cheese. Cover and process until smooth. Pour into chilled bowls. Serve immediately, with optional toppings as desired.
1 cup: 325 cal., 10g fat (7g sat. fat), 15mg chol., 80mg sod., 60g carb. (51g sugars, 4g fiber), 4g pro.

PROSCIUTTO, APPLE & CHEESE STRATA

This is one of my favorite things to make for holidays! It's a wonderful savory dish that incorporates elements of the cuisine I grew up enjoying. Plus, you can prepare it the night before and just throw it in the oven in the morning.
—Danielle Pfanstiehl, Andover, CT

Prep: 20 min. + chilling
Bake: 50 min. + standing • **Makes:** 6 servings

- 6 large eggs
- 1¼ cups 2% milk
- ½ tsp. ground cinnamon
- ¼ tsp. salt
- ¼ tsp. pepper
- 7 cups day-old cubed bread (1-in. cubes)
- ½ lb. sliced prosciutto, cut into 2-in. strips
- 2 medium Pink Lady apples, peeled and thinly sliced
- 1 pkg. (10 oz.) frozen chopped spinach, thawed and squeezed dry
- 1 cup chopped Brie cheese
- 1 cup shredded white cheddar cheese, divided

1. In a large bowl, whisk the eggs, milk, cinnamon, salt and pepper until blended. Stir in bread, prosciutto, apples, spinach, Brie and ½ cup cheddar cheese. Transfer to a greased 13x9-in. baking dish; sprinkle with remaining ½ cup cheddar cheese. Refrigerate, covered, overnight.
2. Preheat oven to 350°. Remove strata from refrigerator while oven heats. Bake, covered, 30 minutes. Uncover and bake until a knife inserted near the center comes out clean, 20-25 minutes longer. Let stand 10 minutes before serving.
1 serving: 478 cal., 25g fat (12g sat. fat), 266mg chol., 1430mg sod., 31g carb. (10g sugars, 3g fiber), 33g pro.

**ROADSIDE DINER
CHEESEBURGER QUICHE**

HAM & CHEESE BREAKFAST STRUDELS

These get the morning off to a great start! Sometimes I assemble the strudels ahead and freeze them individually before baking.
—Jo Groth, Plainfield, IA

- -

Prep: 25 min. • **Bake:** 10 min.
Makes: 6 servings

- 3 Tbsp. butter, divided
- 2 Tbsp. all-purpose flour
- 1 cup whole milk
- ⅓ cup shredded Swiss cheese
- 2 Tbsp. grated Parmesan cheese
- ¼ tsp. salt
- 5 large eggs, lightly beaten
- ¼ lb. ground fully cooked ham (about ¾ cup)
- 6 sheets phyllo dough (14x9-in. size)
- ½ cup butter, melted
- ¼ cup dry bread crumbs

TOPPING

- 2 Tbsp. grated Parmesan cheese
- 2 Tbsp. minced fresh parsley

1. In a small saucepan, melt 2 Tbsp. butter. Stir in the flour until smooth; gradually add milk. Bring to a boil; cook and stir 2 minutes or until thickened. Stir in cheeses and salt.
2. In a large nonstick skillet, melt remaining 1 Tbsp. butter over medium heat. Add eggs to pan; cook and stir until almost set. Stir in ham and the cheese sauce; heat through. Remove from heat.
3. Preheat oven to 375°. Place 1 sheet of the phyllo dough on a work surface. (Keep the remaining phyllo covered with a damp towel to prevent it from drying out.) Brush with melted butter; sprinkle with 2 tsp. bread crumbs. Fold phyllo in half lengthwise; brush again with butter. Spoon ½ cup filling onto phyllo about 2 in. from a short side. Fold side and edges over filling and roll up. Brush with butter. Repeat with remaining phyllo, butter, bread crumbs and filling.
4. Place on a greased baking sheet; sprinkle each with 1 tsp. cheese and 1 tsp. parsley. Bake 10-15 minutes or until golden brown. Serve immediately.

1 strudel: 439 cal., 33g fat (18g sat. fat), 255mg chol., 754mg sod., 20g carb. (4g sugars, 1g fiber), 16g pro.

ROADSIDE DINER CHEESEBURGER QUICHE

Here is an unforgettable quiche that tastes just like its burger counterpart. Easy and appealing, it's perfect for guests and fun for the whole family.
—Barbara J. Miller, Oakdale, MN

- -

Prep: 20 min. • **Bake:** 50 min. + standing
Makes: 8 servings

- 1 sheet refrigerated pie crust
- ¾ lb. ground beef
- 2 plum tomatoes, seeded and chopped
- 1 medium onion, chopped
- ½ cup dill pickle relish
- ½ cup crumbled cooked bacon
- 5 large eggs
- 1 cup heavy whipping cream
- ½ cup 2% milk
- 2 tsp. prepared mustard
- 1 tsp. hot pepper sauce
- ½ tsp. salt
- ¼ tsp. pepper
- 1½ cups shredded cheddar cheese
- ½ cup shredded Parmesan cheese
  Optional: Mayonnaise, additional pickle relish, crumbled cooked bacon, chopped onion and chopped tomato

1. Preheat oven to 375°. Unroll crust into a 9-in. deep-dish pie plate; flute edges and set aside. In a large skillet, cook beef over medium heat until no longer pink, breaking it into crumbles; drain. Stir in the tomatoes, onion, relish and bacon. Transfer to the prepared crust.
2. In a large bowl, whisk the eggs, cream, milk, mustard, pepper sauce, salt and pepper. Pour over beef mixture. Sprinkle with cheeses.
3. Bake until a knife inserted in center comes out clean, 50-60 minutes. If necessary, cover the edges of quiche with foil during the last 15 minutes to prevent overbrowning. Let stand for 10 minutes before cutting. Garnish with optional ingredients as desired.

1 piece: 502 cal., 35g fat (19g sat. fat), 236mg chol., 954mg sod., 24g carb. (8g sugars, 1g fiber), 23g pro.

> "I was on the judging panel when this recipe wowed us all. I love that it actually tastes like a cheeseburger!"
>
> —CHRISTINE RUKAVENA, SENIOR EDITOR

HAM & CHEESE
BREAKFAST
STRUDELS

OVERNIGHT CHERRY DANISH

These rolls with their cherry-filled centers melt in your mouth and store well in the freezer. Just defrost and enjoy!
—Leann Sauder, Tremont, IL

Prep: 1½ hours + chilling • **Bake:** 15 min.
Makes: 3 dozen

  2   **pkg. (¼ oz. each) active dry yeast**
  ½   **cup warm 2% milk (110° to 115°)**
  6   **cups all-purpose flour**
  ⅓   **cup sugar**
  2   **tsp. salt**
  1   **cup cold butter, cubed**
1½   **cups warm half-and-half cream (70° to 80°)**
  6   **large egg yolks, room temperature**
  1   **can (21 oz.) cherry pie filling**
ICING
  3   **cups confectioners' sugar**
  2   **Tbsp. butter, softened**
  ¼   **tsp. vanilla extract**
      Dash salt
  4   **to 5 Tbsp. half-and-half cream**

1. In a small bowl, dissolve the yeast in warm milk. In a large bowl, combine flour, sugar and salt. Cut in butter until crumbly. Add the yeast mixture, cream and egg yolks; stir until mixture forms a soft dough (the dough will be sticky). Refrigerate, covered, overnight.

2. Punch down dough. Turn onto a lightly floured surface; divide into 4 portions. Roll each portion into an 18x4-in. rectangle; cut into 4x1-in. strips.

3. Place 2 strips side by side; twist together. Shape into a ring and pinch ends together. Place 2 in. apart on greased baking sheets. Repeat with remaining strips. Cover with kitchen towels; let rise in a warm place until doubled, about 45 minutes.

4. Preheat oven to 350°. Using the end of a wooden spoon handle, make a ½-in.-deep indentation in the center of each Danish. Fill each with about 1 Tbsp. pie filling. Bake 14-16 minutes or until lightly browned. Remove from pans to wire racks to cool.

5. For icing, in a bowl, beat confectioners' sugar, butter, vanilla, salt and enough cream to reach desired consistency. Drizzle over the Danish.

1 pastry: 218 cal., 8g fat (5g sat. fat), 55mg chol., 188mg sod., 33g carb. (16g sugars, 1g fiber), 3g pro.

BAKED PEACH PANCAKE

This dish makes for a dramatic presentation. I take it right from the oven to the table, fill it with peaches and sour cream and serve it with bacon or ham. Whenever I go home, my mom (the best cook I know) asks me to make this.
—Nancy Wilkinson, Princeton, NJ

Prep: 10 min. • **Bake:** 25 min.
Makes: 6 servings

  2   **cups fresh or frozen sliced peeled peaches**
  4   **tsp. sugar**
  1   **tsp. lemon juice**
  3   **large eggs, room temperature**
  ½   **cup all-purpose flour**
  ½   **cup 2% milk**
  ½   **tsp. salt**
  2   **Tbsp. butter**
      Ground nutmeg
      Sour cream, optional

1. In a small bowl, combine peaches, sugar and lemon juice. In a large bowl, beat eggs until fluffy. Add flour, milk and salt; beat until smooth.

2. Place butter in a 10-in. ovenproof skillet in a 400° oven for 3-5 minutes or until melted. Immediately pour batter into hot skillet. Bake for 20-25 minutes or until pancake has risen and puffed all over.

3. Fill with peach slices and sprinkle with nutmeg. Serve immediately, with sour cream if desired.

1 serving: 149 cal., 7g fat (4g sat. fat), 105mg chol., 272mg sod., 17g carb. (8g sugars, 1g fiber), 5g pro. **Diabetic exchanges:** 1 medium-fat meat, 1 fat, ½ starch, ½ fruit.

OVERNIGHT CHERRY DANISH

CHOCOLATE CHIP SCONES

These scones are delicious warm served with butter, when the chips are melted.
—Diane LaFurno, College Point, NY

Prep: 15 min. • **Bake:** 20 min.
Makes: 6 scones

- 1 **cup all-purpose flour**
- 3 **Tbsp. sugar**
- 1½ **tsp. baking powder**
   Dash salt
- 2 **Tbsp. cold butter**
- 1 **large egg**
- 3 **Tbsp. heavy whipping cream**
- ½ **cup miniature semisweet chocolate chips**

1. Preheat oven to 350°. In a bowl, combine the flour, sugar, baking powder and salt. Cut in butter until the mixture resembles coarse crumbs. In a small bowl, combine egg and cream; stir into dry ingredients just until moistened. Fold in chocolate chips.

2. Turn onto a floured surface; knead gently 6-8 times. Pat into a 6-in. circle. Cut dough into 6 wedges. Separate wedges and place 1 in. apart on an ungreased baking sheet. Bake for 18-20 minutes or until golden brown. Remove from pan to a wire rack. Serve warm.

1 scone: 241 cal., 12g fat (7g sat. fat), 56mg chol., 178mg sod., 32g carb. (15g sugars, 1g fiber), 4g pro.

"Scones are one of my favorite breakfast treats, so I'm thrilled with how quickly these come together."

—SAMMI DIVITO, ASSISTANT EDITOR

CHOCOLATE
CHIP SCONES

BACON & EGG GRAVY

My husband, Ron, created this wonderful breakfast gravy. It's home-style and old-fashioned. Sometimes we ladle the gravy over homemade biscuits. Served with fruit salad, it's a great breakfast.
—Terry Bray, Winter Haven, FL

- -

Takes: 20 min. • **Makes:** 2 servings

- 6 bacon strips, diced
- 5 Tbsp. all-purpose flour
- 1½ cups water
- 1 can (12 oz.) evaporated milk
- 3 hard-boiled large eggs, sliced
  Salt and pepper to taste
- 4 slices bread, toasted

In a skillet, cook bacon over medium heat until crisp; remove to paper towels. Stir flour into the drippings until blended; cook over medium heat until browned, stirring constantly. Gradually add water and milk. Bring to a boil; cook and stir for 2 minutes or until thickened. Add bacon, eggs, salt and pepper. Serve over toast.

1 serving: 934 cal., 61g fat (26g sat. fat), 424mg chol., 1030mg sod., 58g carb. (21g sugars, 2g fiber), 33g pro.

TEST KITCHEN TIP
You can also use this gravy to top waffles, potatoes or fried chicken.

PEPPERONI & SAUSAGE DEEP-DISH PIZZA QUICHE

Try this savory quiche for a hearty change-of-pace breakfast. Needless to say, it's wonderful for lunch and dinner, too.
—Donna Chesney, Naples, FL

- -

Prep: 20 min. • **Cook:** 40 min.
Makes: 8 servings

- 2 cups shredded mozzarella cheese, divided
- 1 cup shredded sharp cheddar cheese
- 4 large eggs
- 4 oz. cream cheese, softened
- ⅓ cup 2% milk
- ¼ cup grated Parmesan cheese
- ½ tsp. garlic powder
- ½ tsp. Italian seasoning
- ½ lb. bulk Italian sausage
- ½ cup pizza sauce
- 1 cup chopped pepperoni
  Fresh basil, optional

1. Preheat the oven to 350°. Sprinkle 1 cup mozzarella and cheddar cheese in a greased 13x9-in. baking dish. In a small bowl, beat eggs, cream cheese, milk, Parmesan, garlic powder and Italian seasoning; pour into dish. Bake for 30 minutes.

2. Meanwhile, in a small skillet, cook the sausage over medium heat until no longer pink, 5-6 minutes, breaking into crumbles; drain. Spread pizza sauce over egg mixture; top with sausage, pepperoni and remaining 1 cup mozzarella cheese. Bake until golden brown and bubbly, 10-15 minutes longer. Let stand 5 minutes before serving. Top with fresh basil if desired.

1 piece: 409 cal., 34g fat (16g sat. fat), 177mg chol., 971mg sod., 5g carb. (2g sugars, 0 fiber), 21g pro.

CINNAMON COFFEE CAKE

I love the excellent texture of this old-fashioned streusel-topped coffee cake. Always a crowd-pleaser, its lovely vanilla flavor enriched by sour cream may remind you of brunch at Grandma's!
—Eleanor Harris, Cape Coral, FL

Prep: 20 min. • **Bake:** 1 hour + cooling
Makes: 20 servings

- 1 cup butter, softened
- 2¾ cups sugar, divided
- 4 large eggs, room temperature
- 2 tsp. vanilla extract
- 3 cups all-purpose flour
- 1 tsp. baking soda
- 1 tsp. salt
- 2 cups sour cream
- 2 Tbsp. ground cinnamon
- ½ cup chopped walnuts

1. In a large bowl, cream the butter and 2 cups sugar until light fluffy, 5-7 minutes. Add 1 egg at a time, beating well after each addition. Beat in vanilla. Combine the flour, baking soda and salt; add alternately with sour cream, beating just enough after each addition to keep batter smooth.
2. Spoon a third of batter into a greased 10-in. tube pan. Combine cinnamon, nuts and remaining ¾ cup sugar; sprinkle a third of the mixture over batter in pan. Repeat the layers 2 more times. Bake at 350° for 60-65 minutes or until a toothpick inserted in center comes out clean. Cool in pan for 15 minutes before removing to a wire rack to cool completely.

1 piece: 340 cal., 16g fat (9g sat. fat), 83mg chol., 299mg sod., 44g carb. (28g sugars, 1g fiber), 5g pro.

CINNAMON
COFFEE CAKE

CHEESY EGG PUFFS

My father loves to entertain, and these buttery egg delights are one of his favorite items to serve at brunch. The leftovers are perfect to reheat in the microwave on busy mornings, so Dad always stashes a few aside for me to take home once the party is over.
—Amy Soto, Winfield, KS

Prep: 15 min. • **Bake:** 35 min.
Makes: 2½ dozen

- ½ lb. sliced fresh mushrooms
- 4 green onions, chopped
- 1 Tbsp. plus ½ cup butter, cubed, divided
- ½ cup all-purpose flour
- 1 tsp. baking powder
- ½ tsp. salt
- 10 large eggs, lightly beaten
- 4 cups shredded Monterey Jack cheese
- 2 cups 4% cottage cheese

1. In a skillet, saute the mushrooms and onions in 1 Tbsp. butter until tender. In a large bowl, combine the flour, baking powder and salt.
2. In another bowl, combine eggs and cheeses. Melt remaining ½ cup butter; add to the egg mixture. Stir into the dry ingredients along with mushroom mixture.
3. Fill greased muffin cups three-fourths full. Bake at 350° for 35-40 minutes or until a knife inserted in the center comes out clean. Carefully run the knife around edge of muffin cups before removing.

2 puffs: 275 cal., 21g fat (12g sat. fat), 194mg chol., 486mg sod., 6g carb. (2g sugars, 0 fiber), 16g pro.

SAUSAGE
BACON BITES

SAUSAGE BACON BITES

These tasty morsels are perfect with almost any egg dish or as finger foods that party guests can just pop into their mouths.
—Pat Waymire, Yellow Springs, OH

- -

Prep: 20 min. + chilling • **Bake:** 35 min.
Makes: about 3½ dozen

- ¾ lb. sliced bacon
- 2 pkg. (8 oz. each) frozen fully cooked breakfast sausage links, thawed
- ½ cup plus 2 Tbsp. packed brown sugar, divided

1. Cut bacon strips widthwise in half; cut sausage links in half. Wrap a piece of bacon around each piece of sausage. Place ½ cup brown sugar in a shallow bowl; roll sausages in sugar. Secure each with a toothpick. Place in a foil-lined 15x10x1-in. baking pan. Cover and refrigerate 4 hours or overnight.
2. Preheat oven to 350°. Sprinkle wrapped sausages with 1 Tbsp. brown sugar. Bake until bacon is crisp, 35-40 minutes, turning once. Sprinkle with remaining brown sugar.
1 piece: 51 cal., 4g fat (1g sat. fat), 6mg chol., 100mg sod., 4g carb. (4g sugars, 0 fiber), 2g pro.

MASHED POTATO DOUGHNUTS

As a special treat in the winter, my parents would make a double batch of these tasty doughnuts to welcome us six kids home from school. This recipe is from my great-aunt and has been handed down through the generations.
—Tammy Evans, Nepean, ON

- -

Prep: 20 min. + chilling • **Cook:** 25 min.
Makes: 2 dozen

- 1 pkg. (¼ oz.) active dry yeast
- 1 cup warm buttermilk (110° to 115°)
- 1½ cups warm mashed potatoes (without added milk and butter)
- 3 eggs
- ⅓ cup butter, melted
- 3 cups sugar, divided
- 4 tsp. baking powder
- 1½ tsp. baking soda
- 1 tsp. salt
- 1 tsp. ground nutmeg
- 6 cups all-purpose flour
  Oil for deep-fat frying
- ½ tsp. ground cinnamon

MASHED POTATO DOUGHNUTS

1. In a large bowl, dissolve yeast in warm buttermilk. Add potatoes, eggs and butter. Add 2 cups sugar, baking powder, baking soda, salt, nutmeg and 3 cups flour. Beat until smooth. Stir in enough remaining flour to form a soft dough. Do not knead. Cover and refrigerate for 2 hours.
2. Turn onto a floured surface; divide into fourths. Roll each portion to ½-in. thickness. Cut with a floured 3-in. doughnut cutter.
3. In an electric skillet or deep-fat fryer, heat oil to 375°. Fry doughnuts, a few at a time, until golden brown on both sides. Drain on paper towels. Combine remaining 1 cup sugar with cinnamon; roll doughnuts in cinnamon-sugar while warm.
1 doughnut: 295 cal., 8g fat (2g sat. fat), 30mg chol., 309mg sod., 52g carb. (26g sugars, 1g fiber), 5g pro.

"Mashed potatoes make the most delicious and moist doughnuts ever. These are so good!"

—SARAH TRAMONTE, ASSOCIATE CULINARY PRODUCER

SHEEPHERDER'S BREAKFAST

My sister-in-law always made this delicious dish when we were camping. Served with toast, juice, and milk or coffee, it's a sure hit with the breakfast crowd. One-dish casseroles like this were a big help while I was raising my nine children, and now I've passed this recipe on to them.
—Pauletta Bushnell, Albany, OR

Takes: 30 min. • **Makes:** 8 servings

- ¾ lb. bacon strips, finely chopped
- 1 medium onion, chopped
- 1 pkg. (30 oz.) frozen shredded hash brown potatoes, thawed
- 8 large eggs
- ½ tsp. salt
- ¼ tsp. pepper
- 1 cup shredded cheddar cheese

1. In a large skillet, cook bacon and onion over medium heat until the bacon is crisp. Drain, reserving ¼ cup drippings in pan.
2. Stir in hash browns. Cook, uncovered, over medium heat until bottom is golden brown, about 10 minutes. Turn potatoes. With the back of a spoon, make 8 evenly spaced wells in potato mixture. Break 1 egg into each well. Sprinkle with salt and pepper.
3. Cook, covered, on low until eggs are set and potatoes are tender, about 10 minutes. Sprinkle with cheese; let stand until cheese is melted.
1 serving: 354 cal., 22g fat (9g sat. fat), 222mg chol., 617mg sod., 22g carb. (2g sugars, 1g fiber), 17g pro.

CINNAMON BREAKFAST BITES

These early-morning treats with a sweet, crispy coating are baked in the oven instead of deep-fried.
—Ruth Hastings, Louisville, IL

Takes: 30 min.
Makes: 6 servings (1½ dozen)

- 1⅓ cups all-purpose flour
- 1 cup crisp rice cereal, coarsely crushed
- 2 Tbsp. plus ½ cup sugar, divided
- 1 Tbsp. baking powder
- ½ tsp. salt
- ¼ cup butter-flavored shortening
- ½ cup milk
- 1 tsp. ground cinnamon
- ¼ cup butter, melted

1. Preheat oven to 425°. In a large bowl, combine the flour, cereal, 2 Tbsp. sugar, baking powder and salt; cut in shortening until mixture resembles coarse crumbs. Stir in milk just until moistened. Shape into 1-in. balls.
2. In a shallow bowl, combine remaining ½ cup sugar with cinnamon. Dip balls in butter, then roll in cinnamon-sugar.
3. Arrange in a single layer in an 8-in. cast-iron skillet or round baking pan. Bake until browned and a toothpick inserted in centers comes out clean, 15-18 minutes.
3 balls: 352 cal., 17g fat (7g sat. fat), 23mg chol., 527mg sod., 47g carb. (22g sugars, 1g fiber), 4g pro.

MOM'S FLUFFY SCRAMBLED EGGS

I make these fluffy scrambled eggs when family comes by for breakfast or when I just want to do something extra special for myself in the morning. My favorite cheese for this recipe is freshly grated white cheddar, but whatever you have in the fridge works!
—Kailey Thompson, Palm Bay, FL

Takes: 30 min. • **Makes:** 8 servings

- 8 bacon strips
- 12 large eggs, beaten
- 6 Tbsp. butter, divided
- 2 cups shredded white cheddar cheese
- ¼ cup minced fresh parsley
- ¼ cup snipped fresh dill
- ½ tsp. salt
- ¼ tsp. pepper
- 8 bread slices, toasted
  Hot pepper sauce

1. In a large nonstick skillet, cook bacon over medium heat until crisp, stirring occasionally. Remove; drain on paper towels and break into 1-in. pieces. Discard drippings. In the same pan, cook and stir eggs over medium heat until almost set. Stir in 2 Tbsp. butter; cook and stir until no liquid egg remains. Add cheese, parsley, dill, salt, pepper and remaining 4 Tbsp. butter; stir gently until cheese is melted.
2. Top toast with eggs and bacon; drizzle with hot pepper sauce.
1 serving: 403 cal., 29g fat (14g sat. fat), 338mg chol., 772mg sod., 14g carb. (2g sugars, 1g fiber), 21g pro.

COCONUT TROPICAL FRUIT SALAD

Add a serving of fruit to breakfast with this delicious medley. Toasted coconut, mango and more bring the flavor of the tropics to any menu.
—Katie Covington, Blacksburg, SC

- -

Takes: 25 min. • **Makes:** 8 servings

- 1 medium mango, peeled and cubed
- 1 medium green apple, cubed
- 1 medium red apple, cubed
- 1 medium pear, cubed
- 1 medium navel orange, peeled and chopped
- 2 medium kiwifruit, peeled and chopped
- 10 seedless red grapes, halved
- 2 Tbsp. orange juice
- 1 firm medium banana, sliced
- ¼ cup sweetened shredded coconut, toasted

In a bowl, combine the first 7 ingredients. Drizzle with orange juice; toss gently to coat. Refrigerate until serving. Just before serving, fold in banana and sprinkle with coconut.
¾ cup: 101 cal., 1g fat (1g sat. fat), 0 chol., 10mg sod., 24g carb. (17g sugars, 3g fiber), 1g pro. **Diabetic exchanges:** 1½ fruit.

TEST KITCHEN TIP

Looking for a flavorful fruit salad that isn't loaded with added sugar? Look no further. Use unsweetened coconut for a no-sugar-added version.

SAUSAGE CHEESE BISCUITS

These biscuits are a brunch-time favorite. I love that they don't require any special or hard-to-find ingredients.
—Marlene Neideigh, Myrtle Point, OR

- -

Takes: 30 min. • **Makes:** 10 servings

- 1 tube (12 oz.) refrigerated buttermilk biscuits (10 count)
- 1 pkg. (8 oz.) frozen fully cooked breakfast sausage links, thawed
- 2 large eggs, beaten
- ½ cup shredded cheddar cheese
- 3 Tbsp. chopped green onions

1. Preheat oven to 400°. Roll out each biscuit into a 5-in. circle; place each in an ungreased muffin cup. Cut sausages into fourths; brown in a skillet. Drain. Divide sausages among cups.
2. In a small bowl, combine eggs, cheese and onions; spoon into cups. Bake until browned, 13-15 minutes.
1 biscuit: 227 cal., 16g fat (6g sat. fat), 57mg chol., 548mg sod., 16g carb. (3g sugars, 0 fiber), 8g pro.

AMISH BREAKFAST CASSEROLE

We enjoyed hearty breakfast casseroles during a nice visit to an Amish inn. When I asked for a recipe, one of the women told me the ingredients right off the top of her head. I modified it to create this version my family loves. Try breakfast sausage in place of bacon.
—Beth Notaro, Kokomo, IN

- -

Prep: 15 min. • **Bake:** 35 min. + standing
Makes: 12 servings

- 1 lb. sliced bacon, diced
- 1 medium sweet onion, chopped
- 6 large eggs, lightly beaten
- 4 cups frozen shredded hash brown potatoes, thawed
- 2 cups shredded cheddar cheese
- 1½ cups 4% cottage cheese
- 1¼ cups shredded Swiss cheese

1. Preheat oven to 350°. In a large skillet, cook bacon and onion over medium heat until bacon is crisp; drain. In a large bowl, combine remaining ingredients; stir in the bacon mixture. Transfer to a greased 13x9-in. baking dish.
2. Bake, uncovered, until a knife inserted in the center comes out clean, 35-40 minutes. Let stand 10 minutes before cutting.
1 serving: 273 cal., 18g fat (10g sat. fat), 153mg chol., 477mg sod., 8g carb. (3g sugars, 1g fiber), 18g pro.

WHOLE WHEAT ENGLISH
MUFFINS, PAGE 74

Breads, Rolls & More

From easy quick breads to bakery-quality yeast rolls and loaves, this chapter has recipes fit for every skill level.

MAPLE BUTTER TWISTS

My stepmother passed along the recipe for this delicious yeast coffee cake that's shaped into pretty rings. When I make it for friends, they always ask for seconds.
—June Gilliland, Hope, IN

- -

Prep: 35 min. + rising
Bake: 25 min. + cooling
Makes: 2 coffee cakes (16 pieces each)

3¼ to 3½ cups all-purpose flour
3 Tbsp. sugar
1½ tsp. salt
1 pkg. (¼ oz.) active dry yeast
¾ cup whole milk
¼ cup butter
2 large eggs, room temperature
FILLING
⅓ cup packed brown sugar
¼ cup sugar
3 Tbsp. butter, softened
3 Tbsp. maple syrup
4½ tsp. all-purpose flour
¾ tsp. ground cinnamon
¾ tsp. maple flavoring
⅓ cup chopped walnuts

GLAZE
½ cup confectioners' sugar
¼ tsp. maple flavoring
2 to 3 tsp. whole milk

1. In a large bowl, combine 1½ cups flour, sugar, salt and yeast. In a saucepan, heat milk and butter to 120°-130°. Add to dry ingredients; beat just until moistened. Add eggs; beat on medium for 2 minutes. Stir in enough remaining flour to form a firm dough. Turn onto a floured surface; knead until smooth and elastic, 5-7 minutes. Place in a greased bowl, turning once to grease top. Cover and let rise in a warm place until doubled, about 70 minutes.
2. In a small bowl, combine the first 7 filling ingredients; beat 2 minutes. Punch dough down; turn onto a lightly floured surface. Divide in half; roll each dough into a 16x8-in. rectangle. Spread filling to within ½ in. of edges. Sprinkle with nuts. Roll up jelly-roll style, starting with a long side.
3. With a sharp knife, cut each roll in half lengthwise. Open halves so cut side is up; gently twist ropes together. Transfer to 2 greased 9-in. round baking pans. Coil into a circle. Tuck ends under; pinch to seal. Cover; let rise in a warm place until doubled, about 45 minutes.
4. Bake at 350° for 25-30 minutes or until golden brown. Cool for 10 minutes; remove from the pans to wire racks. Combine the confectioners' sugar, maple flavoring and enough milk to reach desired consistency; drizzle over warm cakes.

1 piece: 119 cal., 4g fat (2g sat. fat), 21mg chol., 144mg sod., 19g carb. (8g sugars, 0 fiber), 2g pro.

PARMESAN-BACON BUBBLE BREAD

When I needed to put some leftover bread dough to good use, I started with a recipe I often use for bubble bread and substituted savory ingredients for the sweet.
—Lori McLain, Denton, TX

- -

Prep: 20 min. + rising • **Bake:** 20 min.
Makes: 16 servings

1 loaf frozen bread dough, thawed (16 oz.)
¼ cup butter, melted
¾ cup shredded Parmesan cheese
6 bacon strips, cooked and finely crumbled, divided
⅓ cup finely chopped green onions, divided
2 Tbsp. grated Parmesan cheese
2 Tbsp. salt-free herb seasoning blend
1½ tsp. sugar
Optional: Alfredo sauce or marinara sauce

1. Turn dough onto a lightly floured surface; divide and shape into 16 rolls. Place butter in a shallow bowl. In a large bowl, combine the shredded Parmesan, half the bacon, half the green onions, grated Parmesan, seasoning blend and sugar. Dip the dough pieces in melted butter, then toss with the cheese mixture to coat. Stack pieces in a greased 9-in. cast-iron skillet.
2. Cover with a kitchen towel; let rise in a warm place until almost doubled, about 45 minutes. Preheat oven to 350°. Bake until golden brown, 20-25 minutes. Top with remaining bacon and green onions. Serve warm and, if desired, with Alfredo or marinara sauce.

1 piece: 140 cal., 6g fat (3g sat. fat), 14mg chol., 311mg sod., 14g carb. (2g sugars, 1g fiber), 6g pro.

MAPLE BUTTER TWISTS

PARMESAN-BACON
BUBBLE BREAD

HOMEMADE
BUTTERMILK BISCUITS

HOMEMADE BUTTERMILK BISCUITS

The recipe for these four-ingredient biscuits has been handed down for many generations in my family.
—Fran Thompson, Tarboro, NC

- -

Takes: 30 min. • **Makes:** 8 biscuits

½ cup cold butter, cubed
2 cups self-rising flour
¾ cup buttermilk
Melted butter

1. In a large bowl, cut butter into flour until mixture resembles coarse crumbs. Stir in buttermilk just until moistened. Turn onto a lightly floured surface; knead 3-4 times. Pat or lightly roll to ¾-in. thickness. Cut with a floured 2½-in. biscuit cutter.
2. Place on a greased baking sheet. Bake at 425° until golden brown, 11-13 minutes. Brush tops with butter. Serve warm.
Note: As a substitute for each cup of self-rising flour, place 1½ tsp. baking powder and ½ tsp. salt in a measuring cup. Add all-purpose flour to measure 1 cup.
1 biscuit: 222 cal., 12g fat (7g sat. fat), 31mg chol., 508mg sod., 24g carb. (1g sugars, 1g fiber), 4g pro.

ASK SARAH

WHAT IS SELF-RISING FLOUR?

Self-rising flour combines all-purpose flour, salt and a leavening agent such as baking powder. It can not be substituted for all-purpose flour.

HEALTHY AVOCADO PINEAPPLE MUFFINS

These healthy muffins are a real treat for breakfast, luncheon or a coffee break. The avocado adds an extra-special touch. They are delicious served warm from the oven and also freeze well.
—Joan Hallford, North Richland Hills, TX

Prep: 20 min. • **Bake:** 20 min.
Makes: 1 dozen

- ⅔ cup cubed ripe avocado
- 3 large eggs, room temperature
- ¼ cup honey
- 2 Tbsp. canola oil
- 1 can (8 oz.) unsweetened crushed pineapple, undrained
- 2 cups all-purpose flour
- ½ tsp. salt
- ½ tsp. baking powder
- ½ tsp. baking soda
- ½ tsp. ground cinnamon
- ¾ cup toasted chopped pecans, divided

1. Preheat oven to 375°. In a large bowl, beat avocado until only small lumps remain. Add the eggs, honey and oil; beat until blended. Stir in the pineapple. In another bowl, whisk flour, salt, baking powder, baking soda and cinnamon. Add to avocado mixture; stir just until moistened. Fold in ½ cup pecans.
2. Fill 12 greased or foil-lined muffin cups; sprinkle tops with remaining ¼ cup pecans. Bake until a toothpick inserted in center comes out clean, 20-25 minutes. Cool for 5 minutes before removing from pan to a wire rack. Serve warm.
1 muffin: 208 cal., 10g fat (1g sat. fat), 47mg chol., 190mg sod., 26g carb. (9g sugars, 2g fiber), 5g pro. **Diabetic exchanges:** 2 fat, 1½ starch.

ITALIAN CHEESE BREAD

People are astounded to learn that I make this yummy bread from scratch in less than an hour. With this recipe from my brother-in-law, hot homemade bread is an easy alternative to garlic toast. I sometimes serve it as a snack or appetizer.
—Sandra Wingert, Star City, SK

Prep: 20 min. + rising • **Bake:** 15 min.
Makes: 1 loaf (16 pieces)

- 2½ cups all-purpose flour
- 1 Tbsp. quick-rise yeast
- 1 tsp. sugar
- 1 tsp. salt
- 1 cup warm water (120° to 130°)
- 1 Tbsp. canola oil

TOPPING
- ¼ to ⅓ cup prepared Italian salad dressing
- ¼ tsp. salt
- ¼ tsp. garlic powder
- ¼ tsp. dried oregano
- ¼ tsp. dried thyme
- Dash pepper
- 1 Tbsp. grated Parmesan cheese
- ½ cup shredded part-skim mozzarella cheese

1. In a large bowl, combine 2 cups flour, yeast, sugar and salt. Beat in water and oil until blended. Stir in enough remaining flour to form a soft dough.
2. Turn onto a floured surface; knead until smooth and elastic, 1-2 minutes. Place in a greased bowl, turning once to grease the top. Cover and let rise in a warm place for 20 minutes. Preheat oven to 450°.
3. Punch dough down; place on a greased 12-in. pizza pan and pat into a 12-in. circle. Brush with salad dressing. Combine the seasonings; sprinkle over the top. Sprinkle with cheeses.
4. Bake until golden brown, 15 minutes. Serve warm.
1 serving: 171 cal., 5g fat (1g sat. fat), 5mg chol., 428mg sod., 25g carb. (1g sugars, 1g fiber), 5g pro.

ITALIAN CHEESE BREAD

PRALINE-TOPPED
APPLE BREAD

PRALINE-TOPPED APPLE BREAD

Apples and candied pecans make this bread so much better than the usual coffee cakes you see at brunches.
—Sonja Blow, Nixa, MO

- -

Prep: 30 min. • **Bake:** 50 min. + cooling
Makes: 1 loaf (16 pieces)

- 2 cups all-purpose flour
- 2 tsp. baking powder
- ½ tsp. baking soda
- ½ tsp. salt
- 1 cup sugar
- 1 cup sour cream
- 2 large eggs, room temperature
- 3 tsp. vanilla extract
- 1½ cups chopped peeled Granny Smith apples
- 1¼ cups chopped pecans, toasted, divided
- ½ cup butter, cubed
- ½ cup packed brown sugar

1. Preheat oven to 350°. In a large bowl, mix flour, baking powder, baking soda and salt. In another bowl, beat sugar, sour cream, eggs and vanilla until well blended. Stir into flour mixture just until moistened. Fold in apples and 1 cup pecans.

2. Transfer to a greased 9x5-in. loaf pan. Bake until a toothpick inserted in center comes out clean, 50-55 minutes. Cool in pan 10 minutes. Remove to a wire rack to cool completely.

3. In a small saucepan, combine the butter and brown sugar. Bring to a boil, stirring constantly to dissolve sugar; boil 1 minute. Working quickly, pour over bread. Sprinkle with remaining pecans; let stand until set.

Note: To toast nuts, bake in a shallow pan in a 350° oven for 5-10 minutes or cook in a skillet over low heat until lightly browned, stirring occasionally.

1 piece: 288 cal., 16g fat (6g sat. fat), 42mg chol., 235mg sod., 34g carb. (21g sugars, 1g fiber), 4g pro.

EASY YEAST ROLLS

EASY YEAST ROLLS

These tender dinner rolls always disappear in no time. If you've never made homemade yeast bread, this simple dough is the perfect place to start. You can easily cut the recipe in half if you like.
—Wilma Harter, Witten, SD

- -

Prep: 45 min. + rising
Bake: 15 min.
Makes: 4 dozen

- 2 pkg. (¼ oz. each) active dry yeast
- 2 cups warm water (110° to 115°)
- ½ cup sugar
- 1 large egg, room temperature
- ¼ cup canola oil
- 2 tsp. salt
- 6 to 6½ cups all-purpose flour

1. In a bowl, dissolve yeast in warm water. In a large bowl, combine the sugar, egg, oil, salt, yeast mixture and 4 cups flour; beat on medium speed until smooth. Stir in enough remaining flour to form a stiff dough.

2. Turn dough onto a floured surface; knead until smooth and elastic, 6-8 minutes. Place in a greased bowl, turning once to grease the top. Cover and let rise in a warm place until doubled, about 1 hour.

3. Punch down dough. Turn onto a lightly floured surface; divide into 4 portions. Divide and shape each portion into 12 balls. Place 2 in. apart on greased baking sheets. Cover; let rise in a warm place until doubled, about 30 minutes. Preheat oven to 350°.

4. Bake 15-20 minutes or until golden brown. Remove from pans to wire racks.

1 roll: 78 cal., 1g fat (0 sat. fat), 4mg chol., 100mg sod., 14g carb. (2g sugars, 0 fiber), 2g pro.

TEST KITCHEN TIP

To make these in advance, wrap and freeze cooled baked rolls. Defrost at room temperature, wrap in foil and gently warm at 250° before serving.

EASY PEASY BISCUITS

I love that I can make these biscuits and have enough left over to freeze for another meal. They are wonderful served warm with homemade peach preserves.
—Amanda West, Shelbyville, TN

Prep: 25 min. • **Bake:** 10 min.
Makes: 2 dozen

4	cups all-purpose flour
4	Tbsp. baking powder
1	Tbsp. sugar
1	Tbsp. ground flaxseed
1	tsp. sea salt
1	cup solid coconut oil
1½	cups 2% milk

1. Preheat oven to 450°. In a large bowl, whisk the flour, baking powder, sugar, flaxseed and salt. Add coconut oil and cut in with a pastry blender until mixture resembles coarse crumbs. Add milk; stir just until moistened.

2. Turn onto a lightly floured surface; knead gently 8-10 times. Pat or roll dough into a rectangle ½ in. thick; fold dough into thirds (as you would a letter). Pat or roll dough again into a rectangle ½ in. thick; cut with a pizza cutter or knife into 24 biscuits, each about 2½ in. square. Place 1½ in. apart on ungreased baking sheets. Bake until light brown, 8-10 minutes. Serve warm.

Freeze option: Freeze cut biscuit dough on waxed paper-lined baking sheets until firm. Transfer to airtight containers; return to freezer. To use, bake biscuits in a preheated 350° oven until light brown, 15-20 minutes.

1 biscuit: 167 cal., 10g fat (8g sat. fat), 1mg chol., 328mg sod., 17g carb. (1g sugars, 1g fiber), 3g pro.

CALZONE ROLLS

CALZONE ROLLS

Big pizza flavor comes through in these rolls. My recipe makes two pans because you'll need 'em!
—Barb Downie, Peterborough, ON

Prep: 20 min. + rising • **Bake:** 20 min.
Makes: 2 dozen

2¼	tsp. active dry yeast
1⅔	cups water (110° to 115°)
2	Tbsp. nonfat dry milk powder
2	Tbsp. sugar
2	Tbsp. shortening
1¼	tsp. salt
4½	cups all-purpose flour
½	cup chopped onion
½	cup sliced fresh mushrooms
½	cup chopped green pepper
½	cup chopped sweet red pepper
1	Tbsp. olive oil
⅓	cup pizza sauce
½	cup diced pepperoni
1	cup shredded pizza cheese blend
¼	cup chopped ripe olives
2	Tbsp. grated Parmesan cheese

1. In a large bowl, dissolve the yeast in warm water. Add milk powder, sugar, shortening, salt and 3 cups flour. Beat on medium speed until smooth. Stir in enough remaining flour to form a soft dough. Turn dough onto a floured surface; knead until a smooth and elastic, 6-8 minutes. Place in a greased bowl, turning once to grease the top. Cover and let rise in a warm place until doubled, about 1 hour.

2. Meanwhile, in a small skillet, saute the onion, mushrooms and peppers in oil until tender; cool.

3. Punch the dough down. Turn onto a lightly floured surface and divide in half; let rest for 5 minutes. Roll each portion into a 16x10-in. rectangle; spread with pizza sauce. Top with onion mixture, pepperoni, pizza cheese and olives. Roll up each rectangle jelly-roll style, starting with a long side; pinch seam to seal. Cut each into 12 slices (discard end pieces).

4. Place slices cut side down in 2 greased 10-in. cast-iron skillets or 9-in. round baking pans. Sprinkle with Parmesan cheese. Cover and let rise until doubled, about 30 minutes.

5. Bake at 375° until golden, 20-30 minutes. Serve warm.

1 roll: 144 cal., 5g fat (2g sat. fat), 7mg chol., 244mg sod., 21g carb. (2g sugars, 1g fiber), 5g pro.

CHIMICHURRI MONKEY BREAD

The herby goodness of my favorite sauce shines in this nostalgic bread recipe that comes together quickly thanks to refrigerated biscuits. Serve warm as an appetizer with marinara for dipping or as a side to an Italian entree.
—Eden Dranger, Los Angeles, CA

Prep: 20 min. • **Bake:** 20 min.
Makes: 12 servings

- ¼ cup minced fresh parsley
- ¼ cup olive oil
- 2 Tbsp. minced fresh oregano
- 1 Tbsp. white wine vinegar
- 2 garlic cloves, minced
- ¾ tsp. kosher salt
- ¼ tsp. ground cumin
- ¼ tsp. pepper
- ⅛ tsp. crushed red pepper flakes
- 2 tubes (12 oz. each) refrigerated buttermilk biscuits

1. In a shallow bowl, combine the first 9 ingredients. Cut each biscuit in half and shape into a ball. Roll in herb mixture.
2. Place biscuit pieces in a greased 10-in. fluted tube pan. Bake at 375° until golden brown, 18-22 minutes. Cool 10 minutes before inverting onto a serving plate.
1 serving: 209 cal., 11g fat (3g sat. fat), 0 chol., 588mg sod., 25g carb. (3g sugars, 0 fiber), 3g pro..

> "Chimichurri, one of my favorite flavors, translates perfectly into a monkey bread. Watch it disappear at your next party!"
> —SARAH FARMER, EXECUTIVE CULINARY DIRECTOR

OLD-FASHIONED STEAMED MOLASSES BREAD

When I was growing up, the smell of this bread greeted me as I walked in the door from school. I thought everyone baked bread in a slow cooker. My grandmother, my mother and I (and now my daughters) all bake this. It's comfort food at its best!
—Bonnie Geavaras-Bootz, Chandler, AZ

Prep: 20 min. • **Cook:** 3 hours + cooling
Makes: 16 servings

- 2 cups All-Bran
- 1 cup all-purpose flour
- 1 cup whole wheat flour
- 1 cup dried cranberries
- 1½ tsp. baking powder
- 1 tsp. baking soda
- 1 tsp. salt
- ½ tsp. ground cinnamon
- 1 large egg, room temperature
- 1¾ cups buttermilk
- ½ cup molasses
- 2 Tbsp. honey

1. Layer two 24-in. pieces of foil. Starting with a long side, roll up the foil to make a 1-in.-wide strip; shape into a coil. Place on the bottom of a 5-qt. slow cooker to make a rack.
2. Combine the bran, flours, cranberries, baking powder, baking soda, salt and cinnamon. In another bowl, beat egg, buttermilk, molasses and honey. Stir into flour mixture just until blended (do not overbeat). Pour into a greased and floured 2-qt. baking dish. Tightly cover with lightly greased foil. Place in prepared slow cooker. Cook, covered, on high about 3 hours, until a thermometer reads 190-200°.
3. Remove the dish to a wire rack; cool for 10 minutes before inverting loaf onto the rack. Serve warm or cold.
Note: As a substitute for each cup of buttermilk, use 1 Tbsp. white vinegar or lemon juice plus enough milk to measure 1 cup. Stir; let stand 5 minutes.
1 wedge: 157 cal., 1g fat (0 sat. fat), 13mg chol., 351mg sod., 36g carb. (19g sugars, 4g fiber), 4g pro.

CHIMICHURRI MONKEY BREAD

PUMPKIN-FILLED
CRESCENT ROLLS

WHOLE WHEAT
ENGLISH MUFFINS

Whole wheat flour gives these muffins a
hearty taste, but they have a light texture.
They keep well in the refrigerator or freezer.
—Mildred Decker, Sandy, OR

Prep: 20 min. + rising
Bake: 20 min. + cooling
Makes: 10 servings

- 1 pkg. (¼ oz.) active dry yeast
- 3 Tbsp. sugar, divided
- ¼ cup warm water (110° to 115°)
- 1 cup warm 2% milk (110° to 115°)
- 3 Tbsp. butter, softened
- ¾ tsp. salt
- 1 large egg, room temperature
- 1 cup whole wheat flour
- 3 cups all-purpose flour, divided

1. In a large bowl, dissolve yeast and 1 Tbsp.
sugar in warm water; let stand for 5 minutes.
Add the milk, butter, salt, egg, whole wheat
flour, 1 cup all-purpose flour and remaining
2 Tbsp. sugar; beat until smooth. Stir in
enough remaining all-purpose flour to
form a soft dough.
2. Turn onto a lightly floured surface; knead
until smooth and elastic, 6-8 minutes. Place
in a grease bowl, turning once to grease top.
Cover; let rise in a warm place until doubled,
about 1 hour. Preheat oven to 375°.
3. Punch dough down. Turn onto a lightly
floured surface; roll out to ½-in. thickness.
Cover and let rest for 5 minutes. Cut into
4-in. circles. Place 2 in. apart on greased
baking sheets.
4. Bake 8-10 minutes or until bottoms are
browned. Turn muffins over; bake until
second side is browned, about 7 minutes
longer. Remove from pan to a wire rack to
cool. Store in refrigerator. To serve, split
with a fork and toast.
1 serving: 246 cal., 5g fat (3g sat. fat), 34mg
chol., 232mg sod., 43g carb. (6g sugars, 3g
fiber), 7g pro.

TEST KITCHEN TIP

The best way to slice an English
muffin is to poke a few holes
around the edge and open it
with a fork instead of a knife.
This allows the nooks and
crannies to stay intact.

PUMPKIN-FILLED
CRESCENT ROLLS

This recipe, which must date back to 1900
or earlier, derived from my grandmother,
who didn't use traditional measuring cups.
Other fillings that work well are cranberry,
peanut butter or lemon.
—Gary Wanosky, North Ridgeville, OH

Prep: 40 min. + chilling
Bake: 15 min./batch
Makes: 3 dozen

- 4 tsp. active dry yeast
- ¼ cup warm 2% milk (110° to 115°)
- 4 cups all-purpose flour
- ¼ cup sugar
- 1 tsp. salt
- 1 cup butter, cubed
- ½ cup shortening
- 1 cup sour cream
- 4 large egg yolks, room temperature
- 2 tsp. grated lemon zest

FILLING
- ¾ cup canned pumpkin
- ⅓ cup sugar
- 1½ tsp. pumpkin pie spice

1. In a small bowl, dissolve yeast in milk.
In a large bowl, combine 3 cups flour, sugar
and salt; cut in butter and shortening until
crumbly. Add the sour cream, egg yolks,
lemon zest and yeast mixture; mix well.
Stir in enough remaining flour to form a
soft dough.
2. Turn onto a floured surface; knead until
smooth and elastic, 6-8 minutes. Place in a
greased bowl, turning once to grease top.
Cover and refrigerate overnight.
3. Let dough stand at room temperature
for 1 hour. Punch dough down; turn onto
a lightly floured surface. Divide into thirds.
Roll each into a 12-in. circle; cut each circle
into 12 wedges.
4. Combine the filling ingredients; spread a
rounded tsp. of filling over each wedge. Roll
up wedges from wide ends and place point
side down 2 in. apart on greased baking
sheets. Curve ends to form crescents. Cover
and let rise in a warm place for 30 minutes.
5. Preheat oven to 350°. Bake crescents until
golden brown, 13-18 minutes. Remove from
pans to wire racks.
1 roll: 156 cal., 10g fat (5g sat. fat), 41mg
chol., 106mg sod., 15g carb. (4g sugars, 1g
fiber), 2g pro.

**WHOLE WHEAT
ENGLISH MUFFINS**

LEFSE

Lefse is a Scandinavian flatbread made with potatoes. We traditionally make these delicious breads during the holiday season. Serve them topped with butter and a sprinkle of sugar or jelly, then roll them up. It's hard to eat just one.
—Donna Goutermont, Sequim, WA

- -

Prep: 1 hour • **Cook:** 5 min./batch
Makes: 12 servings

- 2 **lbs. potatoes, peeled and cubed**
- ⅓ **cup heavy whipping cream, warmed**
- ¼ **cup shortening or butter, softened**
- 1 **tsp. sugar**
- ¾ **tsp. salt**
- 2 **cups all-purpose flour**

1. Place potatoes in a large saucepan; add water to cover. Bring to a boil. Reduce heat; simmer, covered, until tender, 10-12 minutes. Drain and press through a potato ricer or strainer into a large bowl. Stir in the cream, shortening, sugar and salt. Cool completely.
2. Preheat griddle over medium-high heat. Stir flour into potato mixture. Turn onto a lightly floured surface; knead 6-8 times or until smooth and combined. Divide into 12 portions. Roll each portion between 2 sheets of waxed paper into an 8-in. circle.
3. Place dough on griddle; cook until lightly browned, 2-3 minutes on each side. Remove to a platter; cover loosely with kitchen towel. Repeat with remaining portions. When cool, stack between pieces of waxed paper or paper towels; store in an airtight container.
1 piece: 180 cal., 7g fat (3g sat. fat), 8mg chol., 151mg sod., 27g carb. (1g sugars, 1g fiber), 3g pro.

"My grandma always made lefse when I was growing up, so this is a nostalgic recipe for me. I love this version."

—SHANNON NORRIS, SENIOR FOOD STYLIST

LEFSE

GREEK BREADSTICKS

Get ready for rave reviews with these crispy Greek-inspired appetizers. They're best served hot and fresh from the oven with your favorite tzatziki sauce.
—Jane Whittaker, Pensacola, FL

- -

Prep: 20 min. • **Bake:** 15 min.
Makes: 32 breadsticks

- ¼ cup marinated quartered artichoke hearts, drained
- 2 Tbsp. pitted Greek olives
- 1 pkg. (17.3 oz.) frozen puff pastry, thawed
- 1 carton (6½ oz.) spreadable spinach and artichoke cream cheese
- 2 Tbsp. grated Parmesan cheese
- 1 large egg
- 1 Tbsp. water
- 2 tsp. sesame seeds
  Refrigerated tzatziki sauce, optional

1. Place artichokes and olives in a food processor; cover and pulse until finely chopped. Unfold 1 pastry sheet on lightly floured surface; spread half of the cream cheese over half of pastry. Top with half of the artichoke mixture. Sprinkle with half of the Parmesan cheese. Fold plain half over filling; press gently to seal.
2. Repeat with remaining pastry, cream cheese, artichoke mixture and Parmesan cheese. Whisk egg and water; brush over tops. Sprinkle with sesame seeds. Cut each rectangle into sixteen ¾-in.-wide strips. Twist strips several times; place 2 in. apart on greased baking sheets.
3. Bake at 400° for 12-14 minutes or until golden brown. Serve warm with tzatziki sauce if desired.
1 breadstick: 101 cal., 6g fat (2g sat. fat), 11mg chol., 104mg sod., 9g carb. (0 sugars, 1g fiber), 2g pro.

CHOCOLATE CHAI MINI LOAVES

This bread is irresistible! A friend gets mad when I make it because I give her a loaf, and she can't help but eat the whole thing!
—Lisa Christensen, Poplar Grove, IL

- -

Prep: 25 min. • **Bake:** 35 min. + cooling
Makes: 3 mini loaves (6 pieces each)

- 2 oz. semisweet chocolate, chopped
- ½ cup water
- ½ cup butter, softened
- 1 cup packed brown sugar
- 2 large eggs, room temperature
- 1 tsp. vanilla extract
- 1½ cups all-purpose flour
- 3 Tbsp. chai tea latte mix
- 1 tsp. baking soda
- ½ tsp. salt
- ½ cup sour cream

FROSTING
- 1 cup confectioners' sugar
- 1 Tbsp. butter, softened
- 1 Tbsp. chai tea latte mix
- ½ tsp. vanilla extract
- 4 to 5 tsp. whole milk

1. In a microwave, melt chocolate with the water; stir until smooth. Cool slightly. In a large bowl, cream butter and brown sugar until light and fluffy, 5-7 minutes. Add 1 egg at a time, beating well after each addition. Beat in vanilla, then chocolate mixture.
2. Combine the flour, latte mix, baking soda and salt; add to creamed mixture alternately with sour cream.
3. Transfer to 3 greased 5¾x3x2-in. loaf pans. Bake at 350° 35-40 minutes or until a toothpick inserted in the center comes out clean. Cool for 10 minutes before removing from pans to a wire rack to cool completely.
4. For frosting, combine the confectioners' sugar, butter, latte mix, vanilla and enough milk to achieve desired consistency. Frost tops of loaves.
1 piece: 208 cal., 9g fat (5g sat. fat), 43mg chol., 206mg sod., 30g carb. (21g sugars, 1g fiber), 3g pro.

TEST KITCHEN TIP
Skip the frosting and dust the top of these loaves with confectioners' sugar to cut calories by almost 20%.

CHOCOLATE CHAI MINI LOAVES

GARLIC ROSEMARY
PULL-APART BREAD

GARLIC ROSEMARY PULL-APART BREAD

Eat this bread by itself, dipped in marinara or as part of a meal. For a different flavor, add sun-dried tomatoes, pesto, or an onion soup mix packet instead of the rosemary-garlic combo.
—Christina Trikoris, Clarksville, TN

- -

Prep: 25 min. + rising
Bake: 55 min. + cooling • **Makes:** 16 servings

- 3 tsp. active dry yeast
- 1 tsp. salt
- 5¼ to 6 cups all-purpose flour
- 1 cup water
- 1 cup butter, cubed
- ½ cup 2% milk
- 2 large eggs, room temperature

FLAVORING

- ½ cup butter, melted
- 6 garlic cloves, minced
- 2 Tbsp. minced fresh rosemary or 2 tsp. dried rosemary, crushed
- 1 tsp. salt
- 1 cup grated Parmesan cheese

1. In a large bowl, mix yeast, salt and 2 cups flour. In a small saucepan, heat water, cubed butter and milk to 120°-130°. Add to the dry ingredients; beat on medium speed 2 minutes. Add the eggs; beat on high for 2 minutes. Stir in enough remaining flour to form a soft dough (dough will be sticky).
2. Turn dough onto a floured surface; knead until smooth and elastic, 6-8 minutes. Place in a greased bowl, turning once to grease the top. Cover and let rise in a warm place until doubled, about 1 hour.
3. Punch dough down. Turn onto a lightly floured surface; shape into 1½-in. balls. Combine melted butter, garlic, rosemary and salt. Dip 10 dough balls into butter mixture. Place in a greased 10-in. fluted tube pan; sprinkle with a scant ¼ cup Parmesan cheese. Repeat with remaining balls and Parmesan cheese. Drizzle with any remaining butter mixture. Cover and let rise until doubled, about 45 minutes. Preheat oven to 350°.
4. Bake until golden brown, 55-70 minutes or until a thermometer inserted into bread reads 200°. Cool for 10 minutes before inverting onto a serving plate. Serve warm.
1 serving: 341 cal., 20g fat (12g sat. fat), 74mg chol., 536mg sod., 33g carb. (1g sugars, 1g fiber), 7g pro.

CRANBERRY EGGNOG BRAID

CRANBERRY EGGNOG BRAID

Whether at Thanksgiving, Christmas or New Year's, this is a good party. You can't beat it as a gift, either.
—Mary Lindow, Florence, WI

- -

Prep: 25 min. + rising
Bake: 25 min. + cooling
Makes: 1 loaf (12 pieces)

- 3 to 3½ cups all-purpose flour, divided
- ¼ cup sugar
- ½ tsp. salt
- 1 pkg. (¼ oz.) active dry yeast
- ½ tsp. ground nutmeg
- 1¼ cups eggnog
- ¼ cup butter
- ½ cup dried cranberries

GLAZE

- 1 cup confectioners' sugar
- 1 to 2 Tbsp. eggnog
- ¼ tsp. vanilla extract
  Dash nutmeg

1. In a large bowl, combine 1½ cups of flour, sugar, salt, yeast and nutmeg; set aside. In a saucepan, heat the eggnog and butter to 120°-130° (butter does not need to melt); add to flour mixture. Beat on low until moistened; beat on medium for 3 minutes.
2. Stir in cranberries and enough remaining flour to make a soft dough. Turn onto a floured surface; knead until smooth and elastic, 6-8 minutes. Place in a greased bowl, turning once to grease top. Cover and let rise in a warm place until doubled, about 1 hour.
3. Punch dough down; divide into thirds. Shape each third into a 16-in. rope. Braid ropes on a greased baking sheet; seal the ends. Cover and let rise until nearly doubled, about 30 minutes.
4. Bake at 350° for 25-30 minutes or until golden. Immediately remove from pan to a wire rack to cool completely. Combine the first 3 glaze ingredients; drizzle over braid. Dust with nutmeg.
1 piece: 257 cal., 6g fat (4g sat. fat), 27mg chol., 153mg sod., 46g carb. (21g sugars, 1g fiber), 5g pro.

ALMOND & CRANBERRY COCONUT BREAD

Here's an all-around fantastic bread for any season. The red bursts of cranberry lend every slice extra appeal.
—Rosemary Johnson, Irondale, AL

Prep: 20 min. • **Bake:** 1 hour + cooling
Makes: 2 loaves (16 pieces each)

- 2 cups sweetened shredded coconut
- 1 cup slivered almonds
- 1 cup butter, softened
- 1 cup sugar
- 4 large eggs, room temperature
- 1 cup vanilla yogurt
- 1 tsp. almond extract
- 4½ cups all-purpose flour
- 3 tsp. baking powder
- ½ tsp. salt
- ½ tsp. baking soda
- 1 can (15 oz.) cream of coconut
- 1 cup dried cranberries

1. Place the coconut and almonds in an ungreased 15x10x1-in. pan. Bake at 350° for 10-15 minutes or until lightly toasted, stirring occasionally. Cool.
2. In a large bowl, cream butter and sugar until light and fluffy. Add the eggs, 1 at a time, beating well after each addition. Beat in yogurt and extract until blended. Combine flour, baking powder, salt and baking soda. Add to the creamed mixture alternately with cream of coconut, beating well after each addition. Fold in the cranberries, coconut and almonds.
3. Transfer to 2 greased and floured 9x5-in. loaf pans. Bake at 350° until a toothpick inserted in center comes out clean, 60-70 minutes. Cool 10 minutes before removing from pans to wire racks to cool completely.
1 piece: 273 cal., 13g fat (8g sat. fat), 42mg chol., 176mg sod., 36g carb. (21g sugars, 1g fiber), 4g pro.

BACON-PEANUT BUTTER CORNBREAD MUFFINS

BACON-PEANUT BUTTER CORNBREAD MUFFINS

My family just can't get enough bacon and peanut butter, so I created these quick and easy cornbread muffins using ingredients I regularly keep stocked in my pantry and fridge. The streusel topping adds a delicious sweet-salty crunch! No peanut butter baking chips on hand? For a different flavor twist, use chocolate chips, then drizzle the warm muffins with chocolate syrup instead of caramel.
—Shannon Kohn, Summerville, SC

Prep: 25 min. • **Bake:** 20 min.
Makes: 6 muffins

- 6 Tbsp. softened butter, divided
- ½ cup dry roasted peanuts, chopped
- 1 pkg. (2.1 oz.) ready-to-serve fully cooked bacon, finely chopped, divided
- 1 Tbsp. light brown sugar
- 1 pkg. (8½ oz.) cornbread/muffin mix
- ½ cup buttermilk
- 2 large eggs, room temperature
- ¼ cup creamy peanut butter
- ⅔ cup peanut butter chips
  Caramel ice cream topping, optional

1. Preheat oven to 375°. Grease six 6-oz. ramekins or jumbo muffin cups with 2 Tbsp. butter. For topping, in a small bowl combine 2 Tbsp. butter, peanuts, 3 Tbsp. bacon and brown sugar; set aside.

2. In a large bowl, beat the muffin mix, buttermilk and eggs. Microwave peanut butter and remaining 2 Tbsp. butter until melted; stir into batter. Fold in peanut butter chips and remaining ⅔ cup bacon. Pour into prepared ramekins; sprinkle with topping.
3. Bake until a toothpick inserted in center comes out clean, 20-25 minutes. Cool for 5 minutes before removing from ramekins to a wire rack. Serve warm. If desired, drizzle with caramel ice cream topping.
Note As a substitute for each cup of buttermilk, use 1 Tbsp. white vinegar or lemon juice plus enough milk to measure 1 cup. Stir, then let stand 5 min. Or, use 1 cup plain yogurt or 1¾ tsp. cream of tartar plus 1 cup milk.
1 muffin: 590 cal., 38g fat (15g sat. fat), 94mg chol., 818mg sod., 45g carb. (20g sugars, 5g fiber), 18g pro.

"These are a huge hit with my young adult kids. The topping is crunchy, salty and sweet."

—CATHERINE WARD, PREP KITCHEN MANAGER

FOCACCIA BARESE

This focaccia recipe has been in my mom's family for several generations. It is one of my most requested recipes whenever I am invited to a party—I am not allowed to attend unless I bring it!
—Dora Travaglio, Mount Prospect, IL

Prep: 30 min. + rising • **Bake:** 30 min.
Makes: 8 servings

1⅛ **tsp. active dry yeast**
¾ **cup warm water (110°**
   to 115°), divided
½ **tsp. sugar**
⅓ **cup mashed potato flakes**
1½ **tsp. plus 2 Tbsp. olive oil,**
   divided
¼ **tsp. salt**
1¾ **cups bread flour**
TOPPING
2 **medium tomatoes, thinly sliced**
¼ **cup pitted Greek olives, halved**
1½ **tsp. minced fresh or dried oregano**
½ **tsp. coarse salt**

1. In a large bowl, dissolve yeast in ½ cup warm water. Add the sugar; let stand for 5 minutes. Add potato flakes, 1½ tsp. oil, salt, 1 cup flour and remaining ¼ cup water. Beat until smooth. Stir in enough remaining flour to form a soft dough.
2. Turn onto a floured surface; knead until smooth and elastic, 6-8 minutes. Place in a greased bowl, turning once to grease the top. Cover and let rise in a warm place until doubled, about 1 hour. Punch dough down. Cover and let rest for 10 minutes.
3. Place 1 Tbsp. olive oil in a 10-in. cast-iron or other ovenproof skillet; tilt pan to evenly coat. Add dough; shape to fit pan. Cover and let rise until doubled, about 30 minutes.
4. With fingertips, make several dimples over top of dough. Brush with remaining 1 Tbsp. oil. Blot the tomato slices with paper towels. Arrange tomato slices and olives over dough; sprinkle with oregano and salt.
5. Bake at 375° for 30-35 minutes or until golden brown.
1 piece: 142 cal., 4g fat (1g sat. fat), 0 chol., 269mg sod., 24g carb. (1g sugars, 1g fiber), 4g pro.

TEST KITCHEN TIP

Greek olives, also known as kalamata olives, are rich and fruity in flavor. They can be packed in either a vinegar brine or olive oil.

FOCACCIA BARESE

**CINNAMON
SWIRL BREAD**

CINNAMON SWIRL BREAD

Your family will be impressed with the soft texture and appealing swirls of cinnamon in these lovely breakfast loaves.
—Diane Armstrong, Elm Grove, WI

- -

Prep: 25 min. + rising • **Bake:** 30 min.
Makes: 2 loaves (16 pieces each)

    2 pkg. (¼ oz. each) active dry yeast
    ⅓ cup warm water (110° to 115°)
    1 cup warm 2% milk (110° to 115°)
    1 cup sugar, divided
    2 large eggs, room temperature
    6 Tbsp. butter, softened
    1½ tsp. salt
    5½ to 6 cups all-purpose flour
    2 Tbsp. ground cinnamon

1. In a large bowl, dissolve yeast in warm water. Add milk, ½ cup sugar, eggs, butter, salt and 3 cups flour; beat on medium speed until smooth. Stir in enough remaining flour to form a soft dough.

2. Turn dough onto a floured surface; knead until smooth and elastic, 6-8 minutes. Place in a greased bowl, turning once to grease top. Cover; let rise in a warm place until doubled, about 1 hour.

3. Mix cinnamon and remaining sugar. Punch down the dough. Turn onto a lightly floured surface; divide in half. Roll each portion into an 18x8-in. rectangle; sprinkle each with about ¼ cup cinnamon sugar to within ½ in. of edges. Roll up jelly-roll style, starting with a short side; pinch seam to seal. Place in 2 greased 9x5-in. loaf pans, seam side down.

4. Cover with kitchen towels; let rise in a warm place until doubled, about 1½ hours. Preheat oven to 350°.

5. Bake until golden brown, 30-35 minutes. Remove from pans to wire racks to cool.

1 piece: 132 cal., 3g fat (2g sat. fat), 20mg chol., 141mg sod., 23g carb. (7g sugars, 1g fiber), 3g pro.

COCONUT GARLIC NAAN

One of my favorite comfort foods is naan. I love the airy, chewy inside and the crisp, salty exterior. I drew inspiration from using ingredients like whole wheat flour and coconut oil to create a healthier but even tastier snack. You'll love this nutty bread smeared with garlic confit and sea salt.
—Morgan Harrison, Astoria, NY

- -

Prep: 2 hours + cooling • **Cook:** 5 min./batch
Makes: 8 servings

    ¼ cup coconut oil
    6 garlic cloves, peeled
NAAN
    1 pkg. (¼ oz.) active dry yeast
    ½ cup warm water (110° to 115°)
    ¾ cup whole wheat flour
    ½ cup plain yogurt
    2 Tbsp. coconut oil, divided
    1 tsp. sugar
    1 tsp. salt
    1¼ to 1½ cups all-purpose flour
    1 Tbsp. canola oil

1. Preheat oven to 250°. Place coconut oil and garlic in a small ovenproof bowl. Cover and bake until garlic is soft and golden, about 2 hours. Cool completely.

2. For naan, in a small bowl, dissolve yeast in warm water. In a large bowl, combine whole wheat flour, yogurt, 1 Tbsp. coconut oil, sugar, salt, yeast mixture and ½ cup flour; beat on medium speed until smooth. Stir in enough remaining flour to form a soft dough (dough will be sticky).

3. Turn dough onto a floured surface; knead until smooth and elastic, 6-8 minutes. Place in a greased bowl, turning once to grease the top. Cover and let rise in a warm place until doubled, about 1 hour.

4. Punch down dough. Turn onto a lightly floured surface; divide into 8 pieces. Roll each piece into a ¼-in.-thick oval. In a large skillet, heat canola oil and remaining 1 Tbsp. coconut oil over medium-high heat. Working in batches, cook naan until golden brown, 1-2 minutes. Turn; cook until golden brown, 1-2 minutes longer. Repeat with remaining dough. Serve with garlic confit.

1 piece: 232 cal., 13g fat (10g sat. fat), 2mg chol., 304mg sod., 25g carb. (1g sugars, 2g fiber), 5g pro.

COCONUT
GARLIC NAAN

SAVORY SKILLET POPOVER

This showstopping recipe delivers comfort and flavor and brings a smile. It's the perfect vehicle for using up little bits of leftovers, as long as they are fully cooked and heated in the bottom of the skillet prior to adding the batter and cheese.
—Susan Anderson, Helena, MT

Prep: 25 min. • **Bake:** 20 min.
Makes: 6 servings

- 6 Tbsp. butter
- 2 Tbsp. chopped shallot
- 8 large eggs, room temperature
- ¾ cup 2% milk
- 1 cup plus 2 Tbsp. all-purpose flour
- ½ tsp. kosher salt
- ½ tsp. pepper
- 1 Tbsp. minced fresh thyme
  or 1 tsp. dried thyme
- ¾ cup grated Parmesan cheese

1. Preheat oven to 425°. In a 12-in. cast-iron or other ovenproof skillet, melt butter over medium-high heat. Add shallot; cook and stir until tender, 1-2 minutes.
2. In a large bowl, whisk eggs and milk until blended. Whisk in flour, salt and pepper until smooth; stir in thyme. Pour batter into hot pan; sprinkle with Parmesan.
3. Bake until top is puffed and sides are golden brown and crisp, 20-25 minutes. Serve immediately.
1 piece: 343 cal., 21g fat (11g sat. fat), 290mg chol., 542mg sod., 22g carb. (2g sugars, 1g fiber), 15g pro.

SWISS BEER BREAD

This recipe is a favorite of my family because it isn't greasy like most of the other cheese breads I have tried. It will not last long!
—Debi Wallace, Chestertown, NY

Prep: 15 min. • **Bake:** 50 min. + cooling
Makes: 1 loaf (12 pieces)

- 4 oz. Jarlsberg or Swiss cheese
- 3 cups all-purpose flour
- 3 Tbsp. sugar
- 3 tsp. baking powder
- 1½ tsp. salt
- ½ tsp. pepper
- 1 bottle (12 oz.) beer or
  nonalcoholic beer
- 2 Tbsp. butter, melted

1. Preheat oven to 375°. Divide the cheese in half. Cut half into ¼-in. cubes; shred the remaining cheese. In a large bowl, combine next 5 ingredients. Stir the beer into dry ingredients just until moistened. Fold in cubed and shredded cheese.
2. Transfer to a greased 8x4-in. loaf pan. Drizzle with butter. Bake until a toothpick inserted in the center comes out clean, 50-60 minutes. Cool 10 minutes before removing from pan to a wire rack.
1 piece: 182 cal., 5g fat (3g sat. fat), 11mg chol., 453mg sod., 28g carb. (4g sugars, 1g fiber), 6g pro.

APPLE CIDER BISCUITS

My family enjoys these tender, flaky biscuits warm from the oven. We have a lot of apple trees, so we're always looking for apple recipes. This is a tasty way to use some of our cider.
—Harriet Stichter, Milford, IN

Takes: 30 min. • **Makes:** about 1 dozen

- 2 cups all-purpose flour
- 1 Tbsp. baking powder
- 2 tsp. sugar
- ½ tsp. salt
- ⅓ cup cold butter
- ¾ cup apple cider
- ⅛ tsp. ground cinnamon
  Honey, optional

1. In a bowl, combine flour, baking powder, sugar and salt. Cut in butter until mixture resembles coarse crumbs. Stir in cider just until moistened. Turn onto a lightly floured surface and knead 8-10 times.
2. Roll out to ½-in. thickness; cut with a 2½-in. biscuit cutter. Place on ungreased baking sheets. Sprinkle with cinnamon; pierce tops of biscuits with a fork.
3. Bake at 425° for 12-14 minutes or until golden brown. If desired, serve with honey.
1 biscuit: 131 cal., 5g fat (3g sat. fat), 14mg chol., 252mg sod., 18g carb. (3g sugars, 1g fiber), 2g pro.

BACON PARMESAN POPOVERS

This recipe proves that simple ingredients often result in the best-tasting dishes. These popovers are a nice change from ordinary toast or muffins.
—Donna Gaston, Coplay, PA

Prep: 10 min. • Bake: 30 min.
Makes: 6 popovers

- 2 large eggs, room temperature
- 1 cup 2% milk
- 1 cup all-purpose flour
- 2 Tbsp. grated Parmesan cheese
- ¼ tsp. salt
- 3 bacon strips, diced

1. In a large bowl, beat the eggs and milk. Combine flour, cheese and salt; add to egg mixture and mix well. Cover and let stand at room temperature for 45 minutes.
2. Preheat oven to 450°. In a large skillet, cook bacon over medium heat until crisp. Using a slotted spoon, remove to paper towels to drain. Grease cups of a nonstick popover pan well with some of the bacon drippings; set aside. Stir bacon into batter; fill prepared cups two-thirds full.
3. Bake for 15 minutes. Reduce the heat to 350° (do not open oven door). Bake until deep golden brown, about 15 minutes longer (do not underbake).
4. Run a table knife or small metal spatula around edges of cups to loosen if necessary. Immediately remove popovers from pan; prick with a small sharp knife to allow steam to escape. Serve immediately.
1 popover: 167 cal., 7g fat (3g sat. fat), 73mg chol., 248mg sod., 18g carb. (2g sugars, 1g fiber), 7g pro.

BANANA OAT MUFFINS

Chopped pecans add pleasant crunch to these hearty muffins with rich banana flavor. They're low in cholesterol, but you'd never know it. My husband and I love them.
—Marjorie Mott, Galatia, IL

Takes: 30 min. • Makes: 1 dozen

- ¾ cup all-purpose flour
- ¾ cup quick-cooking oats
- 1 tsp. baking powder
- 1 tsp. ground cinnamon
- ½ tsp. baking soda
- ¼ tsp. ground nutmeg
- 2 egg whites
- 1 cup mashed ripe bananas (about 2 medium)
- ½ cup packed brown sugar
- ¼ cup fat-free milk
- ¼ cup canola oil
- ½ cup chopped pecans

1. In a large bowl, combine the first 6 ingredients. In a small bowl, beat egg whites, bananas, brown sugar, milk and oil. Stir into dry ingredients just until moistened. Stir in pecans.
2. Coat muffin cups with cooking spray; fill two-thirds full with batter. Bake at 400° 15-20 minutes or until a toothpick comes out clean. Cool 5 minutes before removing from pan to a wire rack.
1 serving: 180 cal., 9g fat (1g sat. fat), 0 chol., 102mg sod., 24g carb. (13g sugars, 2g fiber), 3g pro.

QUICK BUTTERMILK CORNBREAD

The tattered recipe card for this cornbread proves it's been a family favorite for years. It's my daughter's top request.
—Judy Sellgren, Grand Rapids, MI

Takes: 30 min. • Makes: 9 servings

- 1¼ cups cornmeal
- 1 cup all-purpose flour
- ⅔ cup packed brown sugar
- ⅓ cup sugar
- 1 tsp. baking soda
- ½ tsp. salt
- 1 large egg, room temperature
- 1 cup buttermilk
- ¾ cup canola oil

1. In a large bowl, combine the cornmeal, flour, sugars, baking soda and salt. In another bowl, whisk the egg, buttermilk and oil; stir into dry ingredients just until moistened. Pour into a greased 9-in. round or square baking pan (pan will be full).
2. Bake at 425° until a toothpick inserted in the center comes out clean, 20-25 minutes. Cool on a wire rack 5 minutes. Serve warm.
Note: As a substitute for each cup of buttermilk, use 1 Tbsp. white vinegar or lemon juice plus enough milk to measure 1 cup. Stir, then let stand 5 min. Or, use 1 cup plain yogurt or 1¾ tsp. cream of tartar plus 1 cup milk.
1 piece: 390 cal., 19g fat (3g sat. fat), 25mg chol., 314mg sod., 50g carb. (25g sugars, 2g fiber), 5g pro.

SAUSAGE & KALE SOUP,
PAGE 104

FAVORITE

Soups & Sandwiches

It's easy to create a classic lunch combo
with this selection of soothing kettle
creations and hearty sammies.

**PRESSURE-COOKER
COLA BBQ CHICKEN**

RAVIOLI SOUP

We adore pasta, so I used it as the inspiration for this unique soup. The meaty tomato base pairs perfectly with the cheesy ravioli pillows.
—Shelley Way, Cheyenne, WY

- -

Prep: 20 min. • **Cook:** 45 min.
Makes: 10 servings (2½ qt.)

- 1   **lb. ground beef**
- 2   **cups water**
- 2   **cans (one 28 oz., one 14½ oz.) crushed tomatoes**
- 1   **can (6 oz.) tomato paste**
- 1½ **cups chopped onions**
- ¼   **cup minced fresh parsley**
- 2   **garlic cloves, minced**
- ¾   **tsp. dried basil**
- ½   **tsp. sugar**
- ½   **tsp. dried oregano**
- ½   **tsp. onion salt**
- ½   **tsp. salt**
- ¼   **tsp. pepper**
- ¼   **tsp. dried thyme**
- 1   **pkg. (9 oz.) refrigerated cheese ravioli**
- ¼   **cup grated Parmesan cheese Additional minced fresh parsley, optional**

1. In a Dutch oven, cook beef over medium heat until no longer pink, 5-7 minutes, breaking it into crumbles; drain. Add water, tomatoes, tomato paste, onions, parsley, garlic, basil, sugar, oregano, onion salt, salt, pepper and thyme; bring to a boil. Reduce heat; cover and simmer for 30 minutes.
2. Cook the ravioli according to package directions; drain. Add to soup and heat through. Stir in the Parmesan cheese. Sprinkle with additional parsley if desired.
1 cup: 235 cal., 8g fat (4g sat. fat), 42mg chol., 542mg sod., 25g carb. (5g sugars, 4g fiber), 17g pro.

PRESSURE-COOKER
COLA BBQ CHICKEN

This recipe is rich with sweet and smoky deliciousness. The meat is juicy and tender, and I like to add a few tasty toppings, like sliced dill pickles and a layer of pepper jack cheese, for a boost of flavor. This can also be cooked in the slow cooker on low for 8 hours.
—Ashley Lecker, Green Bay, WI

- -

Prep: 10 min.
Cook: 10 min.
Makes: 14 servings

- 1   **bottle (18 oz.) barbecue sauce**
- 1   **cup cola**
- 2   **Tbsp. cider vinegar**
- 1   **tsp. garlic powder**
- 1   **tsp. onion powder**
- 1   **tsp. salt**
- ½   **tsp. pepper**
- 2½ **lbs. boneless skinless chicken breasts**
- 14 **hamburger buns, split**
- 14 **slices pepper jack cheese**
- 1   **cup sliced sweet pickles**

1. Place the first 7 ingredients in a 6-qt. electric pressure cooker; add chicken. Lock the lid; close pressure-release valve. Adjust to pressure-cook on high for 7 minutes. Quick-release pressure. A thermometer inserted in chicken should read at least 165°.
2. Remove the chicken; cool slightly. Reserve 2 cups cooking juices; discard the remaining juices. Shred chicken with 2 forks. Combine with reserved juices. Serve on buns with cheese and pickles.
Freeze option: Freeze cooled meat mixture in freezer containers. To use, partially thaw in refrigerator overnight. Heat through in a saucepan, stirring occasionally; add a little water if necessary.
1 sandwich: 367 cal., 10g fat (5g sat. fat), 66mg chol., 971mg sod., 41g carb. (18g sugars, 1g fiber), 26g pro.

RAVIOLI
SOUP

FRENCH ONION SOUP

My daughter and I enjoy spending time together cooking, but our days are busy so we appreciate quick and tasty recipes like this one. Hot and delicious, this soup hits the spot for lunch or dinner.
—Sandra Chambers, Carthage, MS

- -

Prep: 30 min. • **Cook:** 30 min.
Makes: 6 servings

4	cups thinly sliced onions
1	garlic clove, minced
¼	cup butter
6	cups water
8	beef bouillon cubes
1	tsp. Worcestershire sauce
6	slices French bread (¾ in. thick), buttered and toasted
6	slices Swiss cheese

1. In a large covered saucepan, cook the onions and garlic in butter over medium-low heat for 8-10 minutes or until tender and golden, stirring occasionally. Add the water, bouillon and Worcestershire sauce; bring to a boil. Reduce the heat; cover and simmer for 30 minutes.
2. Ladle hot soup into 6 ovenproof bowls. Top each with a piece of French bread. Cut each slice of cheese in half and place both pieces over the bread. Broil until cheese melts. Serve immediately.
1 serving: 244 cal., 15g fat (10g sat. fat), 46mg chol., 1387mg sod., 17g carb. (5g sugars, 2g fiber), 9g pro.

FRENCH ONION SOUP

ASK SARAH

WHAT'S THE BEST WAY TO SLICE AN ONION?

Trim off the root and stem ends; peel. Cut the onion in half from root end to stem end. Place cut side down on a cutting board and thinly slice, starting at the stem end.

HOLIDAY TORTELLINI SOUP

Robust and full of flavor, this tortellini soup freezes well if you want to make it ahead or have leftovers to save for another day.
—Michelle Goggins, Cedarburg, WI

- -

Prep: 15 min. • **Cook:** 35 min.
Makes: 8 servings (2½ qt.)

- 2   Tbsp. olive oil
- 2   oz. pancetta or bacon, finely diced
- 1   medium onion, finely chopped
- 3   garlic cloves, minced
- 1   can (49½ oz.) chicken broth
- 2   tsp. Italian seasoning
- 1   pkg. (9 oz.) refrigerated cheese tortellini
- 1   can (28 oz.) crushed tomatoes in puree
- 8   oz. fresh spinach, rinsed and chopped
      Salt and pepper to taste
- 1   cup freshly shredded Parmesan cheese

1. Heat the oil in a Dutch oven over medium heat. Add pancetta. Cook until crisp. Add the onion; cook 3-4 minutes or until tender. Add garlic; cook 1 minute longer. Add broth and Italian seasoning; bring to a boil and simmer for 5 minutes.
2. Meanwhile, cook tortellini according to package directions; drain. Add tortellini to soup mixture. Stir in crushed tomatoes and simmer 5 minutes. Add spinach and cook just until wilted. Season with salt and pepper. Garnish with Parmesan cheese.
1 cup: 238 cal., 11g fat (4g sat. fat), 28mg chol., 1316mg sod., 26g carb. (7g sugars, 3g fiber), 11g pro.

HEARTY MUFFULETTA

Famous in Louisiana, a muffuletta is a combo of cold cuts, cheese and olive salad layered into an Italian bread shell. I was happy when a friend and co-worker gave me this recipe so I could make it myself. More than a meal, it's a dining experience!
—Ruth Hayward, Lake Charles, LA

- -

Prep: 55 min. + chilling • **Makes:** 10 servings

- ½   cup finely chopped celery
- ½   cup sliced pimiento-stuffed olives, drained
- ½   cup sliced ripe olives, drained
- ½   cup giardiniera
- ⅓   cup finely chopped onion
- ⅓   cup olive oil
- ¼   cup finely chopped green onions
- ¼   cup minced fresh parsley
- 3   Tbsp. lemon juice
- 1   tsp. dried oregano
- 1   garlic clove, minced
- ⅛   tsp. pepper
- 1   round loaf (24 oz.) unsliced Italian bread
- ¼   lb. thinly sliced hard salami
- ¼   lb. provolone cheese
- ¼   lb. thinly sliced deli ham

1. In a bowl, combine first 12 ingredients. Cover and refrigerate at least 8 hours. Drain, reserving 2 Tbsp. liquid.
2. Cut loaf of bread in half horizontally; hollow out top and bottom, leaving a 1-in. shell (discard removed bread or save for another use). Brush cut sides of bread with reserved liquid. Layer bottom of bread shell with salami, half the olive mixture, cheese, remaining olive mixture and ham. Replace bread top. Cut into wedges to serve.
1 piece: 378 cal., 19g fat (5g sat. fat), 25mg chol., 1103mg sod., 38g carb. (2g sugars, 3g fiber), 14g pro.

TEST KITCHEN TIP

Giardiniera is a vegetable mixture available in mild and hot varieties. Look for it in the Italian or pickle section of your grocery store.

HEARTY MUFFULETTA

KENTUCKY
HOT BROWN SLIDERS

KENTUCKY HOT BROWN SLIDERS

I transformed the Hot Brown sandwich, traditionally open-faced, into a party-ready slider. This easy-to-eat finger food was originally meant for a Kentucky Derby get-together, but it's so tasty, I now serve it anytime. Just cover and refrigerate the assembled sandwiches so you can pop them in the oven when company arrives.
—Blair Lonergan, Rochelle, VA

- -

Prep: 20 min. • **Bake:** 30 min.
Makes: 12 servings

- 1 pkg. (12 oz.) Hawaiian sweet rolls
- 3 Tbsp. mayonnaise
- 12 slices deli turkey, folded into quarters
- 12 slices cooked bacon strips, halved widthwise
- 1 jar (4 oz.) diced pimientos, drained, or 2 plum tomatoes, cut into 12 slices
- 6 slices Gruyere cheese, halved
- ¼ cup grated Parmesan cheese
- ½ cup butter, cubed
- 2 Tbsp. finely chopped onion
- 2 Tbsp. brown sugar
- 1½ tsp. Worcestershire sauce
- ¼ tsp. garlic powder

1. Preheat oven to 350°. Without separating rolls, cut package of rolls in half horizontally; arrange bottom halves in a greased 11x7-in. baking pan. Spread the mayonnaise evenly across bottom halves. Top each with turkey, bacon, pimientos, Gruyere and Parmesan cheese. Replace top halves of rolls.
2. In a small skillet, melt butter over medium heat. Add onion; cook and stir until tender, 1-2 minutes. Whisk in the brown sugar, Worcestershire sauce and garlic powder. Cook and stir until the sugar is dissolved; drizzle over sandwiches.
3. Cover and bake 25 minutes. Uncover; bake until golden brown, 5-10 minutes longer.
1 serving: 327 cal., 21g fat (10g sat. fat), 67mg chol., 652mg sod., 20g carb. (9g sugars, 1g fiber), 16g pro.

OVER-THE-RAINBOW MINESTRONE

OVER-THE-RAINBOW MINESTRONE

This vegetarian soup features a rainbow of vegetables. You can use any multicolored pasta in place of the spirals.
—Crystal Schlueter, Northglenn, CO

- -

Prep: 20 min. • **Cook:** 6 hours 20 min.
Makes: 10 servings (3¾ qt.)

- 4 large stems Swiss chard (about ½ lb.) or fresh baby spinach
- 2 Tbsp. olive oil
- 1 medium red onion, finely chopped
- 6 cups vegetable broth
- 2 cans (14½ oz. each) fire-roasted diced tomatoes, undrained
- 1 can (16 oz.) kidney beans, rinsed and drained
- 1 can (15 oz.) garbanzo beans or chickpeas, rinsed and drained
- 1 medium yellow summer squash or zucchini, halved and cut into ¼-in. slices
- 1 medium sweet red or yellow pepper, finely chopped
- 1 medium carrot, finely chopped
- 2 garlic cloves, minced
- 1½ cups uncooked spiral pasta or small pasta shells
- ¼ cup prepared pesto
  Optional toppings: Additional prepared pesto, shredded Parmesan cheese, crushed red pepper flakes and minced fresh basil

1. Cut stems from chard; chop stems and leaves separately. Reserve leaves for adding later. In a large skillet, heat oil over medium heat. Add onion and chard stems; cook and stir until tender, 3-5 minutes. Transfer to a 6-qt. slow cooker.
2. Stir in broth, tomatoes, kidney beans, garbanzo beans, squash, pepper, carrot and garlic. Cook, covered, on low until vegetables are tender, 6-8 hours.
3. Stir in the pasta and reserved chard leaves. Cook, covered, on low until pasta is tender, 20-25 minutes longer; stir in the pesto. If desired, serve with additional pesto, Parmesan cheese, red pepper flakes and fresh basil.
1½ cups: 231 cal., 7g fat (1g sat. fat), 2mg chol., 1015mg sod., 34g carb. (7g sugars, 6g fiber), 9g pro.

CHICKEN CAESAR WRAPS

This classic cold sandwich with tender chicken, Parmesan cheese and chopped Caesar croutons uses just the right amount of dressing. It's a quick and tasty lunch.
—Nancy Pratt, Longview, TX

- -

Takes: 15 min. • **Makes:** 6 wraps

- ¾ **cup reduced-fat creamy Caesar salad dressing**
- ¼ **cup grated Parmesan cheese**
- ½ **tsp. garlic powder**
- ¼ **tsp. pepper**
- 3 **cups cubed cooked chicken breast**
- 2 **cups torn romaine**
- ¾ **cup Caesar salad croutons, coarsely chopped**
- 6 **whole wheat tortillas (8 in.), room temperature**

In a large bowl, combine dressing, cheese, garlic powder and pepper. Add the chicken, romaine and croutons. Spoon ⅔ cup chicken mixture down center of each tortilla; roll up.

1 wrap: 337 cal., 12g fat (2g sat. fat), 57mg chol., 730mg sod., 29g carb. (2g sugars, 4g fiber), 27g pro. **Diabetic exchanges:** 3 lean meat, 2½ starch, ½ fat.

LISA'S ALL-DAY SUGAR & SALT PORK ROAST

My family loves this tender and juicy roast, so we eat it a lot. The salty crust is so delicious mixed into the pulled pork.
—Lisa Allen, Joppa, AL

- -

Prep: 15 min. + marinating • **Cook:** 6¼ hours
Makes: 12 servings

- 1 **cup plus 1 Tbsp. sea salt, divided**
- 1 **cup sugar**
- 1 **bone-in pork shoulder butt roast (6 to 8 lbs.)**
- ¼ **cup barbecue seasoning**
- ½ **tsp. pepper**
- ½ **cup packed brown sugar**
- 12 **hamburger buns or kaiser rolls, split**

1. Combine 1 cup sea salt and granulated sugar; rub onto all sides of roast. Place in a shallow dish; refrigerate, covered, overnight.

2. Preheat oven to 300°. Using a kitchen knife, scrape salt and sugar coating from roast; discard any accumulated juices. Transfer pork to a large shallow roasting pan. Rub with barbecue seasoning; sprinkle with pepper. Roast until tender, 6-8 hours.

3. Increase the oven temperature to 500°. Combine brown sugar and 1 Tbsp. sea salt; sprinkle over cooked pork. Return pork to oven and roast until a crisp crust forms, 10-15 minutes. Remove; when cool enough to handle, shred meat with 2 forks. Serve warm on fresh buns or rolls.

Freeze option: Freeze cooled meat with some of the juices in freezer containers. To use, partially thaw in refrigerator overnight. Heat meat through in a saucepan, stirring occasionally; add water if necessary.

1 sandwich: 534 cal., 24g fat (9g sat. fat), 135mg chol., 2240mg sod., 33g carb. (14g sugars, 1g fiber), 43g pro.

LISA'S ALL-DAY
SUGAR & SALT PORK ROAST

FAMILY-PLEASING TURKEY CHILI

2. Transfer to a 4-qt. slow cooker. Stir in the tomatoes, kidney beans, black beans, broth, corn, tomato paste, chili powder, pepper, cumin and garlic powder.
3. Cover and cook on low until heated through, 4-5 hours. If desired, serve with sour cream and cilantro.

Freeze option: Freeze cooled chili in freezer containers. To use, partially thaw in the refrigerator overnight. Heat through in a saucepan, stirring occasionally; add a little water if necessary.

1½ cups: 349 cal., 7g fat (2g sat. fat), 60mg chol., 725mg sod., 47g carb. (11g sugars, 12g fiber), 27g pro. **Diabetic exchanges:** 3 lean meat, 2 starch, 2 vegetable.

CIABATTA TURKEY BURGERS

Ground turkey creates a lean yet still tasty grilled burger.
—Matthew Hass, Ellison Bay, WI

- -

Takes: 25 min. • **Makes:** 4 servings

- 1 slice white bread, torn into small pieces
- 3 Tbsp. fat-free milk
- 2 tsp. Better Than Bouillon® Roasted Garlic Base
- 2 Tbsp. grated Parmesan cheese
- 2 Tbsp. minced fresh parsley
- 1 tsp. Italian seasoning
- ¼ tsp. pepper
- 1 lb. lean ground turkey
- 4 ciabatta rolls, split
- ½ cup marinara sauce, warmed
   Additional Parmesan cheese and chopped parsley

1. In a large bowl, combine the torn bread, milk and garlic base; let stand until milk is absorbed. Stir in the cheese, parsley and seasonings. Add the turkey; mix lightly but thoroughly. Shape into four ½-in.-thick patties.
2. Place the burgers on an oiled grill rack over medium heat. Grill, covered, until a thermometer reads 165°, 4-5 minutes per side. Place rolls on grill rack, cut side down; grill, covered, until toasted, 1-2 minutes.
3. Serve burgers on rolls. Top with sauce and additional cheese and parsley.

1 burger: 555 cal., 14g fat (3g sat. fat), 81mg chol., 839mg sod., 77g carb. (7g sugars, 4g fiber), 35g pro.

FAMILY-PLEASING TURKEY CHILI

FAMILY-PLEASING TURKEY CHILI

My children really love this recipe—it's one of their favorite comfort foods. The ingredients are relatively inexpensive, and the leftovers are wonderful!
—Sheila Christensen, San Marcos, CA

- -

Prep: 25 min. • **Cook:** 4 hours
Makes: 6 servings (2¼ qt.)

- 1 lb. lean ground turkey
- 1 medium green pepper, finely chopped
- 1 small red onion, finely chopped
- 2 garlic cloves, minced
- 1 can (28 oz.) diced tomatoes, undrained
- 1 can (16 oz.) kidney beans, rinsed and drained
- 1 can (15 oz.) black beans, rinsed and drained
- 1 can (14½ oz.) reduced-sodium chicken broth
- 1¾ cups frozen corn, thawed
- 1 can (6 oz.) tomato paste
- 1 Tbsp. chili powder
- ½ tsp. pepper
- ¼ tsp. ground cumin
- ¼ tsp. garlic powder
   Optional: Reduced-fat sour cream and minced fresh cilantro

1. In a large nonstick skillet, cook the turkey, green pepper and onion over medium heat until meat is no longer pink, breaking it into crumbles. Add the garlic; cook 1 minute longer. Drain.

PHILLY CHEESESTEAK SLIDERS

CHEDDAR BROCCOLI SOUP

Frozen broccoli speeds up the time it takes to prepare this creamy, comforting soup.
—Louise Beatty, Amherst, NY

Takes: 30 min. • **Makes:** 4 servings

- 1 small onion, chopped
- 2 garlic cloves, minced
- 2 Tbsp. butter
- 2 Tbsp. all-purpose flour
- 1 can (14½ oz.) beef broth
- 1½ cups 2% milk
- 1 pkg. (10 oz.) frozen chopped broccoli
- 1 tsp. ground mustard
- 1 tsp. Worcestershire sauce
- ¼ tsp. ground nutmeg
- 1 cup shredded cheddar cheese
  Additional shredded cheddar cheese, optional

1. In a large saucepan, saute onion and garlic in butter until tender. Stir in the flour until blended. Gradually stir in broth; bring to a boil. Cook and stir for 2 minutes.
2. Stir in the milk, broccoli, ground mustard, Worcestershire sauce and nutmeg. Bring to a boil. Reduce heat; simmer, uncovered, for 6-8 minutes or until heated through. Stir in cheese until melted. If desired, serve with additional cheese.
1 cup: 252 cal., 16g fat (11g sat. fat), 52mg chol., 750mg sod., 15g carb. (7g sugars, 3g fiber), 13g pro.

PHILLY CHEESESTEAK SLIDERS

This is a fabulous way to use leftover roast beef, but using sliced roast beef from the deli also works.
—Debra Waggoner, Grand Island, NE

Prep: 20 min. + chilling • **Bake:** 25 min.
Makes: 2 dozen

- 2 large green peppers, sliced
- 1 large sweet onion, sliced
- 1 Tbsp. olive oil
- 2 pkg. (12 oz. each) Hawaiian sweet rolls
- 1½ lbs. sliced deli roast beef
- 12 slices provolone cheese
- ¾ cup butter
- 1½ tsp. dried minced onion
- 1½ tsp. Worcestershire sauce
- 1 tsp. garlic powder

1. In a large skillet, cook green peppers and onion in oil over medium-high heat until tender, 8-10 minutes. Without separating rolls, cut each package in half horizontally; arrange bottom halves in a greased 13x9-in. baking pan. Layer with the roast beef, pepper mixture and cheese; replace top halves of rolls.
2. In a small saucepan, melt butter, dried onion, Worcestershire sauce and garlic powder. Drizzle over rolls. Cover and refrigerate 8 hours or overnight.
3. Preheat oven to 350°. Remove rolls from refrigerator 30 minutes before baking. Bake, uncovered, 15 minutes. Cover with foil; bake until cheese is melted, 10 minutes longer.
1 slider: 247 cal., 14g fat (8g sat. fat), 56mg chol., 413mg sod., 18g carb. (7g sugars, 1g fiber), 14g pro.

"These are a huge hit whenever I make them. The slightly sweet buttery rolls are so delicious with the savory filling."

—MARGARET KNOEBEL, ASSISTANT RECIPE EDITOR

CHEDDAR
BROCCOLI
SOUP

BACON CHEESEBURGER ROLL-UPS

My husband and I both love these roll-ups.
I often serve them with broccoli and cheese.
They must be good because this recipe won
a first-place prize at the Iowa State Fair!
—Jessica Cain, Des Moines, IA

- -

Prep: 25 min. • **Bake:** 20 min.
Makes: 8 servings

1	**lb. ground beef**
6	**bacon strips, diced**
½	**cup chopped onion**
1	**pkg. (8 oz.) Velveeta, cubed**
1	**tube (16.3 oz.) large refrigerated buttermilk biscuits**
1	**large egg, beaten, optional Sesame seeds, optional**
½	**cup ketchup**
¼	**cup yellow mustard**

1. Preheat oven to 400°. In a large skillet,
cook beef, bacon and onion over medium
heat until meat is no longer pink, breaking
it into crumbles; drain. Add cheese; cook
and stir until melted. Remove from heat.
2. Flatten biscuits into 5-in. circles; top each
with ⅓ cup beef mixture. Fold sides and ends
over filling, and roll up. Place seam side down
on a greased baking sheet. If desired, brush
with egg and sprinkle with sesame seeds.
3. Bake until golden brown, 18-20 minutes.
In a small bowl, combine the ketchup and
mustard; serve with roll-ups.
1 roll-up: 429 cal., 24g fat (10g sat. fat),
63mg chol., 1372mg sod., 32g carb.
(11g sugars, 1g fiber), 21g pro.

BACON CHEESEBURGER
ROLL-UPS

CUBAN ROASTED PORK SANDWICHES

For an incredible hot sandwich, slowly roast pork in a seasoned citrus marinade, then layer slices of the meat with pickles, zippy mustard, ham and cheese.
—*Taste of Home* Test Kitchen

Prep: 20 min. + marinating
Bake: 3½ hours + grilling
Makes: 24 servings

- 1 boneless pork shoulder butt roast (5 to 6 lbs.)
- 4 garlic cloves, sliced
- 2 large onions, sliced
- 1 cup orange juice
- 1 cup lime juice
- 2 Tbsp. dried oregano
- 2 tsp. ground cumin
- 1 tsp. salt
- 1 tsp. pepper

SANDWICHES

- 4 loaves (1 lb. each) French bread
- ¾ cup butter, softened
- ½ to 1 cup yellow mustard
- 24 thin sandwich pickle slices
- 2¼ lbs. sliced deli ham
- 2¼ lbs. Swiss cheese, sliced

1. Cut sixteen 1-in. slits in pork; insert garlic slices. In a large bowl, combine the onions, orange juice, lime juice and seasonings. Pour 1½ cups marinade into another large bowl; add pork and turn to coat with marinade. Cover and refrigerate for at least 8 hours or overnight, turning pork occasionally. Cover and refrigerate remaining marinade.
2. Preheat oven to 350°. Drain the pork, discarding drained marinade. Place pork and reserved marinade in a shallow roasting pan. Bake until tender, 3½-4 hours, basting occasionally. Let stand for 15 minutes before slicing.
3. Meanwhile, cut each loaf of bread in half lengthwise; flatten slightly. Spread cut side with butter; spread crust side with mustard. Cut pork into thin slices. Layer pickles, pork, ham and cheese over the mustard. Replace tops so buttered side is outward. Cut each loaf into sixths.
4. Cook in batches on a panini maker or indoor grill for 4-5 minutes or until bread is browned and cheese is melted.
1 sandwich: 590 cal., 27g fat (15g sat. fat), 119mg chol., 1206mg sod., 47g carb. (5g sugars, 2g fiber), 39g pro.

SAUSAGE POTATO SOUP

After a full day of teaching and coaching, I'm often too tired to spend a lot of time preparing dinner. So I rely on this thick, chunky blend that I can have on the table in 30 minutes. The whole family enjoys the wonderful flavor of the smoked sausage.
—Jennifer LeFevre, Hesston, KS

Takes: 30 min. • **Makes:** 6 servings

- ½ lb. smoked kielbasa, diced
- 6 medium potatoes, peeled and cubed
- 2 cups frozen corn
- 1½ cups chicken broth
- 1 celery rib, sliced
- ¼ cup sliced carrot
- ½ tsp. garlic powder
- ½ tsp. onion powder
- ½ tsp. salt
- ¼ tsp. pepper
- 1½ cups whole milk
- ⅔ cup shredded cheddar cheese
- 1 tsp. minced fresh parsley

1. In a large saucepan, cook kielbasa over medium heat until lightly browned, about 5 minutes; drain and set aside. In the same pan, combine the potatoes, corn, broth, celery, carrot and seasonings. Bring to a boil.
2. Reduce the heat; cover and simmer until vegetables are tender, about 15 minutes. Add the milk, cheese, parsley and sausage. Cook and stir over low heat until the cheese is melted and soup is heated through, about 5 minutes.
1 cup: 377 cal., 17g fat (7g sat. fat), 45mg chol., 817mg sod., 44g carb. (8g sugars, 3g fiber), 14g pro.

CUBAN ROASTED PORK SANDWICHES

SALMON SALAD
SANDWICHES

SALMON SALAD SANDWICHES

These are perfect to pack in lunchboxes when your kids can't face another boring sandwich. We love this salmon, cream cheese and dill tucked inside a crusty roll. The carrots and celery add a nice crunch.
—Yvonne Shust, Shoal Lake, MB

Takes: 10 min. • **Makes:** 2 servings

- 3 oz. cream cheese, softened
- 1 Tbsp. mayonnaise
- 1 Tbsp. lemon juice
- 1 tsp. dill weed
- ¼ to ½ tsp. salt
- ⅛ tsp. pepper
- 1 can (6 oz.) pink salmon, drained, bones and skin removed
- ½ cup shredded carrot
- ½ cup chopped celery
  Lettuce leaves
- 2 whole wheat buns, split
  Sliced tomatoes

In a large bowl, beat the cream cheese, mayonnaise, lemon juice, dill, salt and pepper until smooth. Add the salmon, carrot and celery; mix well. Place a lettuce leaf and about ½ cup salmon salad on each bun and top with tomato.

1 sandwich: 463 cal., 29g fat (12g sat. fat), 87mg chol., 1158mg sod., 28g carb. (5g sugars, 5g fiber), 25g pro.

SLOW-COOKER SPLIT PEA SOUP

SLOW-COOKER SPLIT PEA SOUP

When I have leftover ham in the fridge, I like to make this soup. Just throw the ingredients in the slow cooker, turn it on and dinner is done.
—Pamela Chambers, West Columbia, SC

Prep: 15 min. • **Cook:** 8 hours
Makes: 8 servings (2 qt.)

- 1 pkg. (16 oz.) dried green split peas, rinsed
- 2 cups cubed fully cooked ham
- 1 large onion, chopped
- 1 cup julienned or chopped carrots
- 3 garlic cloves, minced
- ½ tsp. dried rosemary, crushed
- ½ tsp. dried thyme
- 1 carton (32 oz.) reduced-sodium chicken broth
- 2 cups water

In a 4- or 5-qt. slow cooker, combine all ingredients. Cover and cook on low for 8-10 hours or until peas are tender.

Freeze option: Freeze cooled soup in freezer containers. To use, thaw overnight in the refrigerator. Heat through in a saucepan over medium heat, stirring occasionally.

1 cup: 260 cal., 2g fat (1g sat. fat), 21mg chol., 728mg sod., 39g carb. (7g sugars, 15g fiber), 23g pro. **Diabetic exchanges:** 2½ starch, 2 lean meat.

TEST KITCHEN TIP

Split peas take a very long time to soften, so you don't have to worry about overcooking them. If you'd like the rest of the vegetables in your soup to retain some bite, add them later into the cooking time.

HEARTY BEEF & BARLEY SOUP

Barley soup is a popular menu item in our house throughout the year. Everyone savors the flavor.
—Elizabeth Kendall, Carolina Beach, NC

- -

Prep: 20 min. • **Cook:** 1 hour 50 min.
Makes: 9 servings (2¼ qt.)

- 1 Tbsp. canola oil
- 1 lb. beef top round steak, cut into ½-in. cubes
- 3 cans (14½ oz. each) beef broth
- 2 cups water
- ⅓ cup medium pearl barley
- ¾ tsp. salt
- ⅛ tsp. pepper
- 1 cup chopped carrots
- ½ cup chopped celery
- ¼ cup chopped onion
- 3 Tbsp. minced fresh parsley
- 1 cup frozen peas

1. In a large saucepan, heat oil over medium heat. Brown the beef on all sides; drain. Stir in broth, water, barley, salt and pepper. Bring to a boil. Reduce the heat; cover and simmer for 1 hour.

2. Add the carrots, celery, onion and parsley; cover and simmer until meat and vegetables are tender, 30-40 minutes. Stir in the peas; heat through.

1 cup: 133 cal., 4g fat (1g sat. fat), 28mg chol., 859mg sod., 10g carb. (2g sugars, 2g fiber), 14g pro. **Diabetic exchanges:** 2 lean meat, ½ starch, ½ fat.

GRANDMOTHER'S CHICKEN & DUMPLINGS

While I was growing up, my grandmother could feed our whole big family with a single chicken—and lots of dumplings.
—Cathy Carroll, Bossier City, LA

- -

Prep: 45 min. + standing • **Cook:** 30 min.
Makes: 10 servings

- 1 large chicken (6 lbs.)
- 2 medium carrots, chopped
- 2 celery ribs, sliced
- 1 large onion, sliced
- 4 qt. water
- 2 Tbsp. white vinegar
- 2 tsp. salt

DUMPLINGS

- 2 cups all-purpose flour
- 1½ tsp. salt
- 1 large egg
- ½ cup reserved chicken broth
- ½ tsp. pepper

1. Place chicken, carrots, celery and onion in a large Dutch oven or stockpot. Add water, vinegar and salt (adding more water, if necessary, to cover chicken). Bring to a boil. Reduce heat; cover and simmer until meat nearly falls from the bones. Remove chicken from broth; allow to cool. Strain broth, discarding vegetables and seasonings.

2. Remove meat from bones; discard skin and bones. Cut meat into bite-sized pieces; set aside and keep warm. Set aside 1 cup broth; cool to lukewarm.

3. To make the dumplings, combine flour and salt. Make a well in flour; add the egg. Gradually stir ¼ cup reserved broth into egg, picking up flour as you go. Continue until flour is used up, adding additional broth as needed until dough is consistency of pie dough. Pour any remaining reserved broth back into stockpot.

4. Turn dough onto a floured surface; knead in additional flour to make a stiff dough. Let the dough rest for 15 minutes. On a floured surface, roll out dough into a 17-in. square. Cut into 1-in. square pieces. Dust with additional flour; let dry 30-60 minutes.

5. Bring the broth to a boil (you should have about 4 qt.). Drop the dumplings into boiling broth. Reduce heat; cover and simmer until a toothpick inserted into center of a dumpling comes out clean (do not lift the cover while simmering), about 10 minutes. Uncover; add reserved chicken. Stir in pepper.

1 cup: 310 cal., 9g fat (2g sat. fat), 114mg chol., 981mg sod., 22g carb. (2g sugars, 1g fiber), 34g pro.

GRANDMOTHER'S
CHICKEN & DUMPLINGS

CHICKEN
PARMESAN
BURGERS

MEXICAN-INSPIRED CHICKEN SOUP

This zesty soup is loaded with chicken, corn and black beans in a mildly spicy red broth. As a busy mom of three young children, I'm always looking for dinner recipes that can be prepared in the morning. The kids love the taco taste of this easy soup.
—Marlene Kane, Lainesburg, MI

Prep: 10 min. • **Cook:** 3 hours
Makes: 6 servings

- 1½ lbs. boneless skinless chicken breasts, cubed
- 2 tsp. canola oil
- ½ cup water
- 1 envelope reduced-sodium taco seasoning
- 1 can (32 oz.) V8 juice
- 1 jar (16 oz.) salsa
- 1 can (15 oz.) black beans, rinsed and drained
- 1 pkg. (10 oz.) frozen corn, thawed
  Optional toppings: Shredded cheddar cheese, sour cream and chopped fresh cilantro

1. In a large nonstick skillet, saute chicken in oil until no longer pink. Add water and taco seasoning; simmer, uncovered, until chicken is well coated.
2. Transfer to a 5-qt. slow cooker. Stir in V8 juice, salsa, beans and corn. Cover and cook on low for 3-4 hours or until heated through. If desired, serve with optional toppings.
1½ cups: 304 cal., 5g fat (1g sat. fat), 63mg chol., 1199mg sod., 35g carb. (11g sugars, 5g fiber), 29g pro.

CHICKEN PARMESAN BURGERS

A restaurant-quality burger that's topped with marinara and loaded with cheese—what's not to love? Fresh basil adds even more flavor if you'd like.
—Brooke Petras, Alpine, CA

Takes: 30 min. • **Makes:** 4 servings

- 3 Tbsp. olive oil, divided
- 1 small onion, finely chopped
- 2 garlic cloves, minced
- ¾ cup marinara sauce, divided
- ½ cup finely chopped or shredded part-skim mozzarella cheese
- ½ cup dry bread crumbs
- 1 tsp. Italian seasoning
- 1 tsp. dried oregano
- ½ tsp. salt
- ½ tsp. pepper
- 1 lb. ground chicken
- 4 slices part-skim mozzarella cheese
- 4 hamburger buns, split and toasted
- ¼ cup shredded Parmesan cheese
  Fresh basil leaves, optional

1. In a large skillet, heat 1 Tbsp. oil over medium-high heat. Add onion; cook and stir until tender, about 3 minutes. Add garlic; cook 1 minute longer. Remove from heat; cool slightly.

2. In a large bowl, combine ¼ cup marinara sauce with chopped mozzarella, bread crumbs, seasonings and onion mixture. Add chicken; mix lightly but thoroughly. With wet hands, shape into four ½-in.-thick patties.
3. In the same skillet, heat remaining 2 Tbsp. oil over medium heat. Cook the burgers until a thermometer reads 165°, 4-5 minutes on each side. Top with sliced mozzarella; cook, covered, until cheese is melted, 1-2 minutes.
4. Serve in buns; top with remaining ½ cup marinara sauce, Parmesan cheese and, if desired, basil leaves.
1 burger: 603 cal., 33g fat (10g sat. fat), 108mg chol., 1275mg sod., 41g carb. (8g sugars, 3g fiber), 38g pro.

> "I especially like making these burgers in summer when I can cook them on the grill and use fresh basil from my garden."
>
> —SARAH TRAMONTE, ASSOCIATE CULINARY EDITOR

**BUFFALO CHICKEN
CALZONES**

SAUSAGE & KALE SOUP

This is my family's absolute favorite soup, and I can have it on the table in less than 45 minutes. I usually double the recipe so the flavors can blend, making the soup even better the next day.
—Dawn Rohn, Riverton, WY

Prep: 15 min. • **Cook:** 25 min.
Makes: 14 servings (3½ qt.)

- 1 lb. smoked kielbasa or
     Polish sausage, cut into ¼-in. slices
- 3 medium Yukon Gold or
     red potatoes, chopped
- 2 medium onions, chopped
- 2 Tbsp. olive oil
- 1 bunch kale, trimmed and torn
- 4 garlic cloves, minced
- ¼ tsp. pepper
- ¼ tsp. salt
- 2 bay leaves
- 1 can (14½ oz.) diced
     tomatoes, undrained
- 1 can (15 oz.) garbanzo beans
     or chickpeas, rinsed and drained
- 1 carton (32 oz.) chicken broth

1. In a Dutch oven over medium-low heat, cook the sausage, potatoes and onions in oil for 5 minutes or until sausage is heated through, stirring occasionally. Add kale; cover and cook for 2-3 minutes or until kale is wilted. Add garlic; cook 1 minute longer.
2. Add the remaining ingredients. Bring to a boil. Reduce the heat; cover and simmer for 9-12 minutes or until potatoes are tender. Discard bay leaves.
1 cup: 187 cal., 11g fat (3g sat. fat), 22mg chol., 706mg sod., 16g carb. (3g sugars, 3g fiber), 7g pro.

BUFFALO CHICKEN CALZONES

I'm always looking for creative ways to jazz up pizza. I created this pizza turnover to incorporate my love of Buffalo chicken wings.
—Ruth Ann Riendeau, Twin Mountain, NH

Prep: 30 min. • **Bake:** 10 min.
Makes: 4 calzones

- 1 can (8 oz.) pizza sauce
- 2 tsp. plus ½ cup Buffalo
     wing sauce, divided
- 1¼ lbs. boneless skinless
     chicken breasts, cubed
- 3 celery ribs, chopped
- 3 Tbsp. butter
     Dash Cajun seasoning
- 2 tubes (13.8 oz. each)
     refrigerated pizza crust
- 1½ cups shredded Monterey
     Jack cheese
- 1 cup crumbled blue cheese
     Cornmeal

1. In a small bowl, combine pizza sauce and 2 tsp. Buffalo wing sauce; set aside. In a large skillet, cook chicken and celery in butter over medium heat for 3-5 minutes or until the chicken is no longer pink; drain if necessary.

Stir in Cajun seasoning and remaining ½ cup Buffalo wing sauce; cover and simmer for 10-15 minutes or until heated through.
2. Preheat oven to 400°. Unroll the pizza dough; divide each portion in half. On a floured surface, roll each into an 8-in. circle. Spread the pizza sauce mixture over half of each circle to within 1 in. of edge. Top with chicken mixture and cheeses. Fold dough over filling; pinch or crimp edges to seal.
3. Sprinkle greased baking sheets with the cornmeal. Place calzones over cornmeal. Bake until golden brown, 10-12 minutes.
½ calzone: 516 cal., 21g fat (11g sat. fat), 82mg chol., 1185mg sod., 51g carb. (8g sugars, 2g fiber), 31g pro.

TEST KITCHEN TIP

You can substitute chicken thighs for chicken breasts. Or, to save time, you can use rotisserie chicken or chopped frozen chicken tenders.

SAUSAGE &
KALE SOUP

CHEDDAR FRENCH DIP SANDWICHES

With leftover roast beef or deli beef, it takes almost no time at all to fix these satisfying hot sandwiches. They're perfect for those hectic days.
—Pollyanna Szwej, Bridgeport, NY

- -

Takes: 20 min. • **Makes:** 4 servings

- ¼ cup butter, cubed
- 2 garlic cloves, minced
- 4 ciabatta rolls, split
- 1 cup shredded cheddar cheese
- 1 lb. thinly sliced roast beef
- 1 can (14½ oz.) beef broth

1. In a small skillet, melt butter. Add garlic; saute for 1 minute. Place rolls on a baking sheet; brush cut sides with garlic butter. Sprinkle with cheese. Broil 3-4 in. from the heat 2-3 minutes or until cheese is melted.
2. In a large saucepan, combine the beef and broth; heat through. Using tongs or a slotted spoon, place beef on rolls. Serve sandwiches with remaining broth for dipping.
1 sandwich: 664 cal., 27g fat (15g sat. fat), 123mg chol., 1885mg sod., 71g carb. (4g sugars, 4g fiber), 40g pro.

HOMEMADE SLOPPY JOES

I simmer a big batch of this hot, tangy sandwich filling and freeze the extras. Then I thaw and reheat it for a quick dinner.
—Sandra Castillo, Janesville, WI

- -

Prep: 10 min. • **Cook:** 30 min.
Makes: 12 servings

- 2 lbs. ground beef
- 2 medium onions, chopped
- 2 to 3 garlic cloves, minced
- 2 cups ketchup
- 1 cup barbecue sauce
- ¼ cup packed brown sugar
- ¼ cup cider vinegar
- 2 Tbsp. prepared mustard
- 1 tsp. Italian seasoning
- 1 tsp. onion powder
- ½ tsp. pepper
- 12 hamburger buns, split

In a large skillet, cook beef, onions and garlic over medium heat until the meat is no longer pink, breaking meat into crumbles; drain. Stir in the ketchup, barbecue sauce, brown sugar, vinegar, mustard, Italian seasoning, onion powder and pepper. Bring to a boil. Reduce the heat; simmer, uncovered, for 20 minutes. Serve on buns.
Freeze option: Freeze cooled meat mixture in freezer containers. To use, partially thaw in the refrigerator overnight. Heat through in a saucepan, stirring occasionally; add water if necessary.
1 sandwich: 368 cal., 11g fat (4g sat. fat), 47mg chol., 1029mg sod., 49g carb. (27g sugars, 1g fiber), 18g pro.

CHICKEN WILD RICE SOUP

This savory soup has a lot of substance, and we enjoy brimming bowls of it all winter long. The men in my family especially love it.
—Virginia Montmarquet, Riverside, CA

- -

Prep: 20 min. • **Cook:** 40 min.
Makes: 14 servings (3½ qt.)

- 2 qt. chicken broth
- ½ lb. fresh mushrooms, chopped
- 1 cup finely chopped celery
- 1 cup shredded carrots
- ½ cup finely chopped onion
- 1 tsp. chicken bouillon granules
- 1 tsp. dried parsley flakes
- ¼ tsp. garlic powder
- ¼ tsp. dried thyme
- ¼ cup butter, cubed
- ¼ cup all-purpose flour
- 1 can (10¾ oz.) condensed cream of mushroom soup, undiluted
- ½ cup dry white wine or additional chicken broth
- 3 cups cooked wild rice
- 2 cups cubed cooked chicken

1. In a large saucepan, combine the first 9 ingredients. Bring to a boil. Reduce heat; cover and simmer for 30 minutes.
2. In Dutch oven, melt the butter; stir in the flour until smooth. Gradually whisk in broth mixture. Bring to a boil; cook and stir for 2 minutes or until thickened. Whisk in the soup and wine. Add the rice and chicken; heat through.
1 cup: 154 cal., 6g fat (3g sat. fat), 27mg chol., 807mg sod., 14g carb. (2g sugars, 2g fiber), 10g pro.

MELT-IN-YOUR-MOUTH SAUSAGES

My family loves this recipe. It's such a good all-around dish, either for sandwiches like these or served with hot cooked spaghetti.
—Ilean Schultheiss, Cohocton, NY

Prep: 10 min. • **Cook:** 4 hours
Makes: 8 servings

- 8 **Italian sausage links (2 lbs.)**
- 1 **jar (26 oz.) meatless spaghetti sauce**
- ½ **cup water**
- 1 **can (6 oz.) tomato paste**
- 1 **large green pepper, thinly sliced**
- 1 **large onion, thinly sliced**
- 1 **Tbsp. grated Parmesan cheese**
- 1 **tsp. dried parsley flakes**
- 8 **brat buns, split**
  Additional Parmesan cheese, optional

1. Place the sausages in a large skillet; cover with water. Bring to a boil. Reduce the heat. Cover and simmer for 10 minutes or until a thermometer reads 160°; drain well.
2. In a 3-qt. slow cooker, combine spaghetti sauce, water, tomato paste, green pepper, onion, cheese and parsley. Add sausages. Cover and cook on low 4-5 hours or until the vegetables are tender. Serve in buns. Sprinkle with additional cheese if desired.
1 sandwich: 557 cal., 29g fat (9g sat. fat), 62mg chol., 1510mg sod., 51g carb. (14g sugars, 4g fiber), 24g pro.

TUNA ARTICHOKE MELTS

After sampling a similar open-faced sandwich at a restaurant, I created my own version of lemon-seasoned tuna salad with artichoke hearts. Serve these melts on the patio for lunch with a friend.
—Evelyn Basinger, Linville, VA

Takes: 15 min. • **Makes:** 2 servings

- 1 **can (6 oz.) light water-packed tuna, drained and flaked**
- ⅓ **cup coarsely chopped water-packed artichoke hearts, rinsed and drained**
- 2 **Tbsp. mayonnaise**
- ½ **cup shredded Mexican cheese blend, divided**
- ¼ **tsp. lemon-pepper seasoning**
- ⅛ **tsp. dried oregano**
- 2 **English muffins, split and toasted**

1. Preheat broiler. In a small bowl, combine the tuna, artichokes, mayonnaise, ¼ cup cheese, lemon pepper and oregano. Spread over English muffin halves.
2. Place on a baking sheet. Broil 4-6 in. from the heat until heated through, 3-5 minutes. Sprinkle with remaining cheese; broil until cheese is melted, 1-2 minutes longer.
2 topped muffin halves: 335 cal., 8g fat (4g sat. fat), 47mg chol., 989mg sod., 31g carb. (3g sugars, 2g fiber), 34g pro.

THAI-INSPIRED ROAST BEEF SANDWICH

We wanted to see how Thai flavors would translate in a plain old peanut butter sandwich. The result is anything but plain—it's just darn delicious.
—*Taste of Home* Test Kitchen

Takes: 5 min. • **Makes:** 1 serving

- 1 **Tbsp. creamy peanut butter**
- 1 **slice crusty white bread**
- 2 **thin slices deli roast beef**
- 1 **tsp. chopped salted peanuts**
- ½ **tsp. grated lime zest**
- ⅛ **tsp. crushed red pepper flakes**

Spread peanut butter over bread. Top with the remaining ingredients.
1 open-faced sandwich: 239 cal., 12g fat (3g sat. fat), 24mg chol., 458mg sod., 19g carb. (4g sugars, 2g fiber), 15g pro.

AUTUMN PORK ROAST,
PAGE 121

Meaty Main Dishes

From beef and lamb to pork and poultry,
this chapter has an assortment of
hearty entrees to fit any occasion.

FOUR-CHEESE CHICKEN FETTUCCINE

As a cattle rancher, my husband is a big fan of beef. For him to comment on a poultry dish is rare. But he always tells me he loves this casserole! I first tasted it at a potluck. Now, I fix it for my family once or twice a month, and I'm asked to take it to most every get-together.

—Rochelle Brownlee, Big Timber, MT

- -

Prep: 20 min.
Bake: 30 min.
Makes: 8 servings

- 8 oz. uncooked fettuccine
- 1 can (10¾ oz.) condensed cream of mushroom soup, undiluted
- 1 pkg. (8 oz.) cream cheese, cubed
- 1 jar (4½ oz.) sliced mushrooms, drained
- 1 cup heavy whipping cream
- ½ cup butter
- ¼ tsp. garlic powder
- ¾ cup grated Parmesan cheese
- ½ cup shredded part-skim mozzarella cheese
- ½ cup shredded Swiss cheese
- 2½ cups cubed cooked chicken

TOPPING

- ⅓ cup seasoned bread crumbs
- 2 Tbsp. butter, melted
- 1 to 2 Tbsp. grated Parmesan cheese

1. Cook the fettuccine according to the package directions.

2. Meanwhile, in a large kettle, combine the soup, cream cheese, mushrooms, cream, butter and garlic powder. Stir in cheeses; cook and stir until melted. Add chicken; heat through. Drain fettuccine; add to the sauce.

3. Transfer to a greased 2½-qt. baking dish. Combine topping ingredients; sprinkle over chicken mixture. Cover and bake at 350° for 25 minutes. Uncover; bake 5-10 minutes longer or until golden brown.

1 serving: 641 cal., 47g fat (27g sat. fat), 167mg chol., 895mg sod., 29g carb. (3g sugars, 2g fiber), 28g pro.

GARLIC BEEF ENCHILADAS

Enchiladas are typically prepared with corn tortillas, but we prefer flour tortillas in this saucy casserole with a subtle kick.

—Jennifer Standridge, Dallas, GA

- -

Prep: 30 min. • **Bake:** 40 min.
Makes: 5 servings

- 1 lb. ground beef
- 1 medium onion, chopped
- 2 Tbsp. all-purpose flour
- 1 Tbsp. chili powder
- 1 tsp. salt
- 1 tsp. garlic powder
- ½ tsp. ground cumin
- ¼ tsp. rubbed sage
- 1 can (14½ oz.) stewed tomatoes, cut up

SAUCE

- ⅓ cup butter
- 4 to 6 garlic cloves, minced
- ½ cup all-purpose flour
- 1 can (14½ oz.) beef broth
- 1 can (15 oz.) tomato sauce
- 1 to 2 Tbsp. chili powder
- 1 to 2 tsp. ground cumin
- 1 to 2 tsp. rubbed sage
- ½ tsp. salt
- 10 flour tortillas (6 in.), warmed
- 2 cups shredded Colby-Monterey Jack cheese, divided
  Optional toppings: Halved grape tomatoes, minced fresh cilantro, sliced jalapeno peppers, chopped or sliced red onion and cubed avocado

1. Preheat the oven to 350°. In a large skillet, cook beef and onion over medium heat until beef is no longer pink, 6-8 minutes, breaking meat into crumbles; drain. Stir in flour and seasonings. Add tomatoes; bring to a boil. Reduce heat; simmer, covered, 15 minutes.

2. In a saucepan, heat butter over medium-high heat. Add garlic; cook and stir 1 minute or until tender. Stir in the flour until blended; gradually whisk in the broth. Bring to a boil; cook and stir for about 2 minutes or until thickened. Stir in the tomato sauce and seasonings; heat through.

3. Pour 1½ cups sauce into an ungreased 13x9-in. baking dish. Place about ¼ cup beef mixture off center on each tortilla; top with 1-2 Tbsp. cheese. Roll up; place over sauce, seam side down. Top with remaining sauce.

4. Bake, covered, 30-35 minutes or until heated through. Sprinkle with remaining cheese. Bake, uncovered, until cheese is melted, 10-15 minutes longer. Serve with toppings as desired.

2 enchiladas: 751 cal., 43g fat (21g sat. fat), 128mg chol., 2536mg sod., 56g carb. (8g sugars, 4g fiber), 38g pro.

FOUR-CHEESE CHICKEN FETTUCCINE

GARLIC BEEF
ENCHILADAS

AIR-FRYER PORK TENDERLOIN

Finally, a way to cook pork tenderloin even faster than the oven! This air-fryer version takes only a few short minutes to make.
—Lynn Faria, Southington, CT

- -

Prep: 10 min. • **Cook:** 20 min. + standing
Makes: 2 servings

1   **pork tenderloin (¾ lb.)**
1   **Tbsp. spicy brown mustard**
2   **tsp. canola oil**
1   **tsp. garlic powder**
1   **tsp. onion powder**
½   **tsp. pepper**

Preheat air fryer to 375°. Trim the silver skin from tenderloin if desired; pat dry. In a small bowl, stir together remaining ingredients; spread over tenderloin. Place in greased air fryer. Cook until a thermometer reads 145°, 18 to 20 minutes. Let stand for 10 minutes before slicing.

5 oz. cooked pork: 257 cal., 11g fat (2g sat. fat), 95mg chol., 145mg sod., 2g carb. (0 sugars, 0 fiber), 34g pro. **Diabetic exchanges:** 5 lean meat, 1 fat.

"This pork is incredibly tender and has fantastic flavor from the spicy brown mustard and seasonings."

—MARGARET KNOEBEL, ASSISTANT RECIPE EDITOR

AIR-FRYER PORK TENDERLOIN

TAKEOUT BEEF FRIED RICE

Transform last night's supper into tonight's dinner for six. Hoisin-flavored chuck roast works wonders in this recipe, but you can use flank steak as well.
—*Taste of Home* Test Kitchen

- -

Takes: 30 min. • **Makes:** 6 servings

- -

- 1 Tbsp. plus 1 tsp. canola oil, divided
- 3 large eggs
- 1 can (11 oz.) mandarin oranges
- 2 medium sweet red peppers, chopped
- 1 cup fresh sugar snap peas, trimmed
- 1 small onion, thinly sliced
- 3 garlic cloves, minced
- ½ tsp. crushed red pepper flakes
- 4 cups cold cooked rice
- 2 cups cooked beef, sliced across grain into bite-sized pieces
- 1 cup beef broth
- ¼ cup reduced-sodium soy sauce
- ½ tsp. salt
- ¼ tsp. ground ginger

1. In a skillet, heat 1 Tbsp. oil over medium-high heat. Whisk eggs until blended; pour into skillet. Mixture should set immediately at edge. As eggs set, push cooked portions toward center, letting uncooked portions flow underneath. When eggs are thickened and no liquid remains, remove to a cutting board and chop. Meanwhile, drain oranges, reserving 2 Tbsp. juice.
2. In the same skillet, heat remaining 1 tsp. oil over medium-high heat. Add peppers, sugar snap peas and onion; cook and stir until crisp-tender, 1-2 minutes. Add garlic and pepper flakes; cook 1 minute longer. Add remaining ingredients and reserved juice; heat through. Gently stir in eggs and drained oranges.
1⅓ cups: 367 cal., 9g fat (2g sat. fat), 136mg chol., 793mg sod., 45g carb. (11g sugars, 3g fiber), 26g pro. **Diabetic exchanges:** 3 starch, 3 lean meat, 1 fat.

MOTHER'S HAM CASSEROLE

One of my mother's favorite dishes, this ham casserole recipe always brings back fond memories of her when I prepare it. It's a terrific use of leftover ham from a holiday dinner. Our five grandchildren love it, and I'm happy to make it for them.
—Linda Childers, Murfreesboro, TN

- -

Prep: 35 min. • **Bake:** 25 min.
Makes: 6 servings

- -

- 2 cups cubed peeled potatoes
- 1 large carrot, sliced
- 2 celery ribs, chopped
- 3 cups water
- 2 cups cubed fully cooked ham
- 2 Tbsp. chopped green pepper
- 2 tsp. finely chopped onion
- 7 Tbsp. butter, divided
- 3 Tbsp. all-purpose flour
- 1½ cups 2% milk
- ¾ tsp. salt
- ⅛ tsp. pepper
- 1 cup shredded cheddar cheese
- ½ cup soft bread crumbs

1. Preheat oven to 375°. In a saucepan, bring the potatoes, carrot, celery and water to a boil. Reduce the heat; cover and cook until tender, about 15 minutes. Drain.
2. In a large skillet, saute ham, green pepper and onion in 3 Tbsp. butter until tender. Add the potato mixture. Transfer to a greased 1½-qt. baking dish.
3. In a large saucepan, melt the remaining 4 Tbsp. butter; stir in flour until smooth. Gradually whisk in the milk, salt and pepper. Bring to a boil; cook and stir for 2 minutes or until thickened. Reduce heat; add cheese and stir until melted.
4. Pour over ham mixture. Sprinkle with bread crumbs. Bake for 25-30 minutes or until heated through.
Note: To make soft bread crumbs, tear bread into pieces and place in a food processor or blender. Cover and pulse until crumbs form. One slice of bread yields ½ to ¾ cup crumbs.
1 cup: 360 cal., 23g fat (14g sat. fat), 87mg chol., 1157mg sod., 21g carb. (5g sugars, 2g fiber), 18g pro.

MOTHER'S HAM CASSEROLE

SLOW-COOKED
SPICY GOULASH

SLOW-COOKED SPICY GOULASH

Ground cumin, chili powder and a can of Mexican diced tomatoes jazz up my goulash recipe. Even the macaroni is prepared in the slow cooker.
—Melissa Polk, West Lafayette, IN

Prep: 25 min. • **Cook:** 5½ hours
Makes: 8 servings

- 1 lb. lean ground beef (90% lean)
- 4 cans (14½ oz. each) Mexican diced tomatoes, undrained
- 2 cans (16 oz. each) kidney beans, rinsed and drained
- 2 cups water
- 1 medium onion, chopped
- 1 medium green pepper, chopped
- ¼ cup red wine vinegar
- 2 Tbsp. chili powder
- 1 Tbsp. Worcestershire sauce
- 2 tsp. beef bouillon granules
- 1 tsp. dried basil
- 1 tsp. dried parsley flakes
- 1 tsp. ground cumin
- ¼ tsp. pepper
- 2 cups uncooked elbow macaroni

1. In a large skillet, cook beef over medium heat until no longer pink, breaking the meat into crumbles; drain. Transfer to a 5-qt. slow cooker. Stir in the tomatoes, beans, water, onion, green pepper, vinegar, chili powder, Worcestershire sauce, bouillon and seasonings. Cover and cook on low for 5-6 hours or until heated through.
2. Stir in macaroni. Cover; cook 30 minutes longer or until macaroni is tender.
1½ cups: 315 cal., 6g fat (2g sat. fat), 35mg chol., 915mg sod., 44g carb. (11g sugars, 9g fiber), 23g pro.

SLOW-COOKER CHEESY WHITE LASAGNA

Here's my best version of my favorite food—lasagna! The recipe is a winner, so it's worth the extra prep. Plan side dishes while the main dish is cooking.
—Suzanne Smith, Bluffton, IN

Prep: 30 min. • **Cook:** 3 hours + standing
Makes: 8 servings

- 1 lb. ground chicken or beef
- 2 tsp. canola oil
- 1¾ cups sliced fresh mushrooms
- 1 medium onion, chopped
- 2 medium carrots, chopped
- 2 garlic cloves, minced
- 2 tsp. Italian seasoning
- ¾ tsp. salt
- ½ tsp. pepper
- ½ cup white wine or chicken broth
- 1 cup half-and-half cream
- 4 oz. cream cheese, softened
- 1 cup shredded white cheddar cheese
- 1 cup shredded Gouda cheese
- 1 large egg, beaten
- 1½ cups 2% cottage cheese
- ¼ cup minced fresh basil or 4 tsp. dried basil
- 9 no-cook lasagna noodles
- 4 cups shredded part-skim mozzarella cheese
  Additional minced fresh basil, optional

1. Fold two 18-in. square pieces of heavy-duty foil into thirds. Crisscross the strips and place on bottom and up sides of a 6-qt. slow cooker. Coat strips with cooking spray.
2. In a 6-qt. stockpot, cook the chicken over medium heat until no longer pink, 6-8 minutes, breaking into crumbles; drain. Remove chicken and set aside.
3. In same pot, heat oil over medium-high heat. Add mushrooms, onion and carrots; cook and stir just until tender, 6-8 minutes. Add garlic, Italian seasoning, salt and pepper; cook 1 minute longer. Stir in the wine. Bring to a boil; cook until liquid is reduced by half, 4-5 minutes. Stir in cream, cream cheese, cheddar and Gouda cheeses. Return chicken to pot. In a large bowl, combine egg, cottage cheese and basil.
4. Spread 1 cup chicken mixture into the slow cooker. Layer with 3 noodles (breaking noodles as necessary to fit), 1 cup chicken mixture, ½ cup cottage cheese mixture and 1 cup mozzarella cheese. Repeat layers twice. Top with remaining chicken mixture and mozzarella. Cook, covered, on low until noodles are tender, 3-4 hours. Remove slow cooker insert and let stand 30 minutes. If desired, sprinkle with more basil. Using foil strips as handles, remove the lasagna to a cutting board or platter.
1 piece: 603 cal., 35g fat (19g sat. fat), 165mg chol., 1086mg sod., 28g carb. (7g sugars, 2g fiber), 40g pro.

SLOW-COOKER CHEESY WHITE LASAGNA

SLOW-COOKED TACO MEAT LOAF

This meat loaf is a hit with my family. My three sons eat two pieces each, which is incredible, considering that they are very picky toddlers. The southwest-style meat loaf is topped with a sweet and tangy sauce.
—Lacey Kirsch, Vancouver, WA

- -

Prep: 20 min. • **Cook:** 3 hours + standing
Makes: 8 servings

- 2 cups crushed tortilla chips
- 1 cup shredded cheddar cheese
- 1 cup salsa
- 2 large eggs, lightly beaten
- ¼ cup sliced ripe olives
- 1 envelope taco seasoning
- 2 lbs. lean ground beef (90% lean)
- ½ cup ketchup
- ¼ cup packed brown sugar
- 2 Tbsp. Louisiana-style hot sauce

1. Cut four 20x3-in. strips of heavy-duty foil; crisscross so they resemble spokes of a wheel. Place strips on the bottom and up the sides of a 3-qt. slow cooker. Coat strips with cooking spray.
2. In a bowl, combine first 6 ingredients. Crumble beef over mixture and mix well. Shape into a round loaf. Place meat loaf in the center of the strips. Cover and cook on low for 3-4 hours or until no pink remains and a thermometer reads 160°.
3. Combine ketchup, brown sugar and hot sauce; pour over meat loaf during the last hour of cooking. Let stand for 10 minutes. Using foil strips as handles, remove the meat loaf to a platter.
1 piece: 345 cal., 16g fat (7g sat. fat), 138mg chol., 936mg sod., 21g carb. (12g sugars, 0 fiber), 27g pro.

> "This is so delicious and easy to transport, I even made it for my sister's birthday dinner on Christmas Eve one year. I like to serve it with polenta."
>
> —CHRISTINE RUKAVENA, SENIOR EDITOR

TROPICAL CHICKEN CAULIFLOWER RICE BOWLS

This fresh favorite is a delicious and healthy dinner with tons of flavor! You can substitute regular rice for the cauliflower rice if desired.
—Bethany DiCarlo, Harleysville, PA

- -

Prep: 40 min. + marinating • **Grill:** 10 min.
Makes: 4 servings

- 1 fresh pineapple, peeled, cored and cubed (about 3 cups), divided
- ½ cup plain or coconut Greek yogurt
- 2 Tbsp. plus ½ cup chopped fresh cilantro, divided
- 3 Tbsp. lime juice, divided
- ¾ tsp. salt, divided
- ¼ tsp. crushed red pepper flakes
- ⅛ tsp. chili powder
- 4 boneless skinless chicken breast halves (6 oz. each)
- 3 cups fresh cauliflower florets (about ½ small cauliflower)
- 1 Tbsp. canola oil
- 1 small red onion, finely chopped
   Optional: Toasted sweetened shredded coconut or lime wedges

1. For the marinade, place 1 cup pineapple, yogurt, 2 Tbsp. each cilantro and lime juice, ¼ tsp. salt, pepper flakes and chili powder in a food processor; process until blended. In a large bowl, toss chicken with marinade; refrigerate, covered, 1-3 hours.
2. In a clean food processor, pulse the cauliflower until it resembles rice (do not overprocess). In a large skillet, heat oil over medium-high heat; saute onion until lightly browned, 3-5 minutes. Add cauliflower; cook and stir until lightly browned, 5-7 minutes. Stir in 1 cup pineapple and remaining 1 Tbsp. lime juice and ½ tsp. salt; cook, covered, over medium heat until the cauliflower is tender, 3-5 minutes. Stir in remaining ½ cup cilantro. Keep warm.
3. Preheat grill or broiler. Drain the chicken, discarding marinade. Place the chicken on an oiled grill rack over medium heat or in a greased foil-lined 15x10x1-in. pan. Grill, covered, or broil 4 in. from heat until a thermometer reads 165°, 4-6 minutes per side. Let stand 5 minutes before slicing.
4. To serve, divide cauliflower mixture among 4 bowls. Top with the chicken, remaining 1 cup pineapple and, if desired, shredded coconut and lime wedges.
1 serving: 325 cal., 10g fat (3g sat. fat), 100mg chol., 529mg sod., 22g carb. (15g sugars, 4g fiber), 38g pro. **Diabetic exchanges:** 5 lean meat, 1 fruit, 1 vegetable, 1 fat.

TROPICAL CHICKEN CAULIFLOWER RICE BOWLS

MUSTARD-CRUSTED PRIME RIB WITH MADEIRA GLAZE

This juicy prime rib is spectacular on its own, but the rich Madeira glaze takes it up a notch to wow at special dinners. What's even better is that it roasts with a bed of tender veggies, so you have the whole meal covered in one pan.

—Kathryn Conrad, Milwaukee, WI

Prep: 20 min. • **Bake:** 2½ hours + standing
Makes: 8 servings

- 1 **bone-in beef rib roast (about 5 lbs.)**
- ½ **cup stone-ground mustard**
- 6 **small garlic cloves, minced**
- 1 **Tbsp. brown sugar**
- ½ **tsp. salt**
- ½ **tsp. coarsely ground pink peppercorns, optional**

VEGETABLES
- 2 **lbs. medium Yukon Gold potatoes, cut into eighths (about 2-in. chunks)**
- 4 **medium carrots, halved lengthwise and cut into 2-in. pieces**
- 1 **medium red onion, cut into eighths (but with root end intact)**
- 1 **medium fennel bulb, cut into eighths**
- 3 **Tbsp. olive oil**
- 1 **Tbsp. balsamic vinegar**
- 1 **tsp. brown sugar**
- ¾ **tsp. salt**
- ½ **tsp. pepper**

MADEIRA GLAZE
- 1 **cup balsamic vinegar**
- ½ **cup Madeira wine**
- 1 **tsp. brown sugar**
  Cracked pink peppercorns, optional

MUSTARD-CRUSTED PRIME RIB WITH MADEIRA GLAZE

1. Let roast stand at room temperature for 1 hour. Preheat oven to 450°. Combine mustard, garlic, brown sugar, salt and, if desired, peppercorns; brush evenly over the top and sides of roast but not over bones (mixture may seem loose but will adhere). Place bone side down on a rack in a shallow roasting pan. Place pan on middle oven rack; immediately reduce heat to 350°. Roast for 1 hour.

2. Toss potatoes, carrots, onion and fennel with next 5 ingredients. Arrange vegetables in a single layer in a 15x10x1-in. baking pan on lowest rack of oven. Roast the meat and vegetables, stirring the vegetables midway through baking, until meat reaches desired doneness (a thermometer should read 135° for medium-rare, 140° for medium and 145° for medium-well), about 1½ hours. Cover the roast loosely with foil during the last 30 minutes to prevent overbrowning. Let stand 15 minutes before carving.

3. Meanwhile, for glaze, combine balsamic vinegar, Madeira wine and brown sugar in a small saucepan. Bring to a boil over medium-high heat; cook until reduced to ½ cup, about 15 minutes. Let glaze cool to room temperature. Serve the roast with vegetables and glaze and, if desired, pink peppercorns and fennel fronds.

1 serving: 575 cal., 25g fat (8g sat. fat), 0 chol., 828mg sod., 44g carb. (18g sugars, 5g fiber), 42g pro.

ASK SARAH

WHAT IS A RIB ROAST?
A rib roast comes from the rib portion of a cow, an area that's extra tender and marbled with fat. It's a very flavorful cut that requires no marinating.

SLOW-COOKER BEEF STEW

BEER & BACON MACARONI & CHEESE

We put a creative spin on classic mac and cheese by adding our favorite beer and bacon. Six tests later, we are happy.
—Cindy Worth, Lapwai, ID

Prep: 25 min. • **Bake:** 15 min.
Makes: 6 servings

- 2 cups uncooked elbow macaroni
- 6 bacon strips, chopped
- 3 garlic cloves, minced
- ¼ cup all-purpose flour
- 1¾ cups 2% milk
- ⅔ cup brown ale or chicken broth
- 1 cup shredded Parmesan cheese
- 1 cup shredded extra-sharp cheddar cheese
- 2 green onions, chopped
- ½ tsp. salt
- ¼ tsp. pepper
  Additional green onions

1. Preheat the oven to 375°. Cook the macaroni according to package directions for al dente; drain.
2. Meanwhile, in a 10-in. cast-iron or other ovenproof skillet, cook bacon over medium heat until crisp. Remove to paper towels. To the same pan, add garlic; cook and stir 30 seconds. Stir in the flour until blended; gradually whisk in milk and beer. Bring to a boil, stirring constantly; cook until thickened, 2-3 minutes. Stir in cheeses until blended. Add macaroni, green onions, salt, pepper and half the bacon; stir to combine. Bake, uncovered, until bubbly, 15-20 minutes. Sprinkle with the remaining bacon and additional green onions. Serve immediately.
1¼ cups: 398 cal., 23g fat (11g sat. fat), 52mg chol., 767mg sod., 28g carb. (5g sugars, 1g fiber), 19g pro.

"The title of this recipe says it all regarding this guy-food favorite. It's really just the best thing ever!"

—MARK HAGEN, EXECUTIVE EDITOR

SLOW-COOKER BEEF STEW

When there's a chill in the air, I love to make this stew. It's loaded with tender chunks of beef, potatoes and carrots.
—Earnestine Wilson, Waco, TX

Prep: 25 min. • **Cook:** 7 hours
Makes: 8 servings (2 qt.)

- 1½ lbs. potatoes, peeled and cubed
- 6 medium carrots, cut into 1-in. lengths
- 1 medium onion, coarsely chopped
- 3 celery ribs, coarsely chopped
- 3 Tbsp. all-purpose flour
- 1½ lbs. beef stew meat, cut into 1-in. cubes
- 3 Tbsp. canola oil
- 1 can (14½ oz.) diced tomatoes, undrained
- 1 can (14½ oz.) beef broth
- 1 tsp. ground mustard
- ½ tsp. salt
- ½ tsp. pepper
- ½ tsp. dried thyme
- ½ tsp. browning sauce, optional
  Minced fresh thyme

1. Layer the potatoes, carrots, onion and celery in a 5-qt. slow cooker. Place flour in a large shallow dish. Add stew meat; turn to coat evenly. In a large skillet, brown meat in oil in batches. Place over vegetables.
2. In a large bowl, combine tomatoes, broth, mustard, salt, pepper, thyme and, if desired, browning sauce. Pour over beef. Cover and cook on low for 7-8 hours, or until the meat and vegetables are tender. If desired, sprinkle with fresh thyme before serving.
1 cup: 272 cal., 12g fat (3g sat. fat), 53mg chol., 541mg sod., 23g carb. (6g sugars, 4g fiber), 19g pro. **Diabetic exchanges:** 2 lean meat, 1½ starch, 1 fat.

BEER & BACON
MACARONI & CHEESE

TURKEY POTPIES

TURKEY POTPIES

With its golden brown crust and scrumptious filling, these comforting potpies will warm you down to your toes. Because it makes two, you can eat one now and freeze the other for later.
—Laurie Jensen, Cadillac, MI

Prep: 40 min. • **Bake:** 40 min. + standing
Makes: 2 pies (6 servings each)

2	medium potatoes, peeled and cut into 1-in. pieces
3	medium carrots, cut into 1-in. slices
1	medium onion, chopped
1	celery rib, diced
2	Tbsp. butter
1	Tbsp. olive oil
6	Tbsp. all-purpose flour
3	cups chicken broth
4	cups cubed cooked turkey
⅔	cup frozen peas
½	cup plus 1 Tbsp. heavy whipping cream, divided
1	Tbsp. minced fresh parsley
1	tsp. garlic salt
¼	tsp. pepper
2	sheets refrigerated pie crust
1	large egg

1. Preheat oven to 375°. In a Dutch oven, saute potatoes, carrots, onion and celery in butter and oil until tender. Stir in flour until blended; gradually add broth. Bring to a boil; cook and stir 2 minutes or until thickened. Stir in turkey, peas, ½ cup cream, parsley, garlic salt and pepper.
2. Spoon into 2 ungreased 9-in. pie plates. Unroll crusts; place over filling. Trim crusts and seal to edge of pie plates. Cut out a decorative center or cut slits in crusts. In a small bowl, whisk egg and remaining 1 Tbsp. cream; brush over crusts.
3. Bake until golden brown, 40-45 minutes. Let stand 10 minutes before cutting.
Freeze option: Cover and freeze unbaked potpies up to 3 months. To use, remove from freezer 30 minutes before baking (do not thaw). Preheat oven to 425°. Place pie on a baking sheet; cover edge loosely with foil. Bake 30 minutes. Reduce oven setting to 350°; remove foil. Bake until golden brown and a thermometer inserted in center reads 165°, 55-60 minutes longer.
1 serving: 287 cal., 15g fat (7g sat. fat), 78mg chol., 542mg sod., 21g carb. (3g sugars, 2g fiber), 17g pro.

AUTUMN PORK ROAST

Although this main meal captures the fabulous flavor of fall, don't hesitate to serve it throughout the year. Your family will flock to the table when they smell this delicious roast. It's a hearty dish that makes everyday dinners more special.
—Kathy Barbarek, Joliet, IL

- -

Prep: 20 min. • **Bake:** 2 hours + standing
Makes: 12 servings

    1   bone-in pork loin roast (5 lbs.)
    8   medium potatoes, peeled
        and quartered
    8   carrots, halved lengthwise
    2   medium onions, quartered
    1   small pumpkin or butternut squash,
        peeled and cut into 1½-in. chunks
    1   cup water
    3   Tbsp. snipped fresh sage
        or 1 Tbsp. rubbed sage
    1   tsp. salt
    ¼   tsp. pepper
    2   Tbsp. butter
    4   medium baking apples, quartered

1. Place roast in a large baking pan. Arrange the potatoes, carrots, onions and pumpkin around roast. Add water to the pan. Sprinkle the meat and vegetables with sage, salt and pepper; dot vegetables with butter.
2. Bake, uncovered, at 400° for 15 minutes. Reduce heat to 350°; bake, uncovered, for 1 hour. Place the apples around roast; cover and bake until a thermometer inserted in pork reads 145°, 45-60 minutes, basting every 30 minutes. Let stand 10 minutes before slicing. If desired, thicken pan juices for gravy.
1 serving: 359 cal., 9g fat (3g sat. fat), 76mg chol., 295mg sod., 41g carb. (11g sugars, 7g fiber), 30g pro. **Diabetic exchanges:** 4 lean meat, 2½ starch.

CHICKEN & DUMPLING CASSEROLE

This savory casserole is one of my husband's favorites. He loves the fluffy dumplings with plenty of gravy poured over them. The basil adds just the right touch of flavor and makes the whole house smell so good while the dish cooks.
—Sue Mackey, Jackson, WI

- -

Prep: 30 min. • **Bake:** 40 min.
Makes: 8 servings

    ½   cup chopped onion
    ½   cup chopped celery
    ¼   cup butter, cubed
    2   garlic cloves, minced
    ½   cup all-purpose flour
    2   tsp. sugar
    1   tsp. salt
    1   tsp. dried basil
    ½   tsp. pepper
    4   cups chicken broth
    1   pkg. (10 oz.) frozen green peas
    4   cups cubed cooked chicken

DUMPLINGS

    2   cups biscuit/baking mix
    2   tsp. dried basil
    ⅔   cup 2% milk

1. Preheat oven to 350°. In a large saucepan, saute onion and celery in butter until tender. Add garlic; cook 1 minute longer. Stir in flour, sugar, salt, basil and pepper until blended. Gradually add broth; bring to a boil. Cook and stir 1 minute or until thickened; reduce heat. Add peas and cook 5 minutes, stirring constantly. Stir in the chicken. Pour into a greased 13x9-in. baking dish.
2. For dumplings, in a small bowl, combine baking mix and basil. Stir in milk with a fork until moistened. Drop by tablespoonfuls into mounds over chicken mixture.
3. Bake, uncovered, 30 minutes. Cover and bake 10 minutes longer or until a toothpick inserted in a dumpling comes out clean.
1 serving: 393 cal., 17g fat (7g sat. fat), 80mg chol., 1313mg sod., 33g carb. (6g sugars, 3g fiber), 27g pro.

CHICKEN & DUMPLING CASSEROLE

ONE-SKILLET LASAGNA

ONE-SKILLET LASAGNA

This is hands-down one of the best skillet lasagna recipes our testing panel has ever tasted. And with classic flavors and cheesy layers, it's definitely kid-friendly.
—*Taste of Home* Test Kitchen

Takes: 30 min. • **Makes:** 6 servings

- ¾ lb. ground beef
- 2 garlic cloves, minced
- 1 can (14½ oz.) diced tomatoes with basil, oregano and garlic, undrained
- 2 jars (14 oz. each) spaghetti sauce
- ⅔ cup condensed cream of onion soup, undiluted
- 2 large eggs, lightly beaten
- 1¼ cups 1% cottage cheese
- ¾ tsp. Italian seasoning
- 9 no-cook lasagna noodles
- ½ cup shredded Colby-Monterey Jack cheese
- ½ cup shredded part-skim mozzarella cheese

1. In a large skillet, cook beef and garlic over medium heat until meat is no longer pink, breaking beef into crumbles; drain. Stir in tomatoes and spaghetti sauce; heat through. Transfer to a large bowl.
2. In a small bowl, combine the soup, eggs, cottage cheese and Italian seasoning.
3. Return 1 cup meat sauce to the skillet; spread evenly. Layer with 1 cup cottage cheese mixture, 1½ cups meat sauce and half the noodles, breaking to fit. Repeat layers of cottage cheese mixture, meat sauce and noodles. Top with remaining meat sauce. Bring to a boil. Reduce heat; cover and simmer for 15-17 minutes or until noodles are tender.
4. Remove from the heat. Sprinkle with shredded cheeses; cover and let stand for 2 minutes or until cheese is melted.
1 serving: 478 cal., 20g fat (8g sat. fat), 128mg chol., 1552mg sod., 43g carb. (15g sugars, 4g fiber), 31g pro.

TEST KITCHEN TIP
Use a sturdy wooden spoon or a spatula to break up the ground beef while it's cooking.

SPICY ROASTED SAUSAGE, POTATOES & PEPPERS

SPICY ROASTED SAUSAGE, POTATOES & PEPPERS

I love to share my cooking, and this hearty sheet-pan dinner has gotten a tasty reputation. People have actually approached me in public to ask for the recipe! I'm always happy to share.
—Laurie Sledge, Brandon, MS

Prep: 20 min. • **Bake:** 30 min.
Makes: 4 servings

- 1 lb. potatoes (about 2 medium), peeled and cut into ½-in. cubes
- 1 pkg. (12 oz.) fully cooked andouille chicken sausage links or flavor of your choice, cut into 1-in. pieces
- 1 medium red onion, cut into wedges
- 1 medium sweet red pepper, cut into 1-in. pieces
- 1 medium green pepper, cut into 1-in. pieces
- ½ cup pickled pepper rings
- 1 Tbsp. olive oil
- ½ to 1 tsp. Creole seasoning
- ¼ tsp. pepper

1. Preheat oven to 400°. In a large bowl, combine the potatoes, sausage, onion, red pepper, green pepper and pepper rings. Mix the oil, Creole seasoning and pepper; drizzle over potato mixture and toss to coat.
2. Transfer to a 15x10x1-in. baking pan coated with cooking spray. Roast until vegetables are tender, stirring occasionally, 30-35 minutes.
1½ cups: 257 cal., 11g fat (3g sat. fat), 65mg chol., 759mg sod., 24g carb. (5g sugars, 3g fiber), 17g pro. **Diabetic exchanges:** 3 lean meat, 1 starch, 1 vegetable, 1 fat.

"This is so simple and can be made on a moment's notice from things I usually have on hand. I often toss in more pickled peppers."

—RASHANDA COBBINS, FOOD EDITOR

THAI PEANUT CHICKEN & NOODLES

This versatile chicken recipe is very similar to chicken pad thai but is easier to make and tastes just as good. Rice noodles can be replaced with mung bean noodles or any type of egg noodles.
—Kristina Segarra, Yonkers, NY

Takes: 30 min.
Makes: 4 servings

- ½ cup water
- ¼ cup soy sauce
- 2 Tbsp. rice vinegar
- 2 Tbsp. creamy peanut butter
- 3 garlic cloves, minced
- 1 to 2 tsp. Sriracha chili sauce
- 1 tsp. sesame oil
- 1 tsp. molasses
- 1 pkg. (6.75 oz.) thin rice noodles
- 2 Tbsp. peanut oil, divided
- 1 lb. chicken tenderloins, cut into ¾-in. pieces
- 1 medium onion, chopped
  Optional: Halved cucumber slices and chopped peanuts

1. For the sauce, whisk together the first 8 ingredients. Bring a large saucepan of water to a boil; remove from heat. Add noodles; let stand until noodles are tender but firm, 3-4 minutes. Drain; rinse with cold water and drain well.
2. In a large skillet, heat 1 Tbsp. peanut oil over medium-high heat; saute the chicken until no longer pink, 5-7 minutes. Remove from pan.
3. In same pan, saute onion in remaining oil over medium-high heat 2-3 minutes or until tender. Stir in the sauce; cook and stir over medium heat until slightly thickened. Add the noodles and chicken; heat through, tossing

to combine. If desired, top with cucumber slices and peanuts. Serve immediately.
2 cups: 444 cal., 13g fat (2g sat. fat), 56mg chol., 1270mg sod., 48g carb. (6g sugars, 2g fiber), 34g pro.

MOZZARELLA-STUFFED MEATBALLS

It's fun to watch my friends eat these meatballs for the first time. They're pleasantly surprised to find melted cheese in the middle. The meatballs are also great in a hot sub sandwich.
—Michaela Rosenthal, Indio, CA

Prep: 20 min. • **Cook:** 15 min.
Makes: 6 servings

- 1 large egg, room temperature, lightly beaten
- ¼ cup prepared Italian salad dressing
- 1½ cups cubed bread
- 2 Tbsp. minced fresh parsley
- 2 garlic cloves, minced
- ½ tsp. dried oregano
- ½ tsp. pepper
- ¼ tsp. salt
- ½ lb. ground pork
- ½ lb. ground sirloin
- 3 oz. fresh mozzarella cheese
- 2 Tbsp. canola oil
- 1 jar (24 oz.) marinara sauce
  Hot cooked pasta

1. In a large bowl, combine the first 8 ingredients. Crumble pork and beef over mixture; mix well. Cut mozzarella into eighteen ½-in. cubes. Divide meat mixture into 18 portions; shape each around a cheese cube.
2. In a large skillet, cook meatballs in oil over medium heat, in batches, until a thermometer inserted in the meat reads 160°; drain. In a large saucepan, heat marinara sauce; add meatballs and heat through. Serve over pasta.
Freeze option: Freeze cooled meatball mixture in freezer containers. To use, partially thaw in refrigerator overnight. Heat through in a covered saucepan, gently stirring and adding a little water if necessary. Serve with pasta.
3 meatballs with about ⅓ cup sauce: 311 cal., 19g fat (6g sat. fat), 84mg chol., 846mg sod., 15g carb. (8g sugars, 3g fiber), 18g pro.

MOZZARELLA-STUFFED MEATBALLS

KASHMIRI LAMB
CURRY STEW

KASHMIRI LAMB
CURRY STEW

When I was growing up, I was taught spicy foods are for lovers. So when I married, this was the first meal I made my husband. Now I make it when we have a disagreement.
—Amber El, Pittsburgh, PA

- -

Prep: 25 min. + marinating • **Cook:** 8 hours
Makes: 11 servings (2¾ qt.)

- 1   cup plain yogurt
- 2   Tbsp. ghee or butter, melted
- ¼   cup lemon juice
- 4   tsp. curry powder
- 1   Tbsp. cumin seeds
- 1   tsp. each coriander seeds, ground ginger, ground cloves, ground cardamom, sugar and salt
- ½   tsp. each ground cinnamon and pepper
- 3   lbs. lamb stew meat, cut into 1-in. cubes
- 1   large onion, sliced
- 1   medium sweet potato, quartered
- 1   medium Yukon Gold potato, quartered
- 1   large tomato, chopped
- 1   cup frozen peas and carrots
- 3   garlic cloves, minced
- 2   dried hot chiles
- ½   cup chicken broth
- 1½   Tbsp. garam masala
        Optional: Hot cooked basmati rice, sliced green onion, mango chutney and raisins

1. In a large dish, combine yogurt, ghee and lemon juice; add curry powder, cumin seeds, coriander, ginger, cloves, cardamom, sugar, salt, cinnamon and pepper. Add the lamb, vegetables, garlic and chiles; turn to coat. Cover and refrigerate up to 24 hours.
2. Transfer lamb mixture and marinade to 6-qt. slow cooker; stir in broth and garam masala. Cook, covered, on low until meat is tender, 8-9 hours. If desired, serve with rice, green onions, mango chutney and raisins.

1 cup: 261 cal., 10g fat (4g sat. fat), 89mg chol., 384mg sod., 15g carb. (5g sugars, 3g fiber), 28g pro. **Diabetic exchanges:** 4 lean meat, 1 starch.

"I love the flavors of this stew and the rich, tender cubes of lamb. It has great flavor and a slight kick."

—SARAH FISCHER, ASSOCIATE FOOD STYLIST

**SHEPHERD'S PIE
TWICE-BAKED POTATOES**

FIESTA CHICKEN

Chili powder and picante sauce add just the right dash of zip to this hearty main dish. It's a snap to assemble, as it uses convenience foods.
—Teresa Peterson, Kasson, MN

- -

Prep: 15 min. • **Bake:** 40 min.
Makes: 8 servings

- 1 can (10¾ oz.) condensed cream of chicken soup, undiluted
- 1 can (10¾ oz.) condensed cream of mushroom soup, undiluted
- 2 small tomatoes, chopped
- ⅓ cup picante sauce
- 1 medium green pepper, chopped
- 1 small onion, chopped
- 2 to 3 tsp. chili powder
- 12 corn tortillas (6 in.), cut into 1-in. strips
- 3 cups cubed cooked chicken
- 1 cup shredded Colby cheese

1. In a large bowl, combine the soups, tomatoes, picante sauce, green pepper, onion and chili powder. In a greased 13x9-in. baking dish, layer half of the tortilla strips, chicken, soup mixture and cheese. Repeat layers.

2. Cover and bake at 350° until bubbly, 40-50 minutes.

Freeze option: Cover and freeze unbaked casserole. To use, partially thaw in the refrigerator overnight. Remove from the refrigerator 30 minutes before baking. Preheat oven to 350°. Bake casserole as directed, increasing time as necessary to heat through and for a thermometer inserted in center to read 165°.

1 serving: 324 cal., 14g fat (5g sat. fat), 65mg chol., 802mg sod., 28g carb. (3g sugars, 4g fiber), 23g pro.

SHEPHERD'S PIE TWICE-BAKED POTATOES

This recipe captures the best of two classic dishes—twice-baked potatoes and shepherd's pie. When served with a green salad, satisfaction is guaranteed even for those with the heartiest of appetites.
—Cyndy Gerken, Naples, FL

- -

Prep: 1¾ hours
Bake: 25 min.
Makes: 6 servings

- 6 large russet potatoes
- 2 Tbsp. olive oil
- 1 lb. ground beef
- 1 medium onion, chopped
- 1 medium green pepper, chopped
- 1 medium sweet red pepper, chopped
- 4 garlic cloves, minced
- 1 pkg. (16 oz.) frozen mixed vegetables
- 3 Tbsp. Worcestershire sauce
- 1 Tbsp. tomato paste
- 1 Tbsp. steak seasoning
- ¼ tsp. salt
- ⅛ tsp. pepper
  Dash cayenne pepper
- 2 tsp. paprika, divided
- ½ cup butter, cubed
- ¾ cup heavy whipping cream
- ¼ cup sour cream
- 1 cup shredded Monterey Jack cheese
- 1 cup shredded cheddar cheese
- ¼ cup shredded Parmesan cheese
- 2 Tbsp. minced chives

TOPPINGS

- ½ cup shredded cheddar cheese
- 1 Tbsp. minced chives
- 1 tsp. paprika

1. Scrub and pierce potatoes; rub with oil. Bake at 375° until tender, about 1 hour.

2. In a large skillet, cook the beef, onion, peppers and garlic over medium heat until beef is no longer pink; drain. Add the mixed vegetables, Worcestershire sauce, tomato paste, steak seasoning, salt, pepper, cayenne and 1 tsp. paprika. Cook and stir until the vegetables are tender.

3. When the potatoes are cool enough to handle, cut a thin slice off the top of each and discard. Scoop out the pulp, leaving thin shells.

4. In a large bowl, mash pulp with butter. Add whipping cream, sour cream, cheeses and chives. Mash potatoes until combined. Spoon 1 cup meat mixture into each shell; top with ½ cup potato mixture. Sprinkle with remaining 1 tsp. paprika.

5. Place on a baking sheet. Bake at 375° for 20 minutes. Sprinkle with cheddar cheese; bake until melted, about 5 minutes longer. Sprinkle with chives and paprika.

Freeze option: Wrap the unbaked stuffed potatoes and freeze in a freezer container. To use, partially thaw in the refrigerator overnight. Bake as directed, adding more time until heated through.

1 stuffed potato: 986 cal., 56g fat (32g sat. fat), 183mg chol., 1066mg sod., 86g carb. (12g sugars, 11g fiber), 37g pro.

FIESTA
CHICKEN

MUSHROOM & BACON SPAGHETTI SQUASH BOWL

I love spaghetti squash but get tired of having it with a tomato-based red sauce. This light cream sauce, along with fresh sage and crispy bacon, will make you and your family excited about spaghetti squash again!
—Emily Montgomery, Montgomery, AL

Prep: 15 min. • **Cook:** 20 min.
Makes: 4 servings

- 1 medium spaghetti squash (about 4 lbs.)
- 12 oz. bacon strips, cut into ¾-in. pieces
- ½ lb. sliced baby portobello mushrooms
- 2 garlic cloves, minced
- ½ tsp. salt
- ¼ tsp. crushed red pepper flakes, optional
- ½ cup dry white wine or chicken broth
- 3 Tbsp. all-purpose flour
- 2½ cups 2% milk
- 2 Tbsp. chopped fresh sage
- ¼ cup shredded Parmesan cheese

1. Cut squash in half lengthwise; discard seeds. Place the squash cut side down on a microwave-safe plate. Microwave, uncovered, on high 15-18 minutes or until tender. Meanwhile, in a large skillet, cook bacon over medium heat until crisp, stirring occasionally. Remove with a slotted spoon; drain on paper towels. Discard drippings, reserving 2 Tbsp. in pan. Add mushrooms to drippings; cook and stir over medium-high heat until tender, 6-8 minutes. Add garlic, salt and, if desired, red pepper flakes; cook 1 minute longer.
2. Stir in the wine. Bring to a boil; cook until liquid is almost evaporated, 4-5 minutes. Stir in flour until blended; gradually whisk in milk. Bring to a boil, stirring constantly; cook and stir until thickened, 2-3 minutes. Remove from the heat; stir in sage.
3. When squash is cool enough to handle, use a fork to separate strands. Serve with mushroom sauce and reserved bacon; sprinkle with Parmesan cheese and, if desired, additional chopped fresh sage.
1 serving: 494 cal., 25g fat (10g sat. fat), 53mg chol., 1085mg sod., 47g carb. (9g sugars, 8g fiber), 23g pro.

MUSHROOM & BACON SPAGHETTI SQUASH BOWL

PENNSYLVANIA POT ROAST

I start this pot roast cooking before I leave for church, adding the vegetables when I get home.
—Donna Wilkinson, Monrovia, MD

Prep: 10 min. • **Cook:** 5 hours
Makes: 6 servings

- 1 boneless pork shoulder butt roast (2½ to 3 lbs.), halved
- 1½ cups beef broth
- ½ cup sliced green onions
- 1 tsp. dried basil
- 1 tsp. dried marjoram
- ½ tsp. salt
- ½ tsp. pepper
- 1 bay leaf
- 6 medium red potatoes, cut into 2-in. chunks
- 4 medium carrots, cut into 2-in. chunks
- ½ lb. medium fresh mushrooms, quartered
- ¼ cup all-purpose flour
- ½ cup cold water
  Browning sauce, optional

1. Place roast in a 5-qt. slow cooker; add the broth, onions and seasonings. Cook, covered, on high for 4 hours. Add the potatoes, carrots and mushrooms. Cook, covered, on high 1 hour longer or until vegetables are tender. Remove meat and vegetables; keep warm. Discard bay leaf.
2. In a saucepan, combine flour and cold water until smooth; stir in 1½ cups cooking juices. Bring to a boil. Cook and stir until thickened, 2 minutes. If desired, add the browning sauce. Serve with the roast and vegetables.

1 serving: 331 cal., 12g fat (4g sat. fat), 78mg chol., 490mg sod., 28g carb. (5g sugars, 4g fiber), 26g pro.

CHORIZO PUMPKIN PASTA

I'm a busy student, and this spicy-sweet pasta makes a perfect quick dinner. Even better, it works on a bigger scale to feed a bunch of friends.
—Christine Yang, Syracuse, NY

Takes: 30 min. • **Makes:** 6 servings

- 3 cups uncooked gemelli or spiral pasta (about 12 oz.)
- 1 pkg. (12 oz.) fully cooked chorizo chicken sausage links or flavor of choice, sliced
- 1 cup canned pumpkin
- 1 cup half-and-half cream
- ¾ tsp. salt
- ¼ tsp. pepper
- 1½ cups shredded Manchego or Monterey Jack cheese
  Minced fresh cilantro, optional

1. Cook pasta according to package directions. Drain, reserving ¾ cup pasta water.
2. Meanwhile, in a skillet, saute sausage over medium heat until lightly browned; reduce heat to medium-low. Add pumpkin, cream, salt and pepper; cook and stir until heated through. Toss with pasta and enough pasta water to moisten; stir in the cheese. If desired, sprinkle with cilantro.

1⅓ cups: 471 cal., 20g fat (11g sat. fat), 92mg chol., 847mg sod., 48g carb. (7g sugars, 3g fiber), 26g pro.

"This elevated mac-and-cheese-type dish feels fancy thanks to the gemelli pasta, Manchego cheese and pumpkin. I often make it meatless by swapping in vegan chorizo."

—ANNAMARIE HIGLEY, ASSOCIATE EDITOR

CHORIZO
PUMPKIN PASTA

SAUSAGE LENTIL STEW

This hearty stew is brimming with protein-packed lentils, vegetables and tasty turkey kielbasa. It's big on flavor but easy on the budget.
—Patti St. Antoine, Broomfield, CO

Prep: 5 min. • **Cook:** 55 min.
Makes: 8 servings

1	lb. fully cooked turkey kielbasa, thinly sliced
2	medium carrots, sliced
2	celery ribs, sliced
1	medium onion, chopped
2	garlic cloves, minced
2	tsp. canola oil
3	cups water
2	medium potatoes, diced
1	can (14½ oz.) chicken broth
1	cup dried lentils, rinsed
¾	tsp. salt
½	tsp. ground cumin
⅛	tsp. cayenne pepper
1	can (28 oz.) diced tomatoes, undrained
1	can (4 oz.) chopped green chiles

In a Dutch oven, cook the kielbasa, carrots, celery, onion and garlic in oil until vegetables are almost tender, about 5 minutes. Stir in water, potatoes, broth, lentils, salt, cumin and cayenne; bring to a boil. Reduce heat; cover and simmer for 40 minutes or until potatoes are tender, stirring occasionally. Add tomatoes and chiles; heat through.
1⅓ cups: 268 cal., 7g fat (3g sat. fat), 30mg chol., 1236mg sod., 34g carb. (0 sugars, 12g fiber), 20g pro. **Diabetic exchanges:** 2 lean meat, 1 starch, 1 vegetable, 1 fat.

TURKEY CORDON BLEU WITH ALFREDO SAUCE

Filled with smoky ham and melted cheese, this turkey is tender and flavorful. But the bacon is what really sets the dish off.
—Sandy Komisarek, Swanton, OH

Prep: 30 min. • **Bake:** 20 min.
Makes: 8 servings

8	slices part-skim mozzarella cheese
8	thin slices deli honey ham
8	turkey breast cutlets
2	cups panko bread crumbs
2	large eggs, lightly beaten
½	cup all-purpose flour
½	tsp. salt
¼	tsp. pepper
¼	cup canola oil
1	jar (15 oz.) Alfredo sauce, warmed
8	bacon strips, cooked and crumbled
¼	cup grated Parmesan cheese

1. Preheat the oven to 350°. Place 1 slice mozzarella cheese and ham on each cutlet. Roll up each from a short side and secure with toothpicks.
2. Place bread crumbs and eggs in separate shallow bowls. In another shallow bowl, combine flour, salt and pepper. Dip turkey in flour mixture, eggs, then bread crumbs.
3. In a large skillet, brown turkey in oil in batches. Place in a greased 13x9-in. baking dish. Bake, uncovered, until turkey juices run clear, 20-25 minutes. Discard toothpicks.
4. Spoon Alfredo sauce over turkey. Sprinkle with bacon and Parmesan cheese.
1 turkey roll-up with about 3 Tbsp. sauce: 455 cal., 24g fat (10g sat. fat), 147mg chol., 910mg sod., 18g carb. (1g sugars, 1g fiber), 39g pro.

CHICKEN PAELLA

Turmeric lends flavor and a pretty golden color to this Spanish-style entree. Haven't tried arborio rice? We know you'll love its creamy texture.
—*Taste of Home* Test Kitchen

Prep: 10 min. • **Cook:** 45 min.
Makes: 2 servings

2	boneless skinless chicken thighs (about ½ lb.), cut into 2-in. pieces
½	cup cubed fully cooked ham
⅓	cup chopped onion
⅓	cup julienned sweet red pepper
1	Tbsp. olive oil, divided
½	cup uncooked arborio rice
½	tsp. ground turmeric
½	tsp. ground cumin
½	tsp. minced garlic
⅛	tsp. salt
1	cup plus 2 Tbsp. chicken broth
¾	cup frozen peas, thawed

1. In a large skillet, saute the chicken, ham, onion and red pepper in 2 tsp. oil until chicken is browned on all sides. Remove with a slotted spoon.
2. In same skillet, saute rice in remaining 1 tsp. oil until lightly browned. Stir in the turmeric, cumin, garlic and salt. Return meat and vegetables to pan; toss lightly. Add broth; bring to a boil. Reduce heat to medium; cover and simmer until rice is tender, 30-35 minutes. Stir in peas.
1½ cups: 516 cal., 17g fat (4g sat. fat), 99mg chol., 1242mg sod., 52g carb. (5g sugars, 4g fiber), 36g pro.

ONE-SKILLET PORK CHOP SUPPER

My husband, Clark, and I reserve this recipe for Sundays after the grandkids have gone home and we're too tired to cook.
—Kathy Thompson, Port Orange, FL

- -

Prep: 10 min. • **Cook:** 30 min.
Makes: 4 servings

- 1 Tbsp. butter
- 4 pork loin chops (½ in. thick and 7 oz. each)
- 3 medium red potatoes, cut into small wedges
- 3 medium carrots, cut into ½-in. slices, or 2 cups fresh baby carrots
- 1 medium onion, cut into wedges
- 1 can (10¾ oz.) condensed cream of mushroom soup, undiluted
- ½ cup water
  Optional: Cracked black pepper and chopped fresh parsley

1. In a large cast-iron or other heavy skillet, heat butter over medium heat. Brown pork chops on both sides; remove from the pan, reserving drippings.
2. In same pan, saute vegetables in drippings until lightly browned. Whisk together soup and water; stir into vegetables. Bring to a boil. Reduce the heat; simmer, covered, just until vegetables are tender, 15-20 minutes.
3. Add the chops; cook, covered, until a thermometer inserted in pork reads 145°, 8-10 minutes. Remove from heat; let stand 5 minutes. If desired, sprinkle with pepper and parsley.
1 serving: 390 cal., 15g fat (6g sat. fat), 97mg chol., 700mg sod., 28g carb. (6g sugars, 4g fiber), 33g pro.

MAMA'S PUERTO RICAN CHICKEN

My mom has a vast repertoire of recipes, and this extra crispy, spiced-up chicken is the best one of the bunch.
—Edwin Robles Jr., Milwaukee, WI

- -

Prep: 20 min. • **Cook:** 45 min.
Makes: 8 servings

- 1 broiler/fryer chicken (about 4 lbs.), cut up
- 1 tsp. ground cumin
- 1 tsp. dried oregano
- 1 tsp. garlic powder, divided
- 1 tsp. salt, divided
- 1 tsp. coarsely ground pepper, divided
- 1 cup dry bread crumbs
- ¾ cup all-purpose flour
- 2 large eggs, beaten
- ¼ cup canola oil
- ¼ cup butter

1. Preheat oven to 350°. Sprinkle chicken with cumin, oregano, ½ tsp. garlic powder, ½ tsp. salt and ½ tsp. pepper. In a shallow bowl, mix bread crumbs with remaining garlic powder, salt and pepper. Place flour and eggs in separate shallow bowls. Dip chicken pieces in flour to coat all sides; shake off excess. Dip in eggs, then in crumb mixture, patting to help coating adhere.
2. In a large skillet, heat oil over medium heat. Stir in butter. Add chicken in batches; cook until golden brown, 2-3 minutes per side. Place chicken on a rack in a shallow roasting pan. Bake, uncovered, until chicken is no longer pink, 30-35 minutes.
1 serving: 421 cal., 20g fat (6g sat. fat), 152mg chol., 507mg sod., 19g carb. (1g sugars, 1g fiber), 38g pro.

HONEY-MAPLE GLAZED HAM

My graham cracker-crusted ham gets a double coating of a honey-maple glaze. The first half melts into the ham while the second forms a sweet caramelized topping.
—Alan Sproles, Knoxville, TN

- -

Prep: 15 min. • **Bake:** 2 hours
Makes: 15 servings

- 1 spiral-sliced fully cooked bone-in ham (7 to 9 lbs.)
- ½ cup maple syrup
- ½ cup butter, softened
- ½ cup packed brown sugar
- ½ cup graham cracker crumbs
- ½ cup honey

1. Preheat oven to 325°. Line a roasting pan with heavy-duty foil. Place ham on a rack in prepared pan. Pour maple syrup over ham, separating slices. In a small bowl, beat the remaining ingredients until blended; spread ¾ cup over ham.
2. Bake, uncovered, for 1½ hours. Spread remaining butter mixture over ham. Bake until a thermometer reads 140°, basting occasionally with the pan drippings, 30-45 minutes longer.
4 oz. cooked ham: 335 cal., 12g fat (6g sat. fat), 109mg chol., 1180mg sod., 27g carb. (24g sugars, 0 fiber), 32g pro.

SPINACH
BURRITOS,
PAGE 152

Fish, Seafood & Meatless

With satisfying vegetarian options
and from-the-sea fare, you and
your family won't miss the meat.

SOUTH SEAS MANGO HALIBUT

This halibut is marinated in aromatic spices, then stir-fried and combined with coconut milk and mangoes. This dish can transform a weeknight meal into a tropical delight!
—*Taste of Home* Test Kitchen

- -

Prep: 15 min. + marinating • **Cook:** 20 min.
Makes: 6 servings

- 2 tsp. ground coriander
- 2 tsp. curry powder
- 1 tsp. chili powder
- ½ tsp. ground allspice
- ¼ tsp. salt
- ⅛ tsp. pepper
- 2 lbs. halibut fillets, cut into 1-in. pieces
- 2 large sweet red peppers, cut into 1-in. pieces
- 1 medium onion, cut into small wedges
- 5 Tbsp. canola oil, divided
- 1 can (13.66 oz.) light coconut milk
- 3 Tbsp. tomato paste
- 2 medium mangoes, peeled and chopped
- 1 pkg. (10 oz.) fresh spinach, torn

1. In a bowl or shallow dish, combine first 6 ingredients. Add the halibut and turn to coat. Cover and refrigerate for 30 minutes. In a large cast-iron or other heavy skillet, stir-fry red peppers and onion in 1 Tbsp. oil until tender, about 5 minutes. Remove from pan; set aside. Add 2 Tbsp. oil to pan; add halibut. Cook and stir until fish just begins to flake easily with fork, 5-8 minutes. Stir in milk, tomato paste, mangoes and reserved pepper mixture. Cook over medium heat for 5 minutes.

2. Meanwhile, in a Dutch oven, cook and stir spinach in remaining 2 Tbsp. oil until wilted, about 2 minutes. Serve fish over spinach.

1⅓ cups: 404 cal., 19g fat (5g sat. fat), 74mg chol., 285mg sod., 27g carb. (20g sugars, 5g fiber), 31g pro.

VEGETARIAN POTATOES AU GRATIN

Fill up on veggies and load up on great flavor with this creamy, hearty entree. The homey bread crumb topping brings it all together deliciously.
—*Taste of Home* Test Kitchen

- -

Prep: 15 min. • **Bake:** 50 min. + standing
Makes: 6 servings

- 3 medium carrots, thinly sliced
- 1 medium green pepper, chopped
- 4 Tbsp. butter, divided
- 3 Tbsp. all-purpose flour
- 1 tsp. dried oregano
- ½ tsp. salt
- 2½ cups 2% milk
- 1 can (15 oz.) black beans, rinsed and drained
- 3 cups shredded Swiss cheese, divided
- 4 medium Yukon Gold potatoes, thinly sliced
- ½ cup seasoned bread crumbs

1. Preheat oven to 400°. In a large saucepan, saute carrots and pepper in 3 Tbsp. butter until tender. Stir in flour, oregano and salt until blended; gradually add milk. Bring to a boil; cook and stir for 2 minutes or until thickened. Stir in beans and 2 cups cheese until cheese is melted.

2. Layer half the potatoes and sauce in a greased 13x9-in. baking dish; repeat layers. Sprinkle with the remaining cheese. In a microwave, melt the remaining butter. Stir in bread crumbs. Sprinkle over top.

3. Cover and bake for 50-55 minutes. Let stand 10 minutes before serving.

1 serving: 557 cal., 25g fat (16g sat. fat), 77mg chol., 749mg sod., 56g carb. (12g sugars, 7g fiber), 27g pro.

SOUTH SEAS
MANGO HALIBUT

CURRY POMEGRANATE PROTEIN BOWL

CURRY POMEGRANATE PROTEIN BOWL

This recipe is as simple as it is beautiful. It combines unique flavors that, when blended together, create a taste sensation that is out of this world. You can try other roasted, salted nuts instead of the soy nuts and use warmed berry jam in place of molasses.
—Mary Baker, Wauwatosa, WI

Prep: 25 min. • **Cook:** 25 min.
Makes: 6 servings

3 cups cubed peeled butternut squash (½-in. cubes)
2 Tbsp. olive oil, divided
½ tsp. salt, divided
¼ tsp. pepper
½ small onion, chopped
1 Tbsp. curry powder
1 Tbsp. ground cumin
1 garlic clove, minced
1 tsp. ground coriander
3 cups water
1 cup dried red lentils, rinsed
½ cup salted soy nuts
½ cup dried cranberries
⅓ cup thinly sliced green onions
⅓ cup pomegranate molasses
½ cup crumbled feta cheese
½ cup pomegranate seeds
¼ cup chopped fresh cilantro

1. Preheat oven to 375°. Place squash on a greased 15x10x1-in. baking pan. Drizzle with 1 Tbsp. oil; sprinkle with ¼ tsp. salt and pepper. Roast until tender, 25-30 minutes, turning once.
2. Meanwhile, in a skillet, heat remaining 1 Tbsp. oil over medium-high heat. Add the onion; cook and stir until crisp-tender, 4-6 minutes. Add the curry powder, cumin, garlic, coriander and remaining ¼ tsp. salt; cook 1 minute longer. Add water and lentils; bring to boil. Reduce heat; simmer, covered, until lentils are tender and water is absorbed, about 15 minutes.
3. Gently stir in soy nuts, cranberries, green onions and roasted squash. Divide among serving bowls. Drizzle with molasses and top with feta, pomegranate seeds and cilantro.
¾ cup: 367 cal., 9g fat (2g sat. fat), 5mg chol., 327mg sod., 60g carb. (23g sugars, 9g fiber), 14g pro.

SALMON SKILLET

Is there anything salmon can't do? It's high in heart-healthy omega-3s and lends itself to simple preparation techniques. And salmon also looks beautiful on the dinner table.
—*Taste of Home* Test Kitchen

Prep: 15 min. • **Cook:** 20 min.
Makes: 4 servings

- 1 lb. small red potatoes, quartered
- 2 pkg. (6 oz. each) fresh baby spinach
- ½ cup all-purpose flour
- 2 tsp. garlic salt, divided
- 2 tsp. paprika
- ½ tsp. pepper
- 4 salmon fillets (6 oz. each)
- 3 Tbsp. butter, divided
- 1 medium onion, halved and thinly sliced
- 1 can (15 oz.) cannellini beans, rinsed and drained
- ¾ cup heavy whipping cream
- ½ tsp. dried thyme

1. Place the potatoes in a Dutch oven and cover with water. Bring to a boil. Reduce heat; cover and cook for 10 minutes or until tender, adding spinach during last 2 minutes of cooking.
2. Meanwhile, combine the flour, 1 tsp. garlic salt, paprika and pepper in a shallow bowl. Coat the salmon with the flour mixture.
3. Cook salmon in 2 Tbsp. butter in a large cast-iron or other heavy skillet over medium heat until fish just begins to flake easily with a fork, 3-5 minutes on each side. Remove and keep warm.
4. Saute the onion in remaining butter in the same pan until tender. Add the beans, cream, thyme and remaining garlic salt. Bring to a boil; cook and stir until thickened, about 2 minutes. Drain potatoes and spinach; add to skillet. Serve with salmon.
1 fillet with 1⅓ cup potato mixture: 695 cal., 42g fat (19g sat. fat), 159mg chol., 955mg sod., 41g carb. (4g sugars, 9g fiber), 39g pro.

CORNBREAD-TOPPED FRIJOLES

My family often requests this economical slow-cooker favorite. It's loaded with fresh southwestern flavors. One batch makes eight servings—but they never last long at our house!
—Suzanne Caldwell, Artesia, NM

Prep: 20 min. • **Cook:** 3 hours
Makes: 8 servings

- 1 medium onion, chopped
- 1 medium green pepper, chopped
- 1 Tbsp. canola oil
- 2 garlic cloves, minced
- 1 can (16 oz.) kidney beans, rinsed and drained
- 1 can (15 oz.) pinto beans, rinsed and drained
- 1 can (14½ oz.) diced tomatoes, undrained
- 1 can (8 oz.) tomato sauce
- 1 tsp. chili powder
- ½ tsp. pepper
- ⅛ tsp. hot pepper sauce

CORNBREAD TOPPING
- 1 cup all-purpose flour
- 1 cup yellow cornmeal
- 1 Tbsp. sugar
- 1½ tsp. baking powder
- ½ tsp. salt
- 2 large eggs, room temperature, lightly beaten
- 1¼ cups fat-free milk
- 1 can (8¼ oz.) cream-style corn
- 3 Tbsp. canola oil

1. In a large skillet, saute onion and green pepper in oil until tender. Add garlic; cook 1 minute longer. Transfer to a greased 5-qt. slow cooker.
2. Stir in beans, tomatoes, tomato sauce, chili powder, pepper and pepper sauce. Cover and cook on high for 1 hour.
3. In a large bowl, combine flour, cornmeal, sugar, baking powder and salt. Combine the eggs, milk, corn and oil; add to dry ingredients and mix well. Spoon evenly over bean mixture.
4. Cover and cook on high 2-3 hours or until a toothpick inserted in the center of cornbread comes out clean.
1 serving: 367 cal., 9g fat (1g sat. fat), 54mg chol., 708mg sod., 59g carb. (10g sugars, 9g fiber), 14g pro.

CORNBREAD-TOPPED FRIJOLES

BLACK BEAN
VEGGIE ENCHILADAS

BLACK BEAN VEGGIE ENCHILADAS

I created this recipe one night when we were in the mood for enchiladas but didn't want all the fat and calories of traditional ones. I used ingredients I had on hand, and now this recipe's a family favorite!
—Nicole Barnett, Northville, MI

- -

Prep: 30 min. • **Bake:** 25 min.
Makes: 6 enchiladas

- 1 small onion, chopped
- 1 small green pepper, chopped
- ½ cup sliced fresh mushrooms
- 2 tsp. olive oil
- 1 garlic clove, minced
- 1 can (15 oz.) black beans, rinsed and drained
- ¾ cup frozen corn, thawed
- 1 can (4 oz.) chopped green chiles
- 2 Tbsp. reduced-sodium taco seasoning
- 1 tsp. dried cilantro flakes
- 6 whole wheat tortillas (8 in.), warmed
- ½ cup enchilada sauce
- ¾ cup shredded reduced-fat Mexican cheese blend
  Optional: Minced fresh cilantro and chopped tomatoes

1. In a large skillet, saute the onion, green pepper and mushrooms in oil until crisp-tender. Add garlic; cook 1 minute longer. Add the beans, corn, chiles, taco seasoning and cilantro; cook for 2-3 minutes or until heated through.
2. Spoon ½ cup bean mixture down center of each tortilla. Roll up and place in a greased 13x9-in. baking dish. Top with enchilada sauce and cheese.
3. Bake, uncovered, at 350° 25-30 minutes or until heated through. Garnish servings with cilantro and tomatoes if desired.
1 enchilada: 292 cal., 8g fat (2g sat. fat), 10mg chol., 759mg sod., 43g carb. (4g sugars, 6g fiber), 13g pro.

AFRICAN PEANUT
SWEET POTATO STEW

AFRICAN PEANUT SWEET POTATO STEW

When I was in college, my mom made an addicting sweet potato stew. I shared it with friends, and now all of us serve it to our own kids. They all love it, of course.
—Alexis Scatchell, Niles, IL

- -

Prep: 20 min. • **Cook:** 6 hours
Makes: 8 servings (2½ qt.)

- 1 can (28 oz.) diced tomatoes, undrained
- 1 cup fresh cilantro leaves
- ½ cup chunky peanut butter
- 3 garlic cloves, halved
- 2 tsp. ground cumin
- 1 tsp. salt
- ½ tsp. ground cinnamon
- ¼ tsp. smoked paprika
- 3 lbs. sweet potatoes (about 6 medium), peeled and cut into 1-in. pieces
- 1 can (15 oz.) garbanzo beans or chickpeas, rinsed and drained
- 1 cup water
- 8 cups chopped fresh kale
  Optional: Chopped peanuts and additional cilantro leaves

1. Place the first 8 ingredients in a food processor; process until pureed. Transfer to a 5-qt. slow cooker; stir in sweet potatoes, beans and water.
2. Cook, covered, on low for 6-8 hours or until the potatoes are tender, adding kale during the last 30 minutes. If desired, top each serving with chopped peanuts and additional cilantro.
1¼ cups: 349 cal., 9g fat (1g sat. fat), 0 chol., 624mg sod., 60g carb. (23g sugars, 11g fiber), 10g pro.

TEST KITCHEN TIP
Meats that are traditionally used in this peanut stew include lamb, chicken and beef.

SPAGHETTI SQUASH WITH BALSAMIC VEGETABLES & TOASTED PINE NUTS

The veggies can be prepared while the squash is cooking in the microwave. That means I can have a satisfying meal on the table in about half an hour.
—Deanna Wolfe, Muskegon, MI

Prep: 20 min. • **Cook:** 15 min.
Makes: 6 servings

- 1 medium spaghetti squash (about 4 lbs.)
- 1 cup chopped carrots
- 1 small red onion, halved and sliced
- 1 Tbsp. olive oil
- 4 garlic cloves, minced
- 1 can (15½ oz.) great northern beans, rinsed and drained
- 1 can (14½ oz.) diced tomatoes, drained
- 1 can (14 oz.) water-packed artichoke hearts, rinsed, drained and halved
- 1 medium zucchini, chopped
- 3 Tbsp. balsamic vinegar
- 2 tsp. minced fresh thyme or ½ tsp. dried thyme
- ¼ tsp. salt
- ¼ tsp. pepper
- ½ cup pine nuts, toasted

1. Cut squash in half lengthwise; discard seeds. Place the squash cut side down on a microwave-safe plate. Microwave, uncovered, on high for 15-18 minutes or until tender.
2. Meanwhile, in a large nonstick skillet, saute the carrots and onion in oil until tender. Add garlic; cook 1 minute. Stir in beans, tomatoes, artichokes, zucchini, vinegar, thyme, salt and pepper. Cook and stir over medium heat until heated through, 8-10 minutes.
3. When squash is cool enough to handle, use a fork to separate strands. Serve with bean mixture. Sprinkle with nuts.
¾ cup bean mixture with ⅔ cup squash and 4 tsp. nuts: 275 cal., 10g fat (1g sat. fat), 0 chol., 510mg sod., 41g carb. (6g sugars, 10g fiber), 11g pro. **Diabetic exchanges:** 2½ starch, 1½ fat, 1 lean meat.

BRUSSELS SPROUTS & TOFU STIR-FRY

I love cooking with Brussels sprouts. This tofu stir-fry recipe is the perfect quick and healthy weeknight meal. You can also make a scrumptious hoagie by stuffing toasted rolls with this tasty mixture.
—Joseph Sciascia, San Mateo, CA

Prep: 20 min. • **Cook:** 25 min.
Makes: 6 servings

- 3 Tbsp. coconut oil, divided
- 1 pkg. (16 oz.) extra-firm tofu, drained and cut into ½-in. cubes
- 2 lbs. fresh Brussels sprouts, trimmed and cut into ¼-in. slices
- 1 medium sweet red pepper, chopped
- 4 green onions, sliced
- 3 garlic cloves, minced
- ¼ cup water
- ¼ cup hoisin sauce
- 2 Tbsp. chili garlic sauce
- ¼ tsp. salt
- ½ cup slivered almonds, toasted
  Hot cooked rice noodles

1. In a large nonstick skillet, heat 1 Tbsp. coconut oil over medium-high heat. Add tofu; stir-fry until browned, 12-15 minutes. Remove from pan and keep warm. Stir-fry the Brussels sprouts in remaining 2 Tbsp. coconut oil for 2 minutes. Add red pepper, green onions and garlic; cover and cook until the vegetables are crisp-tender, 5-7 minutes longer.
2. Stir in water, hoisin sauce, chili garlic sauce and salt. Return tofu to pan; cook and stir until heated through. Stir in the almonds. Serve with noodles.
1⅓ cups: 268 cal., 16g fat (7g sat. fat), 0 chol., 463mg sod., 24g carb. (9g sugars, 8g fiber), 13g pro.

BRUSSELS SPROUTS & TOFU STIR-FRY

1. Peel and slice eggplant lengthwise into fifteen ⅛-in.-thick slices. Place in a colander over a plate; sprinkle with salt and toss. Let stand 30 minutes.

2. Meanwhile, for sauce, in a large saucepan, saute onion in oil. Add garlic; cook 1 minute longer. Stir in remaining sauce ingredients. Bring to a boil. Reduce the heat; simmer, uncovered, until the flavors are blended, stirring occasionally, 20-25 minutes. Rinse and drain eggplant.

3. In a large bowl, combine filling ingredients; set aside.

4. Place the eggs in a shallow bowl. In another shallow bowl, combine bread crumbs, ½ cup Parmesan cheese, garlic, parsley, salt and pepper. Dip eggplant in eggs, then bread crumb mixture.

5. In an electric skillet or deep skillet, heat ½ in. of oil to 375°. Fry eggplant in batches until golden brown, 2-3 minutes on each side. Drain on paper towels.

6. Preheat the oven to 375°. Spoon 1 cup sauce into an ungreased 13x9-in. baking dish. Spread 2 rounded Tbsp. filling over each eggplant slice. Carefully roll up and place seam side down in baking dish. Spoon the remaining sauce over roll-ups. Sprinkle with remaining Parmesan cheese. Cover and bake until bubbly, 30-35 minutes.

3 roll-ups: 726 cal., 48g fat (15g sat. fat), 181mg chol., 3182mg sod., 44g carb. (19g sugars, 7g fiber), 35g pro.

EGGPLANT ROLLATINI

These authentic Italian eggplant roll-ups can take some time to prepare, but the end result is restaurant-quality and just right for a special occasion. Your family will request this dish time and again.
—Nancy Sousley, Lafayette, IN

Prep: 1 hour • **Bake:** 30 min.
Makes: 5 servings

- 1 large eggplant
- 1 Tbsp. salt

SAUCE
- 1 small onion, chopped
- ¼ cup olive oil
- 2 garlic cloves, minced
- 1 can (15 oz.) tomato sauce
- 1 can (14½ oz.) diced tomatoes
- ½ cup chicken broth
- ¼ cup tomato paste
- 2 Tbsp. minced fresh parsley
- 2 tsp. sugar
- ½ tsp. salt
- ½ tsp. dried basil
- ¼ tsp. pepper
- ⅛ tsp. crushed red pepper flakes

FILLING
- 1 carton (15 oz.) ricotta cheese
- 1 cup shredded part-skim mozzarella cheese
- ½ cup grated Parmesan cheese
- ¼ cup minced fresh parsley
- 1 large egg, lightly beaten
- ⅛ tsp. pepper

COATING
- 3 large eggs, lightly beaten
- 1 cup seasoned bread crumbs
- 1 cup grated Parmesan cheese, divided
- 2 garlic cloves, minced
- 2 Tbsp. minced fresh parsley
  Dash each salt and pepper
  Oil for frying

EGGPLANT ROLLATINI

TEST KITCHEN TIP
Sprinkling eggplant with salt helps eliminate any bitterness. Be sure to rinse and dry the eggplant thoroughly before continuing with the recipe.

VEGETARIAN
SKILLET LASAGNA

FAVORITE DEEP-DISH PIZZA

My kids love to get pizza delivered, but it's expensive and not very healthy. I came up with a one-bowl pizza that is healthier than delivery and lets the kids add toppings of their choice. Now everyone's happy.
—Sara Lafountain, Rockville, MD

- -

Prep: 20 min. • **Bake:** 20 min.
Makes: 8 servings

- 1¾ cups whole wheat flour
- 1¾ cups all-purpose flour
- 2 pkg. (¼ oz. each) quick-rise yeast
- 4 tsp. sugar
- 1 tsp. salt
- 1½ cups warm water (120° to 130°)
- ¼ cup olive oil
- 1 can (8 oz.) pizza sauce
- 8 oz. fresh mozzarella cheese, sliced
- 2 cups shredded Italian cheese blend
- ½ tsp. dried oregano
- ½ tsp. Italian seasoning
  Optional: Sliced red onion, chopped green pepper, fresh oregano and crushed red pepper flakes

1. In a large bowl, combine wheat flour, 1 cup all-purpose flour, yeast, sugar and salt. Add the water and oil; beat until smooth. Stir in enough remaining flour to form a soft dough. Press dough onto bottom and up sides of a greased 13x9-in. baking dish.
2. Top with pizza sauce. Place mozzarella slices over sauce. Sprinkle with shredded cheese, oregano and Italian seasoning. If desired, top with the red onion and green pepper. Bake, uncovered, at 400° until golden brown, 20-25 minutes. If desired, top with fresh oregano leaves and crushed red pepper flakes.

1 piece: 449 cal., 20g fat (9g sat. fat), 42mg chol., 646mg sod., 47g carb. (4g sugars, 5g fiber), 19g pro.

VEGETARIAN SKILLET LASAGNA

This easy, flavorful weeknight vegetarian skillet lasagna is sure to satisfy even the meat lovers at your dinner table.
—*Taste of Home* Test Kitchen

- -

Takes: 25 min. • **Makes:** 4 servings

- 2 Tbsp. olive oil
- 2 medium zucchini, halved and sliced
- ½ lb. sliced fresh mushrooms
- ½ cup chopped onion
- 2 garlic cloves, minced
- 1 jar (24 oz.) tomato basil pasta sauce
- ½ cup water
- ¼ tsp. salt
- ¼ tsp. pepper
- ¼ tsp. crushed red pepper flakes
- 6 no-cook lasagna noodles, broken
- ½ cup shredded mozzarella cheese
  Optional: Grated Parmesan cheese and chopped fresh basil leaves

1. Heat olive oil in large cast-iron or other ovenproof skillet over medium-high heat. Add zucchini and mushrooms; cook until softened, 2-3 minutes. Add the onion and garlic; cook until vegetables are tender, 2-3 minutes. Add pasta sauce, water and seasonings. Stir to combine; add broken noodles. Bring to a boil. Reduce the heat; cover and simmer until noodles are tender, about 15 minutes.
2. Top with the mozzarella and, if desired, Parmesan. Broil until cheese melts and starts to brown. If desired, sprinkle with basil.

1½ cups: 355 cal., 14g fat (3g sat. fat), 11mg chol., 955mg sod., 46g carb. (18g sugars, 7g fiber), 13g pro.

TEST KITCHEN TIP
Serve this vegetarian dinner recipe with garlic bread and a fresh tossed salad.

FAVORITE DEEP-DISH PIZZA

CRISPY BAKED TOFU

CRISPY BAKED TOFU

You'll never need another baked tofu recipe! My version is nice and crispy on the outside while remaining super soft on the inside.
—Ralph Jones, San Diego, CA

- -

Prep: 15 min. + standing • **Bake:** 25 min.
Makes: 4 servings

- 1 pkg. (16 oz.) firm or extra-firm tofu
- 2 Tbsp. soy sauce or teriyaki sauce
- 1 Tbsp. olive oil
- 1 Tbsp. toasted sesame oil
- 1 tsp. kosher salt
- 1 tsp. garlic powder
- ½ tsp. pepper
- ¾ cup cornstarch
  Sliced green onions, optional

1. Preheat oven to 400°. Blot tofu dry. Cut into ¾-in. cubes. Place on a clean kitchen towel; cover with another towel. Place a cutting board on top; place a large cast iron skillet on the board. Let stand 10 minutes.
2. In a shallow dish, whisk together the soy sauce, olive oil, sesame oil, salt, garlic powder and pepper. Place the cornstarch in a separate shallow dish. Add tofu to the soy mixture; turn to coat. Add tofu, a few pieces at a time, to the cornstarch; toss to coat. Place on a parchment-lined baking sheet. Bake until the cubes are golden brown and crispy, 25-30 minutes, turning cubes halfway through. Garnish with green onions if desired.
1 serving: 154 cal., 12g fat (2g sat. fat), 0 chol., 949mg sod., 3g carb. (1g sugars, 0 fiber), 10g pro.

"This recipe is baked and uses a minimal amount of oil. It's a great way to cook tofu to add to all your favorite stir-fry dinners, pasta dishes and salads."

—PEGGY WOODWARD, SENIOR FOOD EDITOR

SEA SCALLOPS & FETTUCCINE

When we decided to lose weight, my husband and I tried this recipe and loved it so much we had it every Tuesday. It's so easy, he would fix it on nights I was running late.
—Donna Thompson, Laramie, WY

Takes: 30 min. • **Makes:** 2 servings

- 4 oz. uncooked fettuccine
- 1 Tbsp. olive oil
- ½ medium sweet red pepper, julienned
- 1 garlic clove, minced
- ½ tsp. grated lemon zest
- ¼ tsp. crushed red pepper flakes
- ½ cup reduced-sodium chicken broth
- ¼ cup white wine or additional broth
- 1 Tbsp. lemon juice
- 6 sea scallops (about ¾ lb.)
- 2 tsp. grated Parmesan cheese

1. Cook fettuccine according to package directions; drain.
2. Meanwhile, in a large skillet, heat oil over medium-high heat. Add red pepper, garlic, lemon zest and pepper flakes; cook and stir 2 minutes. Stir in the broth, wine and lemon juice. Bring to a boil. Reduce heat; simmer, uncovered, 5-6 minutes or until the liquid is reduced by half.
3. Cut each scallop horizontally in half; add to skillet. Cook, covered, 4-5 minutes or until the scallops are firm and opaque, stirring occasionally. Serve with fettuccine. Sprinkle with cheese.

1 serving: 421 cal., 10g fat (2g sat. fat), 42mg chol., 861mg sod., 49g carb. (4g sugars, 3g fiber), 30g pro.

FOUR-CHEESE STUFFED SHELLS

More cheese, please! You'll get your fill from saucy jumbo pasta shells loaded with four kinds—ricotta, Asiago, mozzarella and cottage cheese. Do the prep work, then freeze them according to the recipe directions to have a ready-to-bake meal.
—*Taste of Home* Test Kitchen

Prep: 20 min. • **Bake:** 25 min.
Makes: 2 servings

- 6 uncooked jumbo pasta shells
- ½ cup shredded part-skim mozzarella cheese, divided
- ¼ cup shredded Asiago cheese
- ¼ cup ricotta cheese
- ¼ cup 4% cottage cheese
- 1 Tbsp. minced chives
- 1 pkg. (10 oz.) frozen chopped spinach, thawed and squeezed dry
- 1 cup meatless spaghetti sauce

1. Preheat oven to 350°. Cook the pasta according to package directions. Meanwhile, in a small bowl, combine ¼ cup mozzarella cheese, Asiago cheese, ricotta cheese, cottage cheese, chives and ½ cup spinach (save remaining spinach for another use).
2. Spread ½ cup spaghetti sauce into a shallow 1½-qt. baking dish coated with cooking spray. Drain pasta; stuff with cheese mixture. Arrange in prepared dish. Top with remaining spaghetti sauce and mozzarella.
3. Cover and bake until heated through, 25-30 minutes.

Freeze option: Cover and freeze unbaked casserole. To use, partially thaw shells in the refrigerator overnight. Remove from the refrigerator 30 minutes before baking. Preheat oven to 350°. Bake as directed, increasing time as necessary to heat through and for a thermometer inserted in the center of 2 or 3 shells to read 165°.

3 stuffed shells: 376 cal., 14g fat (9g sat. fat), 49mg chol., 959mg sod., 39g carb. (13g sugars, 4g fiber), 25g pro.

FOUR-CHEESE
STUFFED SHELLS

SPICY
ISLAND SHRIMP

SPICY ISLAND SHRIMP

My husband got this recipe while he was living on St. Croix Island. We've served the zippy shrimp dish on several holiday occasions. I'm amazed at how even those who claim not to care for shrimp come out of their shells and devour them when they're prepared this way!
—Teresa Methe, Minden, NE

Prep: 20 min. • **Cook:** 20 min.
Makes: 6 servings

- 1 large green pepper, chopped
- 1 large onion, chopped
- ½ cup butter cubed
- 2¼ lbs. uncooked large shrimp, peeled and deveined
- 2 cans (8 oz. each) tomato sauce
- 3 Tbsp. chopped green onions
- 1 Tbsp. minced fresh parsley
- 1 tsp. salt
- 1 tsp. pepper
- 1 tsp. paprika
- ½ tsp. garlic powder
- ½ tsp. dried oregano
- ½ tsp. dried thyme
- ¼ to ½ tsp. white pepper
- ¼ to ½ tsp. cayenne pepper
    Optional: Hot cooked rice and thinly sliced green onions

1. In a large skillet, saute the green pepper and onion in butter until tender. Reduce heat; add shrimp. Cook 5 minutes or until shrimp turn pink.
2. Stir in tomato sauce, green onions, parsley and seasonings. Bring to a boil. Reduce the heat; simmer, uncovered, for 20 minutes or until slightly thickened. If desired, serve with rice and additional green onions.
1 serving: 293 cal., 17g fat (10g sat. fat), 293mg chol., 1013mg sod., 7g carb. (3g sugars, 2g fiber), 29g pro.

CREAMY PASTA PRIMAVERA

CREAMY PASTA PRIMAVERA

This pasta dish is a wonderful blend of crisp, colorful vegetables and a creamy Parmesan cheese sauce.
—Darlene Brenden, Salem, OR

Takes: 30 min. • **Makes:** 6 servings

- 2 cups uncooked gemelli or spiral pasta
- 1 lb. fresh asparagus, trimmed and cut into 2-in. pieces
- 3 medium carrots, shredded
- 2 tsp. canola oil
- 2 cups cherry tomatoes, halved
- 1 garlic clove, minced
- ½ cup grated Parmesan cheese
- ½ cup heavy whipping cream
- ¼ tsp. pepper

1. Cook the pasta according to package directions. In a large skillet over medium-high heat, saute asparagus and carrots in oil until crisp-tender. Add tomatoes and garlic; cook 1 minute longer.
2. Stir in the cheese, cream and pepper. Drain pasta; toss with asparagus mixture.
1⅓ cups: 275 cal., 12g fat (6g sat. fat), 33mg chol., 141mg sod., 35g carb. (5g sugars, 3g fiber), 10g pro. **Diabetic exchanges:** 2 starch, 2 fat, 1 vegetable.

TEST KITCHEN TIP

To wash asparagus, fill a bowl with cold water and soak it for a few minutes, then rinse off. That will rid the stems of any unpleasant sandiness or dirt.

BEANS & RICE DINNER

On cold or rainy days, this comforting dish really fills the tummy. Sometimes I use pinto beans instead of kidney beans or white rice instead of brown. Add some rolls and a green salad, and dinner is served!
—Lorraine Caland, Shuniah, ON

Takes: 30 min. • **Makes:** 4 servings

- 1 Tbsp. canola oil
- 2 celery ribs, chopped
- 1 medium green pepper, chopped
- 1 medium onion, chopped
- 1 can (28 oz.) diced tomatoes, undrained
- 1 can (16 oz.) kidney beans, rinsed and drained
- 2 cups cooked brown rice
- 2 tsp. Worcestershire sauce
- 1½ tsp. chili powder
- ¼ tsp. pepper
- ¼ cup shredded cheddar cheese
- ¼ cup reduced-fat sour cream
- 2 green onions, chopped

In a large nonstick skillet, heat the oil over medium-high heat. Add celery, green pepper and onion; cook and stir until tender. Stir in the tomatoes, beans, rice, Worcestershire sauce, chili powder and pepper; bring to a boil. Reduce heat; simmer, covered, until heated through, 7-9 minutes. Top with cheese, sour cream and green onions.

1½ cups: 354 cal., 8g fat (3g sat. fat), 13mg chol., 549mg sod., 58g carb. (13g sugars, 12g fiber), 15g pro.

GENERAL TSO'S CAULIFLOWER

Cauliflower florets are deep-fried to a crispy golden brown, then coated with a sauce that has just the right amount of kick. This is a fun alternative to the classic chicken dish.
—Nick Iverson, Denver, CO

Prep: 25 min. • **Cook:** 20 min.
Makes: 4 servings

- Oil for deep-fat frying
- ½ cup all-purpose flour
- ½ cup cornstarch
- 1 tsp. salt
- 1 tsp. baking powder
- ¾ cup club soda
- 1 medium head cauliflower, cut into 1-in. florets (about 6 cups)

SAUCE
- ¼ cup orange juice
- 3 Tbsp. sugar
- 3 Tbsp. soy sauce
- 3 Tbsp. vegetable broth
- 2 Tbsp. rice vinegar
- 2 tsp. sesame oil
- 2 tsp. cornstarch
- 2 Tbsp. canola oil
- 2 to 6 dried pasilla or other hot chiles, chopped
- 3 green onions, white part minced, green part thinly sliced
- 3 garlic cloves, minced
- 1 tsp. grated fresh gingerroot
- ½ tsp. grated orange zest
- 4 cups hot cooked rice

1. In an electric skillet or deep fryer, heat oil to 375°. Combine flour, cornstarch, salt and baking powder. Stir in the club soda just until blended (batter will be thin). Dip the florets, a few at a time, into the batter and fry until the cauliflower is tender and coating is light brown, 8-10 minutes. Drain on paper towels.
2. For sauce, in a small bowl, whisk together the first 6 ingredients; whisk in cornstarch until smooth.
3. In a large saucepan, heat canola oil over medium-high heat. Add chiles; cook and stir until fragrant, 1-2 minutes. Add the white part of onions, garlic, ginger and orange zest; cook until fragrant, about 1 minute. Stir the soy sauce mixture; add to the saucepan. Bring to a boil; cook and stir until thickened, 2-4 minutes.
4. Add cauliflower to sauce; toss to coat. Serve with rice; sprinkle with green onions.

1 cup with 1 cup rice: 584 cal., 17g fat (2g sat. fat), 0 chol., 1628mg sod., 97g carb. (17g sugars, 5g fiber), 11g pro.

GENERAL TSO'S CAULIFLOWER

CREAMY SEAFOOD ENCHILADAS

CREAMY SEAFOOD ENCHILADAS

Shrimp and crab, cooked with a flavorful sauce, make these enchiladas outstanding. I made them for an annual fundraiser, and now they're always in demand. Spice up the recipe to your taste by adding more green chiles and salsa.

—Evelyn Gebhardt, Kasilof, AK

- -

Prep: 20 min. • **Bake:** 30 min.
Makes: 6 servings

¼ cup butter
¼ cup all-purpose flour
1 cup chicken broth
1 can (10¾ oz.) condensed cream of chicken soup, undiluted
1 cup sour cream
½ cup salsa
⅛ tsp. salt

1 cup 4% cottage cheese
1 lb. small shrimp, cooked, peeled and deveined
1 cup cooked or canned crabmeat, drained, flaked and cartilage removed
1½ cups shredded Monterey Jack cheese
1 can (4 oz.) chopped green chiles
1 Tbsp. dried cilantro flakes
12 flour tortillas (6 in.)
Optional: Sliced jalapeno pepper, thinly sliced green onions and chopped cilantro leaves
Additional salsa

1. In a saucepan over low heat, melt butter; stir in flour until smooth. Gradually stir in broth and soup until blended. Bring to a boil; cook and stir until slightly thickened, about 2 minutes. Remove from the heat. Stir in the sour cream, salsa and salt; set aside.

2. Place cottage cheese in a blender; cover and process until smooth. Transfer to a bowl; add shrimp, crab, Monterey Jack cheese, chiles and cilantro.

3. Spread 1½ cups sauce in a greased 13x9-in. baking dish. Place about ⅓ cup seafood mixture down the center of each tortilla. Roll up and place seam side down over sauce. Top the enchiladas with the remaining sauce. Bake, uncovered, at 350° until heated through, 30-35 minutes. If desired, top with sliced jalapeno, green onions and chopped cilantro. Serve with additional salsa.

2 enchiladas: 645 cal., 35g fat (17g sat. fat), 252mg chol., 1812mg sod., 40g carb. (4g sugars, 2g fiber), 42g pro.

HEAVENLY CRAB CAKES

When I switched to a low-fat diet, I thought I'd never be able to have crab cakes again. But then I found this tasty recipe. Now I can enjoy these little patties of paradise without any guilt!

—Laura Letobar, Livonia, MI

- -

Prep: 15 min. + chilling • **Cook:** 15 min.
Makes: 8 servings

1 lb. imitation crabmeat, flaked
1 cup Italian bread crumbs, divided
¼ cup egg substitute
2 Tbsp. fat-free mayonnaise
2 Tbsp. Dijon mustard
1 Tbsp. dill weed
1 Tbsp. lime juice
1 tsp. lemon juice
1 tsp. Worcestershire sauce

1. Combine crabmeat, ½ cup of bread crumbs, egg substitute, mayonnaise, mustard, dill, lime and lemon juices and Worcestershire sauce. Shape into 8 patties. Place remaining bread crumbs in a shallow bowl; dip each patty into crumbs to cover. Refrigerate for 30 minutes.

2. In a large skillet coated with cooking spray, cook the patties over medium heat until browned on both sides, about 15 minutes.

1 serving: 150 cal., 2g fat (0 sat. fat), 14mg chol., 108mg sod., 22g carb. (0 sugars, 0 fiber), 11g pro. **Diabetic exchanges:** 1½ lean meat, 1 starch.

MUSHROOM &
SWEET POTATO
POTPIE

4. Layer sweet potatoes in a circular pattern on top of each ramekin; brush tops with the remaining oil and sprinkle with pepper, salt and additional rosemary. Bake, covered, until potatoes are tender, 20-25 minutes. Remove cover and bake until the potatoes are lightly browned, 8-10 minutes. Let stand 5 minutes before serving.

1 potpie: 211 cal., 10g fat (1g sat. fat), 0 chol., 407mg sod., 26g carb. (10g sugars, 4g fiber), 5g pro.

BISTRO MAC & CHEESE
I like to serve this mac and cheese with a salad and crusty bread. It's a satisfying meal that feels and tastes upscale, but will fit just about any budget. Because the Gorgonzola is so mild in this dish, even the kiddos will go for it.
—Charlotte Giltner, Mesa, AZ

- -

Takes: 25 min. • **Makes:** 8 servings

- 1 pkg. (16 oz.) uncooked elbow macaroni
- 5 Tbsp. butter, divided
- 3 Tbsp. all-purpose flour
- 2½ cups 2% milk
- 1 tsp. salt
- ½ tsp. onion powder
- ½ tsp. pepper
- ¼ tsp. garlic powder
- 1 cup shredded part-skim mozzarella cheese
- 1 cup shredded cheddar cheese
- ½ cup crumbled Gorgonzola cheese
- 3 oz. cream cheese, softened
- ½ cup sour cream
- ½ cup seasoned panko bread crumbs
  Minced fresh parsley, optional

1. Cook macaroni according to package directions; drain. Meanwhile, in a Dutch oven, melt 3 Tbsp. butter over low heat. Stir in flour until smooth; gradually whisk in the milk and seasonings. Bring to a boil, stirring constantly; cook and stir 2 minutes or until thickened.

2. Reduce heat; stir in cheeses until melted. Stir in sour cream. Add the macaroni; toss to coat. In a small skillet, heat remaining butter over medium heat. Add bread crumbs; cook and stir until golden brown. Sprinkle over top. If desired, sprinkle with parsley.

1 cup: 468 cal., 22g fat (14g sat. fat), 68mg chol., 649mg sod., 49g carb. (7g sugars, 2g fiber), 20g pro.

MUSHROOM & SWEET POTATO POTPIE
The last time I was in the U.S., I had an amazing mushroom and beer potpie at a small brewpub. It was so rich and comforting. I tried numerous versions when I got home, and I think I've come pretty close!
—Iben Ravn, Copenhagen, Denmark

- -

Prep: 45 min. • **Bake:** 30 min.
Makes: 8 servings

- ⅓ cup olive oil, divided
- 1 lb. sliced fresh shiitake mushrooms
- 1 lb. sliced baby portobello mushrooms
- 2 large onions, chopped
- 2 garlic cloves, minced
- 1 tsp. minced fresh rosemary, plus more for topping
- 1 bottle (12 oz.) porter or stout beer
- 1½ cups mushroom broth or vegetable broth, divided
- 2 bay leaves
- 1 Tbsp. balsamic vinegar
- 2 Tbsp. reduced-sodium soy sauce
- ¼ cup cornstarch
- 3 to 4 small sweet potatoes, peeled and thinly sliced
- ¾ tsp. coarsely ground pepper
- ½ tsp. salt

1. Preheat oven to 400°. In a Dutch oven, heat 1 Tbsp. oil over medium heat. Add shiitake mushrooms and cook in batches until dark golden brown, 8-10 minutes; remove with a slotted spoon. Repeat with 1 Tbsp. oil and the portobello mushrooms.

2. In same pan, heat 1 Tbsp. oil over medium heat. Add onions; cook and stir 8-10 minutes or until tender. Add the garlic and 1 tsp. rosemary; cook 30 seconds longer. Stir in beer, 1 cup broth, bay leaves, vinegar, soy sauce and sauteed mushrooms.

3. Bring to a boil. Reduce the heat; simmer, uncovered, 10 minutes. In a small bowl, mix the cornstarch and remaining broth until smooth; stir into mushroom mixture. Return to a boil, stirring constantly; cook and stir until thickened, 1-2 minutes. Remove and discard bay leaves; transfer mushroom mixture to 8 greased 8-oz. ramekins. Place on a rimmed baking sheet.

BISTRO
MAC & CHEESE

SPINACH BURRITOS

I made up this recipe a couple of years ago after trying a similar dish in a restaurant. Our oldest son tells me these burritos are awesome! Plus, they're easy.
—Dolores Zornow, Poynette, WI

Prep: 20 min. • **Bake:** 20 min.
Makes: 6 servings

- ½ cup chopped onion
- 2 garlic cloves, minced
- 2 tsp. butter
- 1 pkg. (10 oz.) frozen chopped spinach, thawed and squeezed dry
- ⅛ tsp. pepper
- 6 flour tortillas (10 in.), warmed
- ¾ cup picante sauce, divided
- 2 cups shredded reduced-fat cheddar cheese, divided

1. In a large skillet, saute onion and garlic in butter until tender. Add spinach and pepper; cook for 2-3 minutes or until heated through.
2. Place about 3 tablespoons of the mixture off center on each tortilla; top with 1 Tbsp. picante sauce and 2 Tbsp. cheese. Fold sides and ends over filling and roll up.
3. Place seam side down in a 13x9-in. baking dish coated with cooking spray. Top with the remaining picante sauce and cheese. Bake, uncovered, at 350° for 20-25 minutes or until sauce is bubbly and cheese is melted.

1 burrito: 382 cal., 15g fat (8g sat. fat), 30mg chol., 1049mg sod., 42g carb. (5g sugars, 4g fiber), 19g pro.

ASK SARAH

HOW DO I DRAIN FROZEN, THAWED SPINACH?
Wrap paper towels around spinach and squeeze dry over a colander.

SPINACH BURRITOS

VEGETARIAN PAD THAI

Here's my version of pad thai. It's loaded with crisp, colorful vegetables and zesty flavor. Give fresh and simple a twirl!
—Colleen Doucette, Truro, Nova Scotia

- -

Takes: 30 min. • **Makes:** 4 servings

- 6 oz. uncooked thick rice noodles
- 2 Tbsp. brown sugar
- 3 Tbsp. reduced-sodium soy sauce
- 4 tsp. rice vinegar
- 2 tsp. lime juice
- 2 tsp. olive oil
- 3 medium carrots, shredded
- 1 medium sweet red pepper, cut into thin strips
- 4 green onions, chopped
- 3 garlic cloves, minced
- 4 large eggs, lightly beaten
- 2 cups bean sprouts
- ⅓ cup chopped fresh cilantro
  Chopped peanuts, optional
  Lime wedges

1. Prepare noodles according to package directions. Drain; rinse well and drain again. In a small bowl, mix together brown sugar, soy sauce, vinegar and lime juice.
2. In a large nonstick skillet, heat oil over medium-high heat; stir-fry carrots and pepper until crisp-tender, 3-4 minutes. Add green onions and garlic; cook and stir 2 minutes. Remove from pan.
3. Reduce the heat to medium. Pour the eggs into same pan; cook and stir until no liquid egg remains. Stir in carrot mixture, noodles and sauce mixture; heat through. Add bean sprouts; toss to combine. Top with cilantro and, if desired, peanuts. Serve with lime wedges.
1¼ cups: 339 cal., 8g fat (2g sat. fat), 186mg chol., 701mg sod., 55g carb. (15g sugars, 4g fiber), 12g pro.

PRESSURE-COOKER LENTIL STEW

This vegetarian stew is perfect when you want to take a break from meat. Adding the cream at the end gives it a smoother texture.
—Michelle Collins, Suffolk, VA

- -

Prep: 45 min. • **Cook:** 15 min. + releasing
Makes: 8 servings (2¾ qt.)

- 2 Tbsp. canola oil
- 2 large onions, thinly sliced, divided
- 8 plum tomatoes, chopped
- 2 Tbsp. minced fresh gingerroot
- 3 garlic cloves, minced
- 2 tsp. ground coriander
- 1½ tsp. ground cumin
- ¼ tsp. cayenne pepper
- 3 cups vegetable broth
- 2 cups dried lentils, rinsed
- 2 cups water
- 1 can (4 oz.) chopped green chiles
- ¾ cup heavy whipping cream
- 2 Tbsp. butter
- 1 tsp. cumin seeds
- 6 cups hot cooked basmati or jasmine rice
  Optional: Sliced green onions or minced fresh cilantro

1. Select saute setting on a 6-qt. electric pressure cooker. Adjust for medium heat; add oil. When oil is hot, cook and stir half the onions until crisp-tender, 2-3 minutes. Add tomatoes, ginger, garlic, coriander, cumin and cayenne; cook and stir 1 minute longer. Press cancel. Stir in broth, lentils, water, green chiles and remaining onion.
2. Lock the lid; close the pressure-release valve. Adjust to pressure-cook on high for 15 minutes. Allow the pressure to release naturally. Just before serving, stir in the cream. In a small skillet, heat butter over medium heat. Add cumin seeds; cook and stir until golden brown, 1-2 minutes. Add to lentil mixture.
3. Serve with rice. If desired, sprinkle with green onions or cilantro.
1⅓ cups stew with ¾ cup rice: 497 cal., 16g fat (8g sat. fat), 33mg chol., 345mg sod., 73g carb. (5g sugars, 8g fiber), 17g pro.

PRESSURE-COOKER LENTIL STEW

CAULIFLOWER ALFREDO

My family loves this quick and healthy cauliflower Alfredo sauce on pasta.
—Shelly Bevington, Hermiston, OR

- -

Prep: 20 min. • **Cook:** 20 min.
Makes: 6 servings

- 2 Tbsp. extra virgin olive oil
- 3 garlic cloves, minced
- 1 shallot, minced
- 1 medium head cauliflower, chopped
- 2 vegetable bouillon cubes
- ⅔ cup shredded Parmesan cheese, plus additional for garnish
- ¼ tsp. crushed red pepper flakes
- 1 pkg. (16 oz.) fettuccine
  Chopped fresh parsley

1. In a Dutch oven, heat oil over medium-high heat. Add the garlic and shallot; cook and stir until fragrant, 1-2 minutes. Add the cauliflower, 4 cups water and bouillon; bring to a boil. Cook, covered, 5-6 minutes or until tender. Drain; cool slightly. Transfer to a food processor; add ⅔ cup Parmesan and pepper flakes. Process until pureed smooth.
2. Meanwhile, cook the fettuccine according to package directions for al dente. Drain and place in a large bowl. Add the cauliflower mixture; toss to coat. Sprinkle with parsley and additional Parmesan.
1⅓ cups: 371 cal., 9g fat (3g sat. fat), 6mg chol., 533mg sod., 60g carb. (5g sugars, 5g fiber), 16g pro.

HOMEMADE MEATLESS SPAGHETTI SAUCE

When my tomatoes ripen each summer, the first things I make are BLTs and this delicious homemade spaghetti sauce.
—Sondra Bergy, Lowell, MI

- -

Prep: 20 min. • **Cook:** 3¼ hours
Makes: 2 qt.

- 4 medium onions, chopped
- ½ cup canola oil
- 12 cups chopped peeled fresh tomatoes
- 4 garlic cloves, minced
- 3 bay leaves
- 4 tsp. salt
- 2 tsp. dried oregano
- 1¼ tsp. pepper
- ½ tsp. dried basil
- 2 cans (6 oz. each) tomato paste
- ⅓ cup packed brown sugar
  Hot cooked pasta
  Minced fresh basil, optional

1. In a Dutch oven, saute onions in oil until tender. Add tomatoes, garlic, bay leaves, salt, oregano, pepper and basil. Bring to a boil. Reduce heat; cover and simmer for 2 hours, stirring occasionally.
2. Add the tomato paste and brown sugar; simmer, uncovered, for 1 hour. Discard bay leaves. Serve with pasta and, if desired, basil.
½ cup: 133 cal., 7g fat (1g sat. fat), 0 chol., 614mg sod., 17g carb. (12g sugars, 3g fiber), 2g pro.

FAST BAKED FISH

We always have a good supply of fresh fish, so I make this dish often. It's moist, tender and flavorful.
—Judie Anglen, Riverton, WY

- -

Takes: 25 min. • **Makes:** 4 servings

- 1¼ lbs. fish fillets
- 1 tsp. seasoned salt
  Pepper to taste
  Paprika, optional
- 3 Tbsp. butter, melted

1. Preheat oven to 400°. Place fish in a greased 11x7-in. baking dish. Sprinkle with the seasoned salt, pepper and, if desired, paprika. Drizzle with butter.
2. Cover and bake until fish just begins to flake easily with a fork, 15-20 minutes.
1 serving: 270 cal., 17g fat (7g sat. fat), 110mg chol., 540mg sod., 0 carb. (0 sugars, 0 fiber), 28g pro.

> "I usually use cod or haddock when making this dish. It's a delicious meal with little fuss."
>
> —JULIE SCHNITTKA, SENIOR EDITOR

SLOW-COOKED STUFFED PEPPERS

My favorite kitchen appliance is the slow cooker, and I use mine more than anyone else I know. Here's a tasty dish to try.
—Michelle Gurnsey, Lincoln, NE

- -

Prep: 15 min. • **Cook:** 3 hours
Makes: 4 servings

- 4 medium sweet red peppers
- 1 can (15 oz.) black beans, rinsed and drained
- 1 cup shredded pepper jack cheese
- ¾ cup salsa
- 1 small onion, chopped
- ½ cup frozen corn
- ⅓ cup uncooked converted long grain rice
- 1¼ tsp. chili powder
- ½ tsp. ground cumin
  Reduced-fat sour cream, optional

1. Cut and discard tops from the peppers; remove seeds. In a large bowl, mix beans, cheese, salsa, onion, corn, rice, chili powder and cumin; spoon into peppers. Place in a 5-qt. slow cooker coated with cooking spray.
2. Cook, covered, on low until the peppers are tender and the filling is heated through, 3-4 hours. If desired, serve with sour cream.
1 stuffed pepper: 317 cal., 10g fat (5g sat. fat), 30mg chol., 565mg sod., 43g carb. (6g sugars, 8g fiber), 15g pro. **Diabetic exchanges:** 2 starch, 2 vegetable, 2 lean meat, 1 fat.

SCALLOPS IN SAGE CREAM

I didn't want to hide the ocean freshness of the scallops I bought on the dock from a local fisherman, so I used simple ingredients to complement them.
—Joan Churchill, Dover, NH

- -

Takes: 20 min. • **Makes:** 4 servings

- 1½ lbs. sea scallops
- ¼ tsp. salt
- ⅛ tsp. pepper
- 3 Tbsp. olive oil, divided
- ½ cup chopped shallots
- ¾ cup heavy whipping cream
- 6 fresh sage leaves, thinly sliced
  Hot cooked pasta, optional

1. Sprinkle scallops with salt and pepper. In a large skillet, cook scallops in 2 Tbsp. oil until firm and opaque, 1½-2 minutes on each side. Remove and keep warm.
2. In the same skillet, saute the shallots in the remaining oil until tender. Add cream; bring to a boil. Cook and stir for 30 seconds or until slightly thickened.
3. Return scallops to the pan; heat through. Stir in sage. Serve with pasta if desired.
1 serving: 408 cal., 28g fat (12g sat. fat), 117mg chol., 441mg sod., 9g carb. (1g sugars, 0 fiber), 30g pro.

SALMON QUICHE

This recipe came to me from my mother—it's the kind you request after just one bite! Unlike some quiches, it's also hearty enough to appeal to both big and small appetites.
—Deanna Baldwin, Bermuda Dunes, CA

- -

Prep: 15 min. • **Bake:** 45 min.
Makes: 8 servings

- 1 sheet refrigerated pie crust
- 1 medium onion, chopped
- 1 Tbsp. butter
- 2 cups shredded Swiss cheese
- 1 can (14¾ oz.) salmon, drained, flaked and cartilage removed
- 5 large eggs
- 2 cups half-and-half cream
- ¼ tsp. salt
  Minced fresh parsley, optional

1. Unroll the crust into 9-in. pie plate. Line unpricked pie crust with a double thickness of heavy-duty foil. Bake crust at 450° for 8 minutes. Remove the foil; bake 5 minutes longer. Cool on a wire rack.
2. In a small skillet, saute onion in butter until tender. Sprinkle cheese in the crust; top with salmon and onion.
3. In a small bowl, whisk eggs, cream and salt; pour over the salmon mixture. Bake at 350° for 45-50 minutes or until a knife inserted in center comes out clean. Sprinkle with parsley if desired. Let stand 5 minutes before cutting.
1 piece: 448 cal., 29g fat (15g sat. fat), 219mg chol., 610mg sod., 18g carb. (5g sugars, 0 fiber), 26g pro.

Side Dishes & Salads

Need to round out your everyday and special-occasion dinners? We've got you covered with this show-stopping selection.

FESTIVE TOSSED
SALAD WITH FETA,
PAGE 166

PARTY POTATOES

ORANGE-PISTACHIO QUINOA SALAD

Add this fresh and healthy salad to your holiday spread. Its citrusy, nutty taste is simply delicious.
—Jean Greenfield, San Anselmo, CA

Prep: 15 min. • **Cook:** 15 min. + cooling
Makes: 8 servings

- 1⅓ cups water
- ⅔ cup quinoa, rinsed
- 2 cups chopped romaine lettuce
- 1 can (15 oz.) garbanzo beans or chickpeas, rinsed and drained
- 1 can (15 oz.) mandarin oranges, drained
- 1 medium cucumber, halved and sliced
- 1 cup shelled pistachios, toasted
- ½ cup finely chopped red onion
- 1 medium navel orange
- 2 Tbsp. olive oil
- ½ tsp. salt
- Pinch pepper

1. In a large saucepan, bring water to a boil. Add quinoa. Reduce heat; simmer, covered, 12-14 minutes or until liquid is absorbed. Remove from heat; fluff with a fork. Cool.
2. In a large bowl, combine romaine, beans, mandarin oranges, cucumber, pistachios, onion and cooled quinoa. In a small bowl, finely grate zest from orange. Cut orange crosswise in half; squeeze juice from orange and add to zest. Whisk in oil, salt and pepper. Drizzle over salad; toss to coat.
1 cup: 257 cal., 12g fat (1g sat. fat), 0 chol., 287mg sod., 31g carb. (10g sugars, 6g fiber), 8g pro. **Diabetic exchanges:** 2 starch, 2 fat.

PARTY POTATOES

These creamy, tasty potatoes can be made the day before and stored in the refrigerator until you're ready to pop them in the oven (I often do that). The garlic powder and chives add zip, and the shredded cheese adds color.
—Sharon Mensing, Greenfield, IA

Prep: 15 min. • **Bake:** 50 min.
Makes: 12 servings

- 4 cups mashed potatoes (8 to 10 large) or 4 cups prepared instant potatoes
- 1 cup sour cream
- 1 pkg. (8 oz.) cream cheese, softened
- 1 tsp. minced chives
- ¼ tsp. garlic powder
- ¼ cup dry bread crumbs
- 1 Tbsp. butter, melted
- ½ cup shredded cheddar cheese

1. In a large bowl, combine the potatoes, sour cream, cream cheese, chives and garlic powder. Turn into a greased 2-qt. casserole. Combine bread crumbs with butter; sprinkle over potatoes.
2. Bake at 350° for 50-60 minutes. Top with cheese and serve immediately.
¾ cup: 207 cal., 13g fat (8g sat. fat), 43mg chol., 305mg sod., 16g carb. (1g sugars, 0 fiber), 5g pro.

"Sour cream and cream cheese make these taters rich and tasty! If you prepare them the night before, remove from the fridge 30 minutes before baking and then add a little to the cooking time."

—JULIE SCHNITTKA, SENIOR EDITOR

**ORANGE-PISTACHIO
QUINOA SALAD**

ITALIAN-INSPIRED BRUSSELS SPROUTS

This Brussels sprout recipe features bacon, pine nuts, balsamic glaze and freshly shaved Parmesan cheese. Serve this quick and easy side for special holidays.
—*Taste of Home* Test Kitchen

- -

Prep: 10 min. • **Cook:** 25 min.
Makes: 6 servings

- 2 lbs. Brussels sprouts, halved
- 6 bacon strips, chopped
- 2 Tbsp. olive oil
- ½ tsp. kosher salt
- ½ tsp. pepper
- 3 Tbsp. extra virgin olive oil
- 3 Tbsp. pine nuts
- 2 tsp. minced fresh oregano
- 2 Tbsp. balsamic glaze
- 2 Tbsp. freshly shaved Parmesan cheese

1. Preheat oven to 450°. In a large bowl, toss the Brussels sprouts, bacon, olive oil, salt and pepper. Transfer to a 15x10x1-in. baking sheet. Roast, stirring halfway through cooking, until sprouts are tender and lightly browned, 20-25 minutes.

2. Meanwhile, in a small skillet or saucepan, heat the extra virgin olive oil over low heat. Add pine nuts; cook until fragrant and nuts start to brown, 3-4 minutes. Remove from heat; mix in oregano. Transfer the Brussels sprouts to a serving bowl; add the pine nut mixture and toss to coat. Drizzle with the balsamic glaze and sprinkle with Parmesan; serve warm.

¾ cup: 323 cal., 26g fat (6g sat. fat), 20mg chol., 410mg sod., 16g carb. (5g sugars, 5g fiber), 9g pro.

RICE DRESSING

This yummy rice mixture is a delightful change from our traditional cornbread dressing. To make it a complete meal in itself, I sometimes add finely chopped cooked chicken and a little more broth.
—Linda Emery, Bearden, AR

- -

Prep: 35 min. • **Bake:** 30 min.
Makes: 10 servings

- 4 cups chicken broth, divided
- 1½ cups uncooked long grain rice
- 2 cups chopped onion
- 2 cups chopped celery
- ½ cup butter, cubed
- 2 cans (4 oz. each) mushroom stems and pieces, drained
- 3 Tbsp. minced fresh parsley
- 1½ to 2 tsp. poultry seasoning
- ¾ tsp. salt
- ½ tsp. pepper
- Optional: Fresh sage and thyme

1. In a saucepan, bring 3½ cups broth and rice to a boil. Reduce the heat; cover and simmer until tender, about 20 minutes.

2. Meanwhile, in a skillet, saute onion and celery in butter until tender. Stir in the rice, mushrooms, parsley, poultry seasoning, salt, pepper and the remaining broth. Pour into a greased 13x9-in. baking dish. Bake, uncovered, at 350° for 30 minutes. Garnish with sage and thyme if desired.

¾ cup: 221 cal., 10g fat (6g sat. fat), 26mg chol., 727mg sod., 29g carb. (2g sugars, 1g fiber), 4g pro.

ITALIAN-INSPIRED BRUSSELS SPROUTS

EASY BROCCOLI SALAD

After sampling this salad at a barbecue, I was given the recipe—but without any measurements! I refined the salad at home. Now it's a regular on our table.
—Sara Sherlock, Port Alice, BC

Prep: 15 min. + chilling • **Makes:** 2 servings

- 1½ cups fresh broccoli florets
- ¾ cup shredded cheddar cheese
- 4 bacon strips, cooked and crumbled
- ¼ cup finely chopped onion
- 3 Tbsp. mayonnaise
- 2 Tbsp. white vinegar
- 1 Tbsp. sugar

In a bowl, combine the broccoli, cheese, bacon and onion. In another bowl, whisk mayonnaise, vinegar and sugar. Pour over broccoli mixture and toss to coat. Cover and refrigerate for at least 1 hour before serving.

¾ cup: 420 cal., 35g fat (13g sat. fat), 63mg chol., 585mg sod., 12g carb. (8g sugars, 2g fiber), 15g pro.

ASK SARAH

CAN YOU FREEZE COOKED BACON?

Yes! Place cooked bacon strips on a baking pan lined with waxed paper. Cover with waxed paper and freeze overnight. Pop the frozen strips into an airtight freezer container; freeze up to 6 months.

EASY BROCCOLI SALAD

STEAKHOUSE
MUSHROOM CASSEROLE

STEAKHOUSE MUSHROOM CASSEROLE

This casserole is one of my all-time favorites. Loaded with mushrooms and covered in a rich sauce, it's a home-style side dish that will have everyone scooping up seconds.
—Rosemary Janz, Concord, NC

Prep: 25 min. + chilling • **Bake:** 30 min.
Makes: 8 servings

- 2   lbs. sliced fresh mushrooms
- ¾   cup butter, divided
- 1   cup heavy whipping cream
- 1   large egg yolk
- 1   Tbsp. minced fresh parsley
- 1   Tbsp. lemon juice
- 1   tsp. salt
- ½   tsp. paprika
- 2   cups crushed butter-flavored crackers

1. In a large skillet, saute the mushrooms in batches in ¼ cup butter until mushrooms are tender and liquid is evaporated. In a large bowl, whisk the whipping cream, egg yolk, parsley, lemon juice, salt and paprika. Add mushrooms and stir until blended.
2. Transfer to a greased 8-in. square baking dish. Melt remaining butter; stir in cracker crumbs until blended. Sprinkle over the top. Cover and refrigerate overnight.
3. Remove from refrigerator 30 minutes before baking. Preheat the oven to 350°. Bake, uncovered, until a thermometer reads 160° and topping is golden brown, 30-35 minutes.
¾ cup: 406 cal., 35g fat (19g sat. fat), 103mg chol., 634mg sod., 20g carb. (5g sugars, 2g fiber), 7g pro.

"When I serve this with grilled ribeyes, I could almost skip the steak and just have the mushrooms! They are so good—creamy and flavorful."

—CATHERINE WARD, PREP KITCHEN MANAGER

GORGONZOLA PEAR SALAD

GORGONZOLA PEAR SALAD

This quick, easy recipe really showcases pears. When I have some leftover cooked chicken, I often toss it in with the greens to make a delicious main-dish salad.
—Candace McMenamin, Lexington, SC

Takes: 25 min.
Makes: 6 servings (1¼ cups dressing)

- ⅓   cup white wine vinegar
- 1   can (15 oz.) pear halves, drained
- ½   tsp. salt
- ⅓   cup olive oil
- 6   cups torn mixed salad greens
- 2   medium pears, sliced
- 1   medium tomato, seeded and finely chopped
- ¾   cup chopped walnuts
- ¼   cup crumbled Gorgonzola cheese
     Coarsely ground pepper, optional

1. For dressing, in a blender, combine vinegar, pear halves and salt; cover and process until smooth. While processing, gradually add oil in a steady stream.
2. In a salad bowl, combine greens, sliced pears, tomato, walnuts and cheese. Drizzle with the desired amount of dressing; toss to coat. Serve salad with pepper if desired. Refrigerate any leftover dressing.
1½ cup: 315 cal., 23g fat (4g sat. fat), 4mg chol., 301mg sod., 27g carb. (17g sugars, 5g fiber), 5g pro.

TEST KITCHEN TIP

You can use any pear in this salad. The most common are Bartlett, Anjou and Bosc. But consider Comice pears as well—they're particularly sweet and juicy.

GYRO SALAD WITH TZATZIKI DRESSING

If you're fond of gyros, you'll enjoy this garden-fresh salad that combines ground lamb, crumbled feta cheese, Greek olives, tomatoes and a creamy cucumber dressing.
—*Taste of Home* Test Kitchen

Takes: 30 min. • **Makes:** 6 servings

DRESSING
- 1 cucumber, peeled and coarsely shredded
- ½ tsp. salt
- ½ cup sour cream
- ¾ cup plain yogurt
- 2 Tbsp. white vinegar
- 1 garlic clove, minced
- ½ tsp. dill weed
- ¼ tsp. cracked black pepper

SALAD
- ½ lb. ground lamb or ground beef
- 1 small onion, chopped
- 1 tsp. Greek seasoning or oregano leaves
- 1 pkg. (10 oz.) hearts of romaine salad mix
- 2 tomatoes, chopped
- 1 pkg. (4 oz.) crumbled feta cheese
- ½ cup pitted Greek olives, drained
  Toasted pita bread wedges

1. In a large bowl, sprinkle cucumber with salt; mix well. Let stand 5 minutes. Drain. Stir in the remaining dressing ingredients. Cover and refrigerate.
2. In a large skillet over medium-high heat, cook lamb, onion and Greek seasoning until meat is no longer pink; drain.
3. Arrange the salad mix on a large serving platter; top with tomatoes, cheese, olives and lamb. Spoon dressing over salad. Serve immediately with toasted pita wedges.
1 serving: 236 cal., 16g fat (7g sat. fat), 43mg chol., 807mg sod., 10g carb. (4g sugars, 3g fiber), 14g pro.

SPAGHETTI SQUASH
CASSEROLE BAKE

SPAGHETTI SQUASH CASSEROLE BAKE

One of our daughters shared this recipe—along with squash from her first garden.
—Glenafa Vrchota, Mason City, IA

Prep: 25 min. • **Bake:** 1 hour
Makes: 6 servings

- 1 medium spaghetti squash (about 8 in.)
- 1 Tbsp. butter
- ½ lb. sliced fresh mushrooms
- 1 large onion, chopped
- 2 garlic cloves, minced
- 1 tsp. dried basil
- ½ tsp. dried oregano
- ½ tsp. salt
- ¼ tsp. dried thyme
- ¼ tsp. pepper
- 2 medium tomatoes, chopped
- 1 cup dry bread crumbs
- 1 cup ricotta cheese
- ¼ cup minced fresh parsley
- ¼ cup grated Parmesan cheese

1. Cut the squash in half lengthwise and scoop out the seeds. Place squash, cut side down, in a baking dish. Add ½ in. water and cover tightly with foil. Bake at 375° until squash can be easily pierced with a fork, 20-30 minutes.
2. Meanwhile, melt butter in a large skillet. Add the mushrooms, onion, garlic, basil, oregano, salt, thyme and pepper; saute until onion is tender. Add tomatoes; cook until most of the liquid has evaporated. Set aside.
3. Scoop out flesh of squash, separating strands with a fork. Combine the flesh, tomato mixture, bread crumbs, ricotta cheese and parsley.
4. Transfer to a greased 2-qt. baking dish. Sprinkle with the Parmesan cheese. Bake, uncovered, at 375° until heated through and top is golden brown, about 40 minutes.
¾ cup: 263 cal., 9g fat (5g sat. fat), 24mg chol., 528mg sod., 37g carb. (6g sugars, 5g fiber), 12g pro.

HOLIDAY PRETZEL SALAD

I gave a summer salad a holiday twist by making green, white and red layers. The combination of salty and sweet is a hit!
—Renee Conneally, Northville, MI

- -

Prep: 35 min. + chilling • **Bake:** 10 min.
Makes: 15 servings

- ¾ cup butter, melted
- 3 Tbsp. sugar
- 2 cups crushed pretzels

LIME LAYER
- 1 cup boiling water
- 1 pkg. (3 oz.) lime gelatin
- 1 pkg. (8 oz.) cream cheese, softened
- 1 carton (8 oz.) frozen whipped topping, thawed
- 14 drops green food coloring, optional

CREAM CHEESE LAYER
- 1 pkg. (8 oz.) cream cheese, softened
- ½ cup sugar
- 1 carton (8 oz.) frozen whipped topping, thawed

STRAWBERRY LAYER
- 2 cups boiling water
- 2 pkg. (3 oz. each) strawberry gelatin
- 4 cups sliced fresh strawberries
  Optional: Additional whipped topping, strawberries and miniature pretzels

1. Preheat oven to 350°. Mix the melted butter and sugar; stir in the pretzels. Press onto the bottom of an ungreased 13x9-in. baking dish. Bake for 10 minutes. Cool completely on a wire rack.
2. Meanwhile, for the lime layer, in a large bowl, add boiling water to lime gelatin; stir 2 minutes to completely dissolve. Refrigerate until partially set, about 1 hour. In a bowl, beat cream cheese until smooth. Add cooled lime gelatin mixture; beat until smooth. Fold in the whipped topping; if desired, add green food coloring. Spread over crust. Refrigerate until set but not firm, 25-30 minutes.
3. For the cream cheese layer, in a bowl, beat the cream cheese and sugar until smooth. Fold in the whipped topping.

Spread over lime layer. Refrigerate the 2 layers until set.
4. For strawberry layer, in a large bowl, add boiling water to strawberry gelatin; stir for 2 minutes to completely dissolve. Refrigerate until partially set, about 1 hour. Stir in the strawberries. Gently spoon over the cream cheese layer. Refrigerate, covered, until firm, 2-4 hours. To serve, cut into squares. If desired, top with additional whipped topping, strawberries and pretzels.
1 serving: 407 cal., 25g fat (17g sat. fat), 55mg chol., 368mg sod., 40g carb. (29g sugars, 1g fiber), 5g pro.

PARSNIP-ASPARAGUS AU GRATIN

We pair parsnips with asparagus to create a terrific side dish. The cheesy and buttery crumb topping will entice everyone to eat their veggies!
—*Taste of Home* Test Kitchen

- -

Prep: 30 min. • **Bake:** 40 min.
Makes: 16 servings

- 10 medium parsnips, peeled and cut into 1-in. slices
- ½ tsp. salt
- ⅛ tsp. pepper
- ½ cup butter, divided
- 2 lbs. fresh asparagus, trimmed and cut into 2-in. pieces
- 2 medium onions, chopped
- 4 garlic cloves, minced
- 2 cups soft bread crumbs
- ½ cup grated Parmesan cheese

1. In a large bowl, combine parsnips, salt and pepper. In a microwave, melt 2 Tbsp. butter. Drizzle over parsnips; toss to coat. Transfer to a greased 15x10x1-in. baking pan. Bake at 400° for 20 minutes.
2. Meanwhile, in a microwave, melt 2 Tbsp. butter. Combine the asparagus and melted butter; add to parsnips. Bake 20-25 minutes longer or until vegetables are tender.
3. In a large saucepan, saute the onions in remaining butter until tender. Add the garlic; saute 1 minute longer. Add bread crumbs; cook and stir until lightly toasted. Stir in the cheese. Transfer parsnip mixture to a serving platter; sprinkle with crumb mixture.
⅔ cup: 162 cal., 7g fat (4g sat. fat), 17mg chol., 204mg sod., 23g carb. (7g sugars, 5g fiber), 4g pro. **Diabetic exchanges:** 1½ starch, 1 fat.

HOLIDAY PRETZEL SALAD

FESTIVE TOSSED SALAD WITH FETA

AIR-FRYER FRENCH FRIES

These low-calorie french fries are perfect because I can whip them up at a moment's notice with ingredients I have on hand. They are so crispy, you won't miss the deep fryer!
—Dawn Parker, Surrey, BC

Prep: 10 min. + soaking • **Cook:** 30 min.
Makes: 4 servings

- 3 medium potatoes, cut into ½-in. strips
- 2 Tbsp. coconut or avocado oil
- ½ tsp. garlic powder
- ¼ tsp. salt
- ¼ tsp. pepper
  Chopped fresh parsley, optional

1. Preheat air fryer to 400°. Add potatoes to a large bowl; add enough ice water to cover. Soak for 15 minutes. Drain potatoes; place on towels and pat dry.
2. Combine the potatoes, oil, garlic powder, salt and pepper in second large bowl; toss to coat. In batches, place potatoes in a single layer on tray in greased air-fryer basket. Cook for 15-17minutes or until crisp and golden brown, stirring and turning every 5-7 minutes. If desired, sprinkle with parsley.
¾ cup: 185 cal., 7g fat (6g sat. fat), 0 chol., 157mg sod., 28g carb. (1g sugars, 3g fiber), 3g pro. **Diabetic exchanges:** 2 starch, 1½ fat.

"This was one of the first recipes I made in my air fryer. Sometimes I replace the salt with onion salt for a little extra savory flavor."

—MARK HAGEN, EXECUTIVE EDITOR

FESTIVE TOSSED SALAD WITH FETA

I like to serve this when we're having company because it's fast and easy, and goes with just about anything. Cranberries and feta cheese add a bright touch to the colorful salad. It's a snap to toss together with packaged greens.
—Kate Hilts, Fairbanks, AK

Takes: 10 min.
Makes: 12 servings

- ½ cup olive oil
- ¼ cup balsamic vinegar
- 3 Tbsp. water
- 1 envelope Italian salad dressing mix
- 2 pkg. (10 oz. each) Italian-blend salad greens
- 2 medium tomatoes, seeded and chopped
- 1 small red onion, thinly sliced
- 1 cup (4 oz.) crumbled feta cheese
- ¾ cup dried cranberries

In a jar with a tight-fitting lid, combine the oil, vinegar, water and salad dressing mix; shake well. In a large salad bowl, combine greens, tomatoes, onion, cheese and cranberries. Serve with dressing.
1 cup: 156 cal., 11g fat (2g sat. fat), 5mg chol., 344mg sod., 14g carb. (10g sugars, 2g fiber), 3g pro.

**AIR-FRYER
FRENCH FRIES**

SUCCOTASH

SUCCOTASH

You can't get more southern than succotash. This recipe comes from my mother, who was a fantastic cook. This dish made her famous—at least with everyone who ever tasted it.
—Rosa Boone, Mobile, AL

- -

Prep: 1¾ hours + cooling • **Cook:** 1 hour
Makes: 16 servings

  1 smoked ham hock (about 1½ lbs.)
  4 cups water
  1 can (28 oz.) diced
       tomatoes, undrained
1½ cups frozen lima beans, thawed
  1 pkg. (10 oz.) crowder peas,
       thawed, or 1 can (15½ oz.)
       black-eyed peas, drained
  1 pkg. (10 oz.) frozen corn, thawed
  1 medium green pepper, chopped
  1 medium onion, chopped
  ⅓ cup ketchup
1½ tsp. salt
1½ tsp. dried basil
  1 tsp. rubbed sage
  1 tsp. paprika
  ½ tsp. pepper
  1 bay leaf
  1 cup sliced fresh or frozen okra
       Optional: Snipped fresh dill
       and chives

In a Dutch oven, simmer ham hock in water until tender, about 1½ hours. Cool; remove meat from bone and return to pan. (Discard the bone and broth or save for another use.) Add the tomatoes, beans, peas, corn, green pepper, onion, ketchup and seasonings. Simmer, uncovered, for 45 minutes. Add okra; simmer, uncovered, until tender, about 15 minutes. Discard bay leaf before serving. Garnish with dill and chives if desired.
¾ cup: 79 cal., 0 fat (0 sat. fat), 2mg chol., 442mg sod., 16g carb. (5g sugars, 3g fiber), 4g pro. **Diabetic exchanges:** 1 starch.

QUICK HARVARD BEETS

We grow beets in our own garden, and they're so good in this recipe. They have such a nice flavor and are very pretty.
—Stella Quade, Carthage, MO

Takes: 30 min. • **Makes:** 6 servings

- 3 cups sliced raw beets or 2 cans (16 oz. each) sliced beets
- ½ cup sugar
- 1 Tbsp. all-purpose flour
- ½ cup white vinegar
- ½ tsp. salt
- 2 Tbsp. butter

1. In a saucepan, place the raw beets and enough water to cover. Cook until tender, 15-20 minutes. Drain, reserving ¼ cup liquid. (If using canned beets, drain and reserve ¼ cup juice.)
2. In another saucepan, combine sugar, flour, vinegar and reserved beet juice. Cook over low heat until thickened. Stir in beets, salt and butter. Simmer for 10 minutes.
½ cup: 133 cal., 4g fat (2g sat. fat), 10mg chol., 280mg sod., 24g carb. (21g sugars, 2g fiber), 1g pro.

EVERYTHING STUFFING

My family goes crazy for the stuffing I make in my slow cooker. It freezes well so we can enjoy it long after the holiday has passed.
—Bette Votral, Bethlehem, PA

Prep: 30 min. • **Cook:** 3 hours
Makes: 9 servings

- ½ lb. bulk Italian sausage
- 4 cups seasoned stuffing cubes
- 1½ cups crushed cornbread stuffing
- ½ cup chopped toasted chestnuts or pecans
- ½ cup minced fresh parsley
- 1 Tbsp. minced fresh sage or 1 tsp. rubbed sage
- ⅛ tsp. salt
- ⅛ tsp. pepper
- 1¾ cups sliced baby portobello mushrooms
- 1 pkg. (5 oz.) sliced fresh shiitake mushrooms
- 1 large onion, chopped
- 1 medium apple, peeled and chopped
- 1 celery rib, chopped
- 3 Tbsp. butter
- 1 can (14½ oz.) chicken broth

1. In a large skillet, cook the Italian sausage over medium heat until no longer pink, breaking it into crumbles; drain. Transfer to a large bowl. Stir in the stuffing cubes, cornbread stuffing, chestnuts, parsley, sage, salt and pepper.
2. In the same skillet, saute the mushrooms, onion, apple and celery in butter until tender. Stir into stuffing mixture. Add enough broth to reach desired moistness. Transfer to a 4-qt. slow cooker. Cover and cook on low for 3 hours, stirring once.
¾ cup: 267 cal., 13g fat (4g sat. fat), 21mg chol., 796mg sod., 30g carb. (5g sugars, 3g fiber), 8g pro.

> "Flat-out delightful! Every bite is loaded with flavor and would work well with any main dish."

—RAEANN THOMPSON, SENIOR ART DIRECTOR

EVERYTHING STUFFING

SPICED CARROTS
WITH PISTACHIOS

SPICED CARROTS WITH PISTACHIOS

Give a classic carrot side dish a little extra crunch. This quick and easy recipe is gluten free and vegetarian. It'll satisfy everyone at the table for holiday gatherings.
—*Taste of Home* Test Kitchen

- -

Takes: 30 min. • **Makes:** 8 servings

- 2 **lbs. carrots, sliced**
- ¼ **cup butter**
- ¼ **cup packed brown sugar**
- ½ **tsp. apple pie spice**
- ¼ **tsp. salt**
- ⅛ **tsp. white pepper**
- ½ **cup golden raisins**
- ⅓ **cup pistachios**

1. Place carrots in a large saucepan; add 1 in. of water. Bring to a boil. Reduce heat; cover and simmer for 8-10 minutes or until crisp-tender. Drain and set aside.
2. In the same pan, combine butter, brown sugar, pie spice, salt and pepper; cook and stir until butter is melted. Add carrots, raisins and pistachios; cook and stir over medium heat for 5 minutes or until glazed.

½ cup: 181 cal., 8g fat (4g sat. fat), 15mg chol., 223mg sod., 26g carb. (18g sugars, 4g fiber), 3g pro.

DID YOU KNOW?
Golden raisins are dried differently then brown raisins, resulting in a fruity, lighter taste and a plump, juicy texture.

MUSHROOM STEAK SALAD WITH WALNUT VINAIGRETTE

MUSHROOM STEAK SALAD WITH WALNUT VINAIGRETTE

When I want to serve a romantic dinner for my husband and me, I fix this elegant yet easy salad. I just add crusty French bread and a glass of wine.
—Candace McMenamin, Lexington, SC

- -

Takes: 30 min. • **Makes:** 2 servings

- 8 **oz. boneless beef sirloin steak (¾ in. thick)**
- 3 **Tbsp. olive oil, divided**
- 1 **cup each sliced fresh baby portobello, shiitake and button mushrooms**
- 2 **Tbsp. balsamic vinegar**
- 1 **Tbsp. minced fresh thyme or 1 tsp. dried thyme**
- 2 **Tbsp. walnut oil**
- 2 **Tbsp. finely chopped walnuts**
- 3 **cups torn mixed salad greens**
- 1 **shallot, sliced**
- 2 **Tbsp. crumbled goat cheese**

1. In a large skillet over medium heat, cook steak in 1 Tbsp. olive oil until meat reaches desired doneness (for medium-rare, a thermometer should read 135°; medium, 140°; medium-well, 145°), 4-6 minutes on each side. Remove from skillet; let stand for 5 minutes before slicing.
2. Meanwhile, in the same skillet, saute the mushrooms until tender. In a small bowl, combine vinegar and thyme. Whisk in walnut oil and remaining olive oil. Stir in walnuts.
3. Divide salad greens and shallot between 2 serving bowls. Cut steak into slices. Top salads with steak and mushrooms. Drizzle with dressing; sprinkle with cheese.

1 serving: 602 cal., 48g fat (9g sat. fat), 75mg chol., 151mg sod., 14g carb. (5g sugars, 4g fiber), 31g pro.

ORZO WITH PARMESAN & BASIL

Dried basil adds rich herb flavor to this creamy and delicious skillet side dish that's table-ready in just minutes!
—Anna Chaney, Antigo, WI

- -

Takes: 20 min. • **Makes:** 4 servings

- 1 cup uncooked orzo pasta or pearl couscous
- 2 Tbsp. butter
- 1 can (14½ oz.) chicken broth
- ½ cup grated Parmesan cheese
- 2 tsp. dried basil
- ⅛ tsp. pepper
  Thinly sliced fresh basil, optional

1. In a large cast-iron or other heavy skillet, saute orzo in butter until lightly browned, 3-5 minutes.

2. Stir in broth. Bring to a boil. Reduce heat; cover and simmer until liquid is absorbed and orzo is tender, 10-15 minutes. Stir in the cheese, basil and pepper. If desired, top with fresh basil.

½ cup: 285 cal., 10g fat (5g sat. fat), 26mg chol., 641mg sod., 38g carb. (2g sugars, 1g fiber), 11g pro.

Corn & Pepper Orzo: Omit the Parmesan cheese, basil and pepper. Prepare orzo as directed. In a large skillet coated with cooking spray, saute 1 chopped large red sweet pepper and 1 chopped medium onion in 1 Tbsp. olive oil. Stir in 2 cups thawed frozen corn, 2 tsp. Italian seasoning and ⅛ tsp. each salt and pepper. Drain orzo; toss with vegetable mixture. Yield: 6 servings.

NOODLE KUGEL

NOODLE KUGEL

I make this traditional dish along with other Jewish specialties for an annual Hanukkah/Christmas party with our friends.
—Lauren Kargen, Buffalo, NY

- -

Prep: 20 min. • **Bake:** 50 min. + standing
Makes: 15 servings

- 1 pkg. (1 lb.) egg noodles
- ½ cup butter, melted
- 8 large eggs
- 2 cups sugar
- 2 cups sour cream
- 2 cups 4% cottage cheese

TOPPING

- ¾ cup cinnamon graham cracker crumbs (about 4 whole crackers)
- 3 Tbsp. butter, melted

1. Cook the noodles according to package directions; drain. Toss with butter; set aside. In a large bowl, beat the eggs, sugar, sour cream and cottage cheese until well blended. Stir in noodles.

2. Transfer to a greased 13x9-in. baking dish. Combine the cracker crumbs and butter; sprinkle over top.

3. Bake casserole, uncovered, at 350° until a thermometer reads 160°, 50-55 minutes. Let stand for 10 minutes before cutting. Serve warm or cold.

1 cup: 432 cal., 19g fat (11g sat. fat), 191mg chol., 261mg sod., 54g carb. (30g sugars, 1g fiber), 12g pro.

TEST KITCHEN TIP
Kugel is best enjoyed right away, but if you're planning a special event, it can be made ahead and stored for up to 2 days in the refrigerator. It can also be frozen for up to 2 months, but be sure to wrap it very well.

RICE NOODLE SALAD

This salad is easy, sweet, spicy, nutty and light. Many friends request this for get-togethers, and our family enjoys it at least once a month for dinner. To make it a main dish, I add marinated and grilled teriyaki chicken.
—Krista Frank, Rhododendron, OR

Takes: 25 min. • **Makes:** 10 servings

- 1 pkg. (8.8 oz.) thin rice noodles
- 2 cups fresh spinach, cut into strips
- 1 large carrot, shredded
- ½ cup pineapple tidbits
- ¼ cup minced fresh cilantro
- 1 green onion, chopped

SESAME PEANUT DRESSING
- ¼ cup unsalted peanuts
- ¼ cup water
- ¼ cup lime juice
- 2 Tbsp. soy sauce
- 1 Tbsp. brown sugar
- 1 Tbsp. canola oil
- 1 tsp. sesame oil
- ½ tsp. ground ginger
- ¼ tsp. crushed red pepper flakes
  Optional: Salted peanuts and additional lime juice

1. Cook the noodles according to package directions. Meanwhile, in a large salad bowl, combine the spinach, carrot, pineapple, cilantro and onion.

2. In a blender, combine dressing ingredients; cover and process until blended. Drain the noodles and rinse in cold water; drain well. Add to spinach mixture. Drizzle with dressing and toss to coat. If desired, sprinkle with the peanuts and additional lime juice.

¾ cup: 149 cal., 4g fat (1g sat. fat), 0 chol., 238mg sod., 26g carb. (4g sugars, 1g fiber), 2g pro. **Diabetic exchanges:** 1½ starch, 1 fat.

FAMILY-FAVORITE CARAMELIZED ONIONS

This recipe was given to me by my mother-in-law. After a few tweaks, these onions are better than ever and, to my husband's disappointment, there are rarely any leftovers. The good news is that they can easily be made ahead and reheated.
—Sharon Gibson, Hendersonville, NC

Prep: 10 min. • **Cook:** 45 min.
Makes: 8 servings

- 3 Tbsp. butter
- ⅓ cup packed brown sugar
- 1 Tbsp. lemon juice
- ¼ tsp. pepper
- 4 jars (15 oz. each) whole onions, drained

In a large skillet over medium heat, melt the butter; stir in brown sugar, lemon juice and pepper. Cook and stir until sugar is dissolved, 1-2 minutes. Add onions. Reduce the heat to medium-low; cook until deep golden brown, 45-50 minutes, stirring occasionally.

¼ cup: 135 cal., 4g fat (3g sat. fat), 11mg chol., 769mg sod., 23g carb. (18g sugars, 4g fiber), 1g pro.

RICE NOODLE SALAD

SPICED ACORN SQUASH

Working full time, I found I didn't always have time to cook the meals my family loved, so I re-created many of the dishes in the slow cooker. This treatment for squash is one of our favorites.
—Carol Greco, Centereach, NY

Prep: 15 min. • **Cook:** 3½ hours
Makes: 4 squash halves

- ¾ cup packed brown sugar
- 1 tsp. ground cinnamon
- 1 tsp. ground nutmeg
- 2 small acorn squash, halved and seeded
- ¾ cup raisins
- 4 Tbsp. butter
- ½ cup water

1. In a small bowl, mix the brown sugar, cinnamon and nutmeg; spoon into squash halves. Sprinkle with raisins. Top each with 1 Tbsp. butter. Wrap each half individually in heavy-duty foil, sealing tightly.
2. Pour water into a 5-qt. slow cooker. Place squash halves in slow cooker, cut side up (packets may be stacked). Cook, covered, on high 3½-4 hours or until squash is tender. Open foil carefully to allow steam to escape.
Squash half: 433 cal., 12g fat (7g sat. fat), 31mg chol., 142mg sod., 86g carb. (63g sugars, 5g fiber), 3g pro.

FRIED CABBAGE

When I was young, my family grew our own cabbage. It was fun to put them to use in the kitchen, just as I did with this comforting side. It's so delicious with potatoes, deviled eggs and cornbread.
—Bernice Morris, Marshfield, MO

Takes: 20 min. • **Makes:** 6 servings

- 2 Tbsp. butter
- 1 tsp. sugar
- ½ tsp. salt
- ¼ tsp. crushed red pepper flakes
- ⅛ tsp. pepper
- 6 cups coarsely chopped cabbage
- 1 Tbsp. water

In a large skillet, melt butter over medium heat. Stir in sugar, salt, pepper flakes and pepper. Add cabbage and water. Cook until tender, 5-6 minutes, stirring occasionally.
1 cup: 59 cal., 4g fat (2g sat. fat), 10mg chol., 251mg sod., 6g carb. (3g sugars, 2g fiber), 1g pro. **Diabetic exchanges:** 1 vegetable, 1 fat.

ROASTED CAULIFLOWER

Roasting is a simple way to prepare cauliflower. Seasoned with a wonderful blend of herbs, this side is easy enough for weeknight dinners.
—Leslie Palmer, Swampscott, MA

Takes: 30 min. • **Makes:** 4 servings

- 3 cups fresh cauliflowerets
- 2 Tbsp. lemon juice
- 4½ tsp. olive oil
- 1 garlic clove, minced
- 1 tsp. dried parsley flakes
- ½ tsp. dried thyme
- ½ tsp. dried tarragon
- ¼ tsp. pepper
- ¼ cup grated Parmesan cheese

In a bowl, combine first 8 ingredients; toss to coat. Transfer to an ungreased 15x10x1-in. baking pan. Bake at 425° until tender, 15-20 minutes, stirring occasionally. Sprinkle with cheese.
¾ cup: 107 cal., 7g fat (2g sat. fat), 4mg chol., 120mg sod., 9g carb. (4g sugars, 4g fiber), 5g pro. **Diabetic exchanges:** 2 vegetable, 1 fat.

MASHED CAULIFLOWER WITH PARMESAN

I couldn't shake my mashed potato habit—until I tried cauliflower mashed to a similar consistency. I started making my own, and my family loves it.
—Meredith Howard, Franklin, KY

- -

Takes: 30 min. • **Makes:** 6 servings

- 1 large head cauliflower (about 2½ lbs.), broken into florets
- 1 cup shredded Parmesan cheese, divided
- ⅓ cup heavy whipping cream or half-and-half cream
- 1 Tbsp. butter
- ½ tsp. pepper
  Minced fresh parsley, optional

1. Place 1 in. of water and the cauliflower in a large saucepan; bring to a boil over high heat. Cook, covered, until cauliflower is soft, 10-12 minutes. Drain.
2. Mash cauliflower to desired consistency. Stir in ½ cup cheese, cream, butter and pepper. Sprinkle with remaining ½ cup cheese and, if desired, parsley.
⅔ cup: 154 cal., 11g fat (7g sat. fat), 33mg chol., 290mg sod., 8g carb. (3g sugars, 3g fiber), 8g pro.

HOMEMADE CRANBERRY RELISH

The baked cranberry compote couldn't be easier to prepare and tastes terrific on top of sliced Thanksgiving turkey. The recipe comes courtesy of my sister-in-law.
—Betty Johnson, Eleva, WI

- -

Prep: 5 min. • **Bake:** 1 hour + chilling
Makes: 4 cups

- 4 cups fresh or frozen cranberries
- 2 cups sugar
- 1 cup orange marmalade
- 1 cup chopped walnuts, toasted
- 3 Tbsp. lemon juice

1. Preheat oven to 350°. In an ungreased 13 x 9-in. baking dish, combine cranberries and sugar. Cover and bake for 1 hour.
2. In a large bowl, combine the orange marmalade, walnuts and lemon juice. Stir in cranberry mixture. Cover and refrigerate until chilled.
¼ cup: 206 cal., 4g fat (0 sat. fat), 0 chol., 12mg sod., 42g carb. (39g sugars, 1g fiber), 2g pro.

BROCCOLI RICE CASSEROLE

This hearty broccoli rice casserole is my usual choice to make for a potluck. With the green broccoli and the rich cheese sauce, it's pretty to serve. And it makes a tasty side dish for almost any kind of meat.
—Margaret Mayes, La Mesa, CA

- -

Prep: 10 min. • **Bake:** 25 min.
Makes: 8 servings

- 1 Tbsp. butter
- 1 small onion, chopped
- ½ cup chopped celery
- 3 cups frozen chopped broccoli, thawed
- 1 cup cheese dip
- 1 can (10½ oz.) condensed cream of mushroom soup, undiluted
- 1 can (5 oz.) evaporated milk
- 3 cups cooked rice

Preheat oven to 325°. In a large skillet, melt the butter over medium-high heat. Add the onion, celery and broccoli; cook and stir until crisp-tender, 3-5 minutes. Stir in the cheese dip, soup and milk until smooth. Spoon the rice into a greased 8-in. square baking dish. Pour the cheese mixture over the rice; do not stir. Bake, uncovered, until bubbly, 25-30 minutes.
1 cup: 241 cal., 11g fat (6g sat. fat), 32mg chol., 782mg sod., 28g carb. (5g sugars, 3g fiber), 8g pro.

Cookies, Brownies & Bars

These bite-sized bundles packed with chocolate, fruit, oats and more will satisfy a sweet tooth in no time!

BLOND BUTTERSCOTCH
BROWNIES, PAGE 188

**DELUXE CHOCOLATE
MARSHMALLOW BARS**

ORANGE GINGERBREAD TASSIES

I make big Christmas cookie plates every year, and it's fun to have something with a different shape to include. These have a delicious flavor with the gingerbread and orange and are really easy! They're also yummy with lemon zest if you prefer that over the orange. Decorate with some candied orange peel if you have it.
—Elisabeth Larsen, Pleasant Grove, UT

- -

Prep: 20 min. + chilling
Bake: 15 min. + cooling
Makes: 2 dozen

  ½ cup butter, softened
  4 oz. cream cheese, softened
  ¼ cup molasses
  1 tsp. ground ginger
  ½ tsp. ground cinnamon
  ½ tsp. ground allspice
  ¼ tsp. ground cloves
  1 cup all-purpose flour
  ½ cup white baking chips
  ¼ cup heavy whipping cream
  2 Tbsp. butter
  4 tsp. grated orange zest
    Candied orange peel, optional

1. Beat first 7 ingredients until light and fluffy. Gradually beat in flour. Refrigerate, covered, until firm enough to shape, about 1 hour.
2. Preheat oven to 350°. Shape dough into 1-in. balls; press evenly onto bottom and up sides of ungreased mini-muffin cups. Bake until golden brown, 15-18 minutes. Press the centers with the handle of a wooden spoon to reshape as necessary. Cool completely in pan before removing to wire rack.
3. In a microwave-safe bowl, heat baking chips, cream and butter until blended, stirring occasionally. Stir in orange zest; cool completely. Spoon into the crusts. Refrigerate until filling is soft-set. If desired, garnish with orange peel.
1 cookie: 91 cal., 6g fat (4g sat. fat), 13mg chol., 43mg sod., 9g carb. (5g sugars, 0 fiber), 1g pro.

DELUXE CHOCOLATE MARSHMALLOW BARS

I've been asked to share this chocolaty layered recipe more than any other in my collection. It's a longtime favorite of our three daughters, and I can't even begin to count how many times I've made them!
—Esther Shank, Harrisonburg, VA

- -

Prep: 25 min. • **Bake:** 15 min. + cooling
Makes: 3 dozen

  ¾ cup butter, softened
  1½ cups sugar
  3 large eggs, room temperature
  1 tsp. vanilla extract
  1⅓ cups all-purpose flour
  3 Tbsp. baking cocoa
  ½ tsp. baking powder
  ½ tsp. salt
  ½ cup chopped nuts, optional
  4 cups miniature marshmallows
TOPPING
  1⅓ cups semisweet chocolate chips
  1 cup peanut butter
  3 Tbsp. butter
  2 cups Rice Krispies

1. Preheat oven to 350°. In a small bowl, cream butter and sugar until light and fluffy, 5-7 minutes. Add eggs, 1 at a time, beating well after each addition. Beat in vanilla. Combine flour, cocoa, baking powder and salt; gradually add to the creamed mixture. Stir in nuts if desired. Spread into a greased 15x10x1-in. baking pan.
2. Bake until set, 15-18 minutes or until set. Sprinkle with marshmallows; bake 2-3 minutes longer or until melted. Place pan on a wire rack. Using a knife dipped in water, spread marshmallows evenly over the top. Cool completely.
3. For topping, combine chocolate chips, peanut butter and butter in a small saucepan. Cook and stir over low heat until blended. Remove from heat; stir in Rice Krispies. Immediately spread over bars. Chill until set.
1 bar: 196 cal., 11g fat (5g sat. fat), 28mg chol., 128mg sod., 24g carb. (16g sugars, 1g fiber), 3g pro.

ORANGE
GINGERBREAD TASSIES

SEA SALT MINT WHITE MOCHA COOKIES

This recipe came from my mom's Grandma Alice, who taught her how to bake. Grandma Alice always had a fresh plate of warm cookies on her counter. I learned some of her recipes by heart. I've been making these since high school!
—Kristin Bowers, Rancho Palos Verdes, CA

- -

Prep: 20 min. • **Bake:** 15 min./batch
Makes: 26 cookies

- 1 cup butter-flavored shortening
- ¾ cup sugar
- ¾ cup packed brown sugar
- 2 large eggs, room temperature
- 1 tsp. mint extract
- 1½ cups all-purpose flour
- 1 Tbsp. instant espresso powder
- 1 tsp. sea salt
- 1 tsp. baking soda
- 2 cups old-fashioned oats
- 1 pkg. (10 to 12 oz.) white baking chips

1. Preheat the oven to 350°. In a large bowl, cream shortening and sugars until light and fluffy, 5-7 minutes. Beat in eggs and extract. In another bowl, whisk the flour, espresso powder, salt and baking soda; gradually beat into creamed mixture. Stir in oats and white baking chips.

2. Drop dough by scant ¼ cupfuls 2 in. apart onto parchment-lined baking sheets. Bake until edges begin to brown, 12-15 minutes. Cool on pans 5 minutes. Remove to wire racks to cool. Store in an airtight container.

1 cookie: 229 cal., 12g fat (4g sat. fat), 17mg chol., 140mg sod., 28g carb. (19g sugars, 1g fiber), 3g pro.

TEST KITCHEN TIP

Do not remove the cookies from the baking sheet too soon after baking. They are more fragile when they are warm.

SEA SALT MINT WHITE MOCHA COOKIES

DATE OATMEAL BARS

In no time at all, you can treat your family to these bars. They'll be surprised at how light and tasty the snacks are.
—Helen Cluts, Eden Prairie, MN

Prep: 20 min. • **Bake:** 20 min. + cooling
Makes: 16 servings

- 1 cup chopped dates
- ½ cup water
- ¼ cup sugar
- 1½ cups quick-cooking oats
- 1 cup all-purpose flour
- 1 cup packed brown sugar
- ½ tsp. baking soda
- ¼ tsp. salt
- ⅓ cup butter, melted
- 1 large egg white, room temperature

1. Preheat oven to 350°. Place dates, water and sugar in a small saucepan; bring to a boil, stirring constantly. Reduce the heat; simmer, uncovered, until thickened, about 5 minutes, stirring constantly.

2. In a large bowl, mix oats, flour, brown sugar, baking soda and salt; stir in melted butter and egg white. Press half the mixture into an 8-in. square baking pan coated with cooking spray. Spread carefully with date mixture; top with remaining oat mixture.

3. Bake until lightly browned, 20-25 minutes. Cool in pan on a wire rack. Cut into bars.

1 bar: 182 cal., 4g fat (3g sat. fat), 10mg chol., 114mg sod., 35g carb. (23g sugars, 2g fiber), 2g pro. **Diabetic exchanges:** 1½ starch, 1 fat, ½ fruit.

TEST KITCHEN TIP

Store your date bars in an airtight container at room temperature with pieces of waxed paper or parchment between layers, so they don't stick to one another.

CARAMEL HEAVENLIES

Before I cut these bars into triangles, I trim the edges so all the cookies look the same. My husband and daughter love this part because they get to eat the scraps.
—Dawn Burns, Lake St. Louis, MO

Prep: 20 min. • **Bake:** 15 min. + cooling
Makes: 3 dozen

- 12 whole graham crackers
- 2 cups miniature marshmallows
- ¾ cup butter, cubed
- ¾ cup packed brown sugar
- 1 tsp. ground cinnamon
- 1 tsp. vanilla extract
- 1 cup sliced almonds
- 1 cup sweetened shredded coconut

1. Preheat oven to 350°. Line a 15x10x1-in. baking pan with foil, letting foil extend over sides by 1 in.; lightly coat foil with cooking spray. Arrange graham crackers in prepared pan; sprinkle with marshmallows.

2. In a small saucepan, combine the butter, brown sugar and cinnamon; cook and stir over medium heat until the butter is melted and sugar is dissolved. Remove from heat; stir in vanilla.

3. Spoon butter mixture over marshmallows. Sprinkle with the almonds and coconut. Bake for 14-16 minutes or until browned. Cool completely in pan on a wire rack.

4. Using foil, lift out of the pan. Cut into triangles; discard foil.

1 piece: 110 cal., 7g fat (3g sat. fat), 10mg chol., 68mg sod., 13g carb. (8g sugars, 1g fiber), 1g pro.

DATE OATMEAL BARS

WHITE CHOCOLATE CRANBERRY BLONDIES

The family often requests these bars, but for a fancier presentation, cut them into triangles and drizzle white chocolate over each one individually.
—Erika Busz, Kent, WA

Prep: 35 min. • **Bake:** 20 min. + cooling
Makes: 3 dozen

- ¾ cup butter, cubed
- 1½ cups packed light brown sugar
- 2 large eggs, room temperature
- ¾ tsp. vanilla extract
- 2¼ cups all-purpose flour
- 1½ tsp. baking powder
- ¼ tsp. salt
- ⅛ tsp. ground cinnamon
- ½ cup dried cranberries
- 6 oz. white baking chocolate, coarsely chopped

FROSTING
- 1 pkg. (8 oz.) cream cheese, softened
- 1 cup confectioners' sugar
- 1 Tbsp. grated orange zest, optional
- 6 oz. white baking chocolate, melted
- ½ cup dried cranberries, chopped

1. Preheat the oven to 350°. In a large microwave-safe bowl, melt the butter; stir in the brown sugar. Cool slightly.
2. Add eggs, 1 egg at a time, beating well after each addition. Beat in the vanilla. In another bowl, whisk together flour, baking powder, salt and cinnamon; stir into butter mixture. Stir in cranberries and chopped chocolate (batter will be thick). Spread into a greased 13x9-in. pan.
3. Bake until golden brown and a toothpick inserted in center comes out clean (do not overbake), 18-21 minutes. Cool completely on a wire rack.
4. For the frosting, beat the cream cheese, confectioners' sugar and, if desired, orange zest until smooth. Gradually beat in half of the melted white chocolate; spread over blondies. Sprinkle with cranberries; drizzle with remaining melted chocolate.
5. Cut into triangles. Store in an airtight container in the refrigerator.
1 blondie: 198 cal., 9g fat (6g sat. fat), 27mg chol., 100mg sod., 28g carb. (22g sugars, 0 fiber), 2g pro.

CARAMEL SNICKERDOODLE BARS

CARAMEL SNICKERDOODLE BARS

What did I do when I couldn't decide between two of my favorite desserts? I combined them! This snickerdoodle-blondie hybrid is even better with my other favorite ingredient: caramel.
—Niki Plourde, Gardner, MA

Prep: 30 min. • **Bake:** 25 min. + chilling
Makes: 4 dozen

- 1 cup butter, softened
- 2 cups packed brown sugar
- 2 large eggs, room temperature
- 2 tsp. vanilla extract
- 2½ cups all-purpose flour
- 2 tsp. baking powder
- 1 tsp. salt
- ¼ cup sugar
- 3 tsp. ground cinnamon
- 2 cans (13.4 oz. each) dulce de leche
- 12 oz. white baking chocolate, chopped
- ⅓ cup heavy whipping cream
- 1 Tbsp. light corn syrup

1. Preheat oven to 350°. Line a 13x9-in. baking pan with parchment, letting ends extend 1 in. over the sides.
2. In a large bowl, cream butter and brown sugar until light and fluffy, 5-7 minutes. Beat in eggs and vanilla. In another bowl, whisk flour, baking powder and salt; gradually beat into creamed mixture. Spread onto bottom of prepared pan.
3. In a small bowl, mix sugar and cinnamon; sprinkle 2 Tbsp. mixture over batter. Bake until edges are light brown, 25-30 minutes. Cool completely in pan on a wire rack.
4. Spread dulce de leche over crust. In a small saucepan, combine white baking chocolate, cream and corn syrup; cook and stir over low heat until smooth. Cool slightly. Spread over the dulce de leche. Sprinkle with remaining cinnamon sugar. Refrigerate, covered, at least 1 hour.
5. Lifting with parchment, remove from pan. Cut into bars. Refrigerate leftovers.
Note: This recipe was tested with Nestle La Lechera dulce de leche; look for it in the international foods section. If using Eagle Brand dulce de leche (caramel flavored sauce), thicken according to package directions before using.
1 bar: 197 cal., 8g fat (5g sat. fat), 27mg chol., 137mg sod., 28g carb. (23g sugars, 0 fiber), 2g pro.

CARDAMOM CHEESECAKE BARS

Fans of cheesecake will love these bite-sized desserts. Crunchy and smooth, they are so perfect for the holidays—or any other time.
—Judi Oudekerk, Buffalo, MN

Prep: 35 min. • **Bake:** 35 min. + chilling
Makes: 16 servings

- ¾ cup graham cracker crumbs
- 2 Tbsp. butter, melted
- 2 pkg. (8 oz. each) cream cheese, softened
- ½ cup sugar
- 2 tsp. ground cardamom, divided
- 1 tsp. vanilla extract
- 2 large eggs, room temperature, lightly beaten
- ⅓ cup all-purpose flour
- ⅓ cup quick-cooking oats
- ⅓ cup packed brown sugar
- ¼ cup cold butter
- ⅓ cup sliced almonds

1. In a small bowl, combine graham cracker crumbs and melted butter. Press onto the bottom of a greased 9-in. square baking pan. In a large bowl, beat the cream cheese, sugar, 1 tsp. cardamom and extract until smooth. Add the eggs; beat on low speed just until combined. Pour over crust.
2. In a small bowl, combine flour, oats, brown sugar and remaining cardamom. Cut in cold butter until crumbly. Stir in sliced almonds. Sprinkle over top.
3. Bake at 350° for 35-40 minutes or until center is almost set and topping is golden brown. Cool on a wire rack 1 hour. Cover and refrigerate for at least 2 hours before serving. Cut into 16 bars.
1 bar: 232 cal., 16g fat (9g sat. fat), 69mg chol., 149mg sod., 18g carb. (12g sugars, 1g fiber), 4g pro.

GINGERBREAD BISCOTTI

Sweet cranberries and crunchy almonds pair well with the mild gingerbread flavor in these cookies.
—*Taste of Home* Test Kitchen

Prep: 25 min. • **Bake:** 35 min. + cooling
Makes: 3 dozen

- 3 large eggs, room temperature
- 1 cup sugar
- ⅓ cup canola oil
- ¼ cup molasses
- 3¾ cups all-purpose flour
- 3 tsp. baking powder
- 3 tsp. ground ginger
- 2¼ tsp. ground cinnamon
- ¼ tsp. ground nutmeg
- ¾ cup slivered almonds
- ½ cup dried cranberries

1. Preheat oven to 375°. In a large bowl, beat eggs, sugar, oil and molasses until blended. Combine the flour, baking powder, ginger, cinnamon and nutmeg; gradually beat into egg mixture. Turn onto a floured surface. Knead in almonds and cranberries.
2. Divide dough in half; shape each portion into a 14x3-in. rectangle. Transfer to a greased baking sheet. Bake until lightly browned, 24-26 minutes. Cool 5 minutes.
3. Transfer to a cutting board; with a serrated knife, cut each rectangle into 18 slices. Place slices cut side down on greased baking sheets. Bake until firm and crisp, 10-15 minutes, turning once. Remove to wire racks to cool. Store in an airtight container.
1 cookie: 118 cal., 4g fat (1g sat. fat), 18mg chol., 40mg sod., 19g carb. (8g sugars, 1g fiber), 2g pro.

GINGERBREAD BISCOTTI

COCONUT KEY LIME THUMBPRINTS

4. Bake until edges are golden brown, 12-14 minutes. Reshape indentations as needed. Cool on pans 5 minutes. Remove to wire racks to cool completely.
5. To serve, fill each cookie with about 1½ tsp. curd. In a microwave, melt white chocolate and shortening; stir until smooth. Drizzle over cookies. Refrigerate leftover filled cookies.

1 cookie: 182 cal., 11g fat (7g sat. fat), 29mg chol., 76mg sod., 21g carb. (13g sugars, 1g fiber), 2g pro.

CHERRY BARS

Whip up a pan of these festive bars in just 20 minutes with staple ingredients and pie filling. Between the easy preparation and the pretty colors, they're destined to become a holiday classic.
—Jane Kamp, Grand Rapids, MI

Prep: 20 min. • **Bake:** 35 min. + cooling
Makes: 5 dozen

   1   cup butter, softened
   2   cups sugar
   1   tsp. salt
   4   large eggs, room temperature
   1   tsp. vanilla extract
   ¼   tsp. almond extract
   3   cups all-purpose flour
   2   cans (21 oz. each) cherry pie filling
GLAZE
   1   cup confectioners' sugar
   ½   tsp. vanilla extract
   ½   tsp. almond extract
   2   to 3 Tbsp. 2% milk

1. Preheat oven to 350°. In a large bowl, cream butter, sugar and salt until light and fluffy, 5-7 minutes. Add eggs, 1 at a time, beating well after each addition. Beat in extracts. Gradually add flour.
2. Spread 3 cups dough into a greased 15x10x1-in. baking pan. Spread with pie filling. Drop remaining the dough by teaspoonfuls over the filling. Bake 35-40 minutes or until golden brown. Cool completely in pan on a wire rack.
3. In a small bowl, mix confectioners' sugar, extracts and enough milk to reach desired consistency; drizzle over top.

1 bar: 112 cal., 3g fat (2g sat. fat), 21mg chol., 72mg sod., 19g carb. (9g sugars, 0 fiber), 1g pro.

COCONUT KEY LIME THUMBPRINTS

This is the cookie recipe I created for the Las Vegas World Food Championships in 2013. It's similar to a shortbread thumbprint cookie, but with lots more personality.
—Amy Freeze, Avon Park, FL

Prep: 40 min. + cooling
Bake: 15 min./batch + cooling
Makes: about 2½ dozen

   2   Tbsp. cornstarch
   ⅔   cup Key lime juice
   ¾   cup sugar
   2   large egg yolks
COOKIES
   1   cup butter, softened
   ½   cup confectioners' sugar
   ⅛   tsp. salt
   1   tsp. vanilla extract
   ½   tsp. coconut extract
   2   cups all-purpose flour
   2   large egg whites

   2   tsp. water
   2½ cups sweetened shredded coconut
DRIZZLE
   4   oz. white baking chocolate, chopped
   1   Tbsp. shortening

1. For lime curd, in a small saucepan, whisk the cornstarch and lime juice until smooth. Whisk in sugar and egg yolks; cook and stir over medium heat until boiling. Transfer to a bowl; cool slightly. Press plastic wrap onto surface of curd; refrigerate until cold.
2. Preheat oven to 400°. Cream butter, confectioners' sugar and salt until light and fluffy, 5-7 minutes. Beat in extracts. Gradually beat in flour.
3. In a small bowl, whisk together the egg whites and water. Place the coconut in a separate bowl. Shape dough into 1¼-in. balls. Dip in the egg whites, then roll in coconut, coating well. Place 2 in. apart on parchment-lined baking sheets. Press a deep indentation in center of each with the handle of a wooden spoon.

FRENCH BUTTER COOKIES

PUMPKIN BARS

What could be more appropriate fall treat than a big pan of pumpkin-flavored bars? Actually, my family loves these any time of year!
—Brenda Keller, Andalusia, AL

- -

Prep: 20 min. • **Bake:** 25 min. + cooling
Makes: 2 dozen

   4 **large eggs, room temperature**
1⅔ **cups sugar**
   1 **cup canola oil**
   1 **can (15 oz.) pumpkin**
   2 **cups all-purpose flour**
   2 **tsp. ground cinnamon**
   2 **tsp. baking powder**
   1 **tsp. baking soda**
   1 **tsp. salt**
ICING
   6 **oz. cream cheese, softened**
   2 **cups confectioners' sugar**
 ¼ **cup butter, softened**
   1 **tsp. vanilla extract**
   1 **to 2 Tbsp. 2% milk**

1. In a bowl, beat the eggs, sugar, oil and pumpkin until well blended. Combine flour, cinnamon, baking powder, baking soda and salt; gradually add to pumpkin mixture and mix well. Pour into an ungreased 15x10x1-in. baking pan. Bake at 350° for 25-30 minutes or until set. Cool completely.
2. For icing, beat the cream cheese, confectioners' sugar, butter and vanilla in a bowl. Add enough milk to achieve spreading consistency. Spread icing over bars. Store in the refrigerator.
1 bar: 260 cal., 13g fat (3g sat. fat), 45mg chol., 226mg sod., 34g carb. (24g sugars, 1g fiber), 3g pro.

> "I make this at least once a month in fall and winter. It's such a delicious and easy weekday treat. I love that the bars stay moist and fresh-tasting for days."
>
> —KARA DENNISON, COPY EDITOR

FRENCH BUTTER COOKIES

The Brittany region of France is known for its use of butter. These French butter cookies, also known as sable Breton, shine the spotlight on the famous ingredient. This recipe is mildly sweet, rich, crisp and has a hint of salt. You won't be able to resist having a second—or third.
—*Taste of Home* Test Kitchen

- -

Prep: 15 min. + chilling
Bake: 15 min./batch + cooling
Makes: 2 dozen

 ⅔ **cup European-style salted butter, softened**
 ½ **cup sugar**
   3 **large egg yolks, room temperature, divided use**
   1 **tsp. vanilla extract**
   2 **cups all-purpose flour**
 ¼ **tsp. salt**
   2 **Tbsp. water**

1. Cream the butter and sugar until light and fluffy, 5-7 minutes. Beat in 2 egg yolks and vanilla. Gradually beat in flour and salt. Divide dough into 2 portions; shape each into a disk. Cover; refrigerate until firm enough to roll, about 30 minutes.
2. Preheat oven to 350°. Working with 1 portion of dough at a time, roll to ¼-in. thickness between parchment. Cut with floured 2-in. round cookie cutter. Place 1 in. apart on ungreased baking sheets. Whisk the remaining egg yolk and water; brush over cookies. Create a cross-hatch design by dragging the tines of a fork across the cookie.
3. Bake until the edges are light golden, 12-15 minutes. Cool on pans 5 minutes. Remove to wire racks to cool completely.
1 cookie: 107 cal., 6g fat (3g sat. fat), 37mg chol., 42mg sod., 12g carb. (4g sugars, 0 fiber), 1g pro.

PUMPKIN BARS

BLOND BUTTERSCOTCH BROWNIES

Toffee and chocolate dot the golden brown batter of these delightful brownies. I do a lot of cooking for the police officers I work with, and they always line up for these treats.
—Jennifer Ann Sopko, Battle Creek, MI

- -

Prep: 15 min. • **Bake:** 20 min. + cooling
Makes: 2 dozen

- 2 cups all-purpose flour
- 2 cups packed brown sugar
- 2 tsp. baking powder
- ¼ tsp. salt
- ½ cup butter, melted and cooled
- 2 large eggs, room temperature
- 1 tsp. vanilla extract
- 1 cup semisweet chocolate chunks
- 4 Heath candy bars (1.4 oz. each), coarsely chopped

1. In a large bowl, combine flour, brown sugar, baking powder and salt. In another bowl, beat the butter, eggs and vanilla until smooth. Stir into dry ingredients just until combined (batter will be thick).
2. Spread into a 13x9-in. baking pan coated with cooking spray. Sprinkle with chocolate chunks and the chopped candy bars; press gently into batter.
3. Bake at 350° until a toothpick inserted in the center comes out clean, 20-25 minutes. Cool on a wire rack. Cut into bars.
1 piece: 218 cal., 9g fat (5g sat. fat), 29mg chol., 126mg sod., 35g carb. (26g sugars, 1g fiber), 2g pro.

ASK SARAH

WHEN ARE BARS DONE BAKING?

They should be set and slightly browned. Insert a toothpick in the center of the pan; if it comes out clean, the bars are done.

BLOND BUTTERSCOTCH BROWNIES

FROSTED BUTTER RUM BRICKLE BITES

Rum, butter and toffee bits turned these cookies into my husband's new favorite. If you'd like them less sweet, skip the frosting and sprinkle with confectioners' sugar while the cookies are still warm.
—Cindy Nerat, Menominee, MI

Prep: 35 min. • **Bake:** 10 min./batch + cooling
Makes: about 4 dozen

- 1 cup butter, softened
- ¾ cup confectioners' sugar
- 2 tsp. rum extract
- ½ tsp. salt
- 2 cups all-purpose flour
- 1 pkg. (8 oz.) brickle toffee bits

ICING
- ⅓ cup butter, cubed
- 2 cups confectioners' sugar
- ½ tsp. rum extract
- 2 to 3 Tbsp. 2% milk

1. Preheat oven to 375°. Beat the first 4 ingredients until blended. Beat in flour. Stir in toffee bits. Shape dough into 1-in. balls; place 2 in. apart on parchment-lined baking sheets.
2. Bake until the edges are light brown and toffee bits begin to melt, 8-10 minutes. Cool on pans 5 minutes. Remove to wire racks to cool completely.
3. In a small heavy saucepan, melt butter over medium heat. Heat until golden brown, about 5 minutes, stirring constantly. Remove from the heat; stir in confectioners' sugar, rum extract and enough milk to reach desired consistency. Spread over cookies.
1 cookie: 112 cal., 6g fat (4g sat. fat), 15mg chol., 89mg sod., 13g carb. (9g sugars, 0 fiber), 1g pro.

JUMBO BROWNIE COOKIES

Bring these deeply fudgy cookies to a party, and you're sure to make a friend. A little espresso powder in the dough makes them over-the-top good.
—Rebecca Cababa, Las Vegas, NV

Prep: 20 min. • **Bake:** 15 min./batch
Makes: about 1½ dozen

- 2⅔ cups 60% cacao bittersweet chocolate baking chips
- ½ cup unsalted butter, cubed
- 4 large eggs, room temperature
- 1½ cups sugar
- 4 tsp. vanilla extract
- 2 tsp. instant espresso powder, optional
- ⅔ cup all-purpose flour
- ½ tsp. baking powder
- ¼ tsp. salt
- 1 pkg. (11½ oz.) semisweet chocolate chunks

1. Preheat oven to 350°. In a large saucepan, melt chocolate chips and butter over low heat, stirring until smooth. Remove from the heat; cool until mixture is warm.
2. In a small bowl, whisk the eggs, sugar, vanilla and, if desired, espresso powder until blended. Whisk into the chocolate mixture. In another bowl, mix the flour, baking powder and salt; add to chocolate mixture, mixing well. Fold in chocolate chunks; let stand until mixture thickens slightly, about 10 minutes.
3. Drop by ¼ cupfuls 3 in. apart onto parchment-lined baking sheets. Bake until set, 12-14 minutes. Cool on pans 1-2 minutes. Remove cookies to wire racks to cool.
1 cookie: 350 cal., 19g fat (11g sat. fat), 60mg chol., 65mg sod., 48g carb. (40g sugars, 3g fiber), 4g pro.

JUMBO BROWNIE COOKIES

DOUBLE-CHOCOLATE
PRETZEL TURTLE COOKIES

DOUBLE-CHOCOLATE PRETZEL TURTLE COOKIES

My father loves turtles, so I decided to turn them into a cookie. They were a big hit. The generous size makes them ideal for giving as gifts, and they're always the first to go at potlucks.
—Melissa Keenan, Larchmont, NY

Prep: 15 min. • **Bake:** 10 min./batch
Makes: 1 dozen

½ cup butter, softened
½ cup packed brown sugar
⅓ cup sugar
1 large egg, room temperature
1 tsp. vanilla extract
1 cup all-purpose flour
⅔ cup baking cocoa
½ tsp. baking powder
½ tsp. baking soda
½ tsp. salt
1 cup (6 oz.) Rolo candies, halved
½ cup coarsely crushed pretzels
½ cup coarsely chopped pecans

1. Preheat oven to 350°. In a large bowl, cream butter and sugars until light and fluffy, 5-7 minutes. Beat in egg and vanilla. In another bowl, whisk flour, cocoa, baking powder, baking soda and salt; gradually beat into creamed mixture. Stir in Rolos, pretzels and pecans.
2. Drop dough by ¼ cupfuls 2 in. apart onto parchment-lined baking sheets. Bake until cookies look crackled, 12-14 minutes.
3. Allow cookies to cool completely on pans. Store between pieces of waxed paper in an airtight container.
1 cookie: 295 cal., 15g fat (7g sat. fat), 38mg chol., 321mg sod., 38g carb. (24g sugars, 2g fiber), 4g pro.

SHORTBREAD LEMON BARS

SHORTBREAD LEMON BARS

I've put together two family cookbooks over the years, and this recipe ranks among my favorites. The special lemon bars have a yummy shortbread crust and refreshing flavor. I'm never afraid to make this dessert for guests because I know it will be a hit with everyone.
—Margaret Peterson, Forest City, IA

Prep: 25 min. • **Bake:** 15 min. + chilling
Makes: 3 dozen

1½ cups all-purpose flour
½ cup confectioners' sugar
1 tsp. grated lemon zest
1 tsp. grated orange zest
¾ cup cold butter, cubed

FILLING
4 large eggs, room temperature
2 cups sugar
⅓ cup lemon juice
¼ cup all-purpose flour
2 tsp. grated lemon zest
2 tsp. grated orange zest
1 tsp. baking powder

TOPPING
2 cups sour cream
⅓ cup sugar
½ tsp. vanilla extract

1. Preheat oven to 350°. In a food processor, combine the flour, confectioners' sugar, and lemon and orange zest. Add butter; cover and process until mixture forms a ball.
2. Pat into a greased 13x9-in. baking pan. Bake until set and the edges are lightly browned, 12-14 minutes.
3. In a large bowl, combine all the filling ingredients. Pour over hot crust. Bake until set and lightly browned, 14-16 minutes. In a small bowl, combine topping ingredients. Spread over filling.
4. Bake until topping is set, 7-9 minutes longer. Cool on a wire rack. Refrigerate overnight. Cut into the bars just before serving. Store in the refrigerator.
1 bar: 172 cal., 9g fat (5g sat. fat), 51mg chol., 70mg sod., 20g carb. (15g sugars, 0 fiber), 2g pro.

BLACK-BOTTOM BANANA BARS

These bars stay very moist, and their rich banana and chocolate taste is even better the second day. My mother-in-law gave me this recipe, and it's a big favorite with both my husband and two sons.
—Renee Wright, Ferryville, WI

- -

Prep: 20 min. • **Bake:** 25 min.
Makes: 3 dozen

- ½ cup butter, softened
- 1 cup sugar
- 1 large egg
- 1 tsp. vanilla extract
- 1½ cups mashed ripe bananas (about 3 medium)
- 1½ cups all-purpose flour
- 1 tsp. baking powder
- 1 tsp. baking soda
- ½ tsp. salt
- ¼ cup baking cocoa

1. In a large bowl, cream butter and sugar until light and fluffy, 5-7 minutes. Beat in egg and vanilla. Stir in the bananas. Combine flour, baking powder, baking soda and salt; add to the creamed mixture and mix well.
2. Divide batter in half. Add cocoa to half; spread into a greased 13x9-in. baking pan. Spoon the remaining batter on top and, if desired, swirl with a knife to marble batter.
3. Bake at 350° until a toothpick inserted in the center comes out clean, about 25 minutes. Cool on a wire rack.
1 bar: 76 cal., 3g fat (2g sat. fat), 12mg chol., 104mg sod., 12g carb. (7g sugars, 1g fiber), 1g pro.

SCOTTISH SHORTBREAD

My mother, who is of Scottish heritage, passed this recipe, as with most of my favorite recipes, on to me. When I entered Scottish Shortbread at our local fair, it won a red ribbon.
—Rose Mabee, Selkirk, MB

- -

Prep: 15 min.
Bake: 20 min./batch + cooling
Makes: about 4 dozen

- 2 cups butter, softened
- 1 cup packed brown sugar
- 4 to 4½ cups all-purpose flour

1. Preheat oven to 325°. Cream butter and brown sugar until light and fluffy, 5-7 minutes. Add 3¾ cups flour; mix well. Turn dough onto a floured surface; knead for 5 minutes, adding enough remaining flour to form a soft dough.
2. On a sheet of parchment paper, roll dough to a 16x9-in. rectangle. Transfer to a baking sheet, and cut into 3x1-in. strips. Prick each cookie multiple times with a fork. Refrigerate at least 30 minutes or overnight.
3. Separate cookies and place 1 in. apart on ungreased baking sheets. Bake until cookies are lightly browned, 20-25 minutes. Transfer to wire racks to cool completely.
1 cookie: 123 cal., 8g fat (5g sat. fat), 20mg chol., 62mg sod., 12g carb. (5g sugars, 0 fiber), 1g pro.

"Shortbread cookie lovers will really enjoy the buttery-ness of these tender, crumbly cookies. They can also be dipped in chocolate—delicious!"

—MARK NEUFANG, CULINARY ASSISTANT

SCOTTISH SHORTBREAD

CARROT SPICE THUMBPRINT COOKIES

4. For the frosting, beat the butter, cream cheese, confectioners' sugar and extract until blended. To serve, fill each cookie with about 1½ tsp. of frosting; sprinkle with additional confectioners' sugar. Refrigerate leftover filled cookies.

1 cookie: 167 cal., 9g fat (3g sat. fat), 17mg chol., 146mg sod., 21g carb. (14g sugars, 1g fiber), 2g pro.

HONEY-PECAN SQUARES

When I left Texas, a neighbor gave me pecans from his trees. I send these to him, and he's always happy to receive them.
—Lorraine Caland, Shuniah, ON

- -

Prep: 15 min. • **Bake:** 30 min.
Makes: 2 dozen

- 1 cup unsalted butter, softened
- ¾ cup packed dark brown sugar
- ½ tsp. salt
- 3 cups all-purpose flour

FILLING

- ½ cup unsalted butter, cubed
- ½ cup packed dark brown sugar
- ⅓ cup honey
- 2 Tbsp. sugar
- 2 Tbsp. heavy whipping cream
- ¼ tsp. salt
- 2 cups chopped pecans, toasted
- ½ tsp. maple flavoring or vanilla extract

1. Preheat oven to 350°. Line a 13x9-in. baking pan with parchment, letting ends extend up sides of pan. In a large bowl, cream the butter, brown sugar and salt until light and fluffy, 5-7 minutes. Gradually beat in flour. Press onto the bottom of prepared pan. Bake 16-20 minutes or until lightly browned.

2. In a small saucepan, combine the first 6 filling ingredients; bring to a boil. Cook 1 minute. Remove from the heat; stir in pecans and maple flavoring. Pour over the crust.

3. Bake 10-15 minutes or until bubbly. Cool in pan on a wire rack. Lifting with parchment, transfer to a cutting board; cut into bars.

Note: To toast nuts, bake in a shallow pan in a 350° oven for 5-10 minutes or cook in a skillet over low heat until lightly browned, stirring occasionally.

1 bar: 292 cal., 19g fat (8g sat. fat), 32mg chol., 81mg sod., 29g carb. (17g sugars, 1g fiber), 3g pro.

CARROT SPICE THUMBPRINT COOKIES

Carrot cake is a family favorite, and these delicious cookies taste just like it with shredded carrots, dried cranberries, toasted walnuts, cinnamon and cloves. And they're topped with a rich cream cheese frosting. Who could resist? Each cookie is like eating a piece of carrot cake, but with no fork needed!
—Susan Bickta, Kutztown, PA

- -

Prep: 30 min. • **Bake:** 10 min./batch + cooling
Makes: 5 dozen

- 1 cup margarine, softened
- 1 cup sugar
- ½ cup packed brown sugar
- 2 large eggs, room temperature
- 2 tsp. vanilla extract
- 3 cups all-purpose flour
- 1½ tsp. ground cinnamon
- 1 tsp. baking powder
- ¾ tsp. salt
- ½ tsp. baking soda
- ⅛ tsp. ground cloves
- 1½ cups shredded carrots
- ⅔ cup chopped walnuts, toasted
- ½ cup dried cranberries

FROSTING

- ½ cup butter, softened
- 4 oz. cream cheese, softened
- 2 cups confectioners' sugar
- 1 tsp. vanilla extract
  Additional confectioners' sugar

1. Preheat oven to 375°. In a large bowl, cream together margarine and sugars until light and fluffy, 5-7 minutes. Beat in eggs and vanilla. In another bowl, whisk flour, cinnamon, baking powder, salt, baking soda and cloves; gradually beat into creamed mixture. Stir in carrots, walnuts and cranberries.

2. Drop dough by rounded tablespoonfuls 2 in. apart onto parchment-lined baking sheets. Press a deep indentation in center of each with the back of a ½-tsp. measure.

3. Bake until the edges begin to brown, 10-12 minutes. Reshape indentations as needed. Cool on pans 5 minutes. Remove to wire racks to cool completely.

GINGERBREAD AMARETTI COOKIES

These are classic Italian cookies with a new gingerbread twist! Don't overbake—they should be slightly chewy.
—Tina Zaccardi, Eastchester, NY

Prep: 20 min. • **Bake:** 10 min./batch
Makes: 2 dozen

- 1   can (8 oz.) almond paste
- ¾   cup sugar
- 1   Tbsp. baking cocoa
- 1   tsp. ground ginger
- ½   tsp. ground cinnamon
     Dash ground cloves
- 2   large egg whites, room temperature
- 2   Tbsp. molasses
- 1   cup pearl or coarse sugar

1. Preheat oven to 375°. Crumble the almond paste into a food processor; add the sugar, baking cocoa and spices. Pulse until combined. Add egg whites and molasses; process until smooth.
2. Drop by tablespoonfuls into pearl sugar; roll to coat. Place 2 in. apart on parchment-lined baking sheets. Bake until set, 10-12 minutes. Cool 1 minute before removing from pans to wire racks. Store in an airtight container.
1 cookie: 107 cal., 3g fat (0 sat. fat), 0 chol., 6mg sod., 21g carb. (19g sugars, 1g fiber), 1g pro.

LEMON BUTTER COOKIES

These tender cutout cookies have a slight lemon flavor that makes them stand out from the rest. They're very easy to roll out compared to other sugar cookies I've worked with. I know you'll enjoy them as much as we do.
—Judy McCreight, Springfield, IL

Prep: 20 min. + chilling • **Bake:** 10 min./batch
Makes: about 13 dozen

- 1   cup butter, softened
- 2   cups sugar
- 2   large eggs, room temperature, lightly beaten
- ¼   cup whole milk
- 2   tsp. lemon extract
- 4½   cups all-purpose flour
- 2   tsp. baking powder
- ½   tsp. salt
- ¼   tsp. baking soda
     Colored sugar, optional

1. In a large bowl, cream butter and sugar until light and fluffy, 5-7 minutes. Beat in the eggs, milk and extract. Combine dry ingredients; gradually add to creamed mixture and mix well. Cover and chill for 2 hours.
2. Preheat the oven to 350°. Roll out the dough on a lightly floured surface to ⅛-in. thickness. Cut with a 2-in. cookie cutter dipped in flour. Place cutouts 2 in. apart on ungreased baking sheets. Sprinkle with colored sugar if desired.
3. Bake until the edges just begin to brown, 8-9 minutes. Remove to wire racks to cool.
2 cookies: 70 cal., 3g fat (2g sat. fat), 12mg chol., 55mg sod., 11g carb. (5g sugars, 0 fiber), 1g pro.

MIXED NUT BARS

One pan of these bars goes a long way. They get a nice flavor from butterscotch chips.
—Bobbi Brown, Waupaca, WI

Prep: 10 min. • **Bake:** 20 min. + cooling
Makes: 2½ dozen

- 1½   cups all-purpose flour
- ¾   cup packed brown sugar
- ¼   tsp. salt
- ½   cup plus 2 Tbsp. cold butter, divided
- 1   cup butterscotch chips
- ½   cup light corn syrup
- 1   can (11½ oz.) mixed nuts

1. Preheat oven to 350°. In a small bowl, combine flour, brown sugar and salt. Cut in ½ cup butter until mixture resembles coarse crumbs. Press into a greased 13x9-in. baking pan. Bake for 10 minutes.
2. Meanwhile, in a microwave, melt butterscotch chips and remaining butter; stir until smooth. Stir in the corn syrup.
3. Sprinkle nuts over crust; top with butterscotch mixture. Bake until set, about 10 minutes. Cool on a wire rack. Cut into bars.
1 bar: 201 cal., 12g fat (5g sat. fat), 10mg chol., 98mg sod., 22g carb. (15g sugars, 1g fiber), 3g pro.

CRISP SUGAR COOKIES

My grandmother always had sugar cookies in her pantry. We grandchildren would empty that big jar quickly because those cookies were the absolute best!
—Evelyn Poteet, Hancock, MD

- -

Prep: 15 min. + chilling • **Bake:** 10 min./batch
Makes: 8 dozen

- 1 cup butter, softened
- 2 cups sugar
- 2 large eggs, room temperature
- 1 tsp. vanilla extract
- 5 cups all-purpose flour
- 1½ tsp. baking powder
- 1 tsp. baking soda
- ½ tsp. salt
- ¼ cup 2% milk

1. In a large bowl, cream butter and sugar until light and fluffy, 5-7 minutes. Add eggs and vanilla. Combine flour, baking powder, baking soda and salt; add to creamed mixture alternately with milk. Cover; refrigerate 15-30 minutes or until easy to handle.
2. Preheat oven to 350°. On a floured surface, roll out dough to ⅛-in. thickness. Cut into desired shapes using a 2-in. cookie cutter. Place 2 in. apart on greased baking sheets.
3. Bake 10 minutes or until edges are lightly browned. Remove from pans to wire racks to cool completely.
2 cookies: 117 cal., 4g fat (2g sat. fat), 19mg chol., 105mg sod., 18g carb. (8g sugars, 0 fiber), 2g pro.

CRANBERRY BOG BARS

Sweet and chewy, these fun bars combine the flavors of oats, cranberries, brown sugar and pecans. I like to sprinkle the squares with confectioners' sugar before serving.
—Sally Wakefield, Gans, PA

- -

Prep: 25 min. • **Bake:** 25 min.
Makes: 2 dozen

- 1¼ cups butter, softened, divided
- 1½ cups packed brown sugar, divided
- 3½ cups old-fashioned oats, divided
- 1 cup all-purpose flour
- 1 can (14 oz.) whole-berry cranberry sauce
- ½ cup finely chopped pecans

1. In a large bowl, cream 1 cup butter and 1 cup brown sugar until light and fluffy, 5-7 minutes. Combine 2½ cups oats and the flour. Gradually add to creamed mixture until crumbly. Press into a greased 13x9-in. baking pan. Spread with cranberry sauce.
2. In a microwave-safe bowl, melt remaining butter; stir in pecans and remaining brown sugar and oats. Sprinkle over the cranberry sauce. Bake at 375° until lightly browned, 25-30 minutes. Cool on a wire rack. Cut into bars.
1 bar: 239 cal., 12g fat (6g sat. fat), 25mg chol., 88mg sod., 32g carb. (18g sugars, 2g fiber), 2g pro.

CINNAMON PECAN BARS

I'm a special education teacher, and we bake these bars in my life skills class. It is an easy recipe that my special-needs students have fun preparing.
—Jennifer Peters, Adams Center, NY

- -

Prep: 10 min. • **Bake:** 25 min.
Makes: 2 dozen

- 1 pkg. butter pecan cake mix (regular size)
- ½ cup packed dark brown sugar
- 2 large eggs, room temperature
- ½ cup butter, melted
- ½ cup chopped pecans
- ½ cup cinnamon baking chips

1. Preheat oven to 350°. In a large bowl, combine cake mix and brown sugar. Add eggs and melted butter; mix well. Stir in pecans and baking chips. Spread into a greased 13x9-in. baking pan.
2. Bake until golden brown, 25-30 minutes. Cool in pan on a wire rack. Cut into bars.
1 bar: 185 cal., 9g fat (4g sat. fat), 26mg chol., 190mg sod., 25g carb. (17g sugars, 0 fiber), 2g pro.

EGGNOG
PUMPKIN PIE,
PAGE 216

Cakes & Pies

These wow-worthy cakes and cupcakes, as well as from-scratch pies and tarts, will turn any gathering into a celebration!

CREAM-FILLED
PUMPKIN
CUPCAKES

CREAM-FILLED PUMPKIN CUPCAKES

Here's a deliciously different use for pumpkin. Bursting with flavor and plenty of eye-catching appeal, these sweet and spicy filled cupcakes are bound to dazzle your family.
—Ali Johnson, Petersburg, PA

- -

Prep: 35 min. • **Bake:** 20 min. + cooling
Makes: 1½ dozen

- 2 cups sugar
- ¾ cup canola oil
- 1 can (15 oz.) pumpkin
- 4 large eggs, room temperature
- 2 cups all-purpose flour
- 2 tsp. baking soda
- 1 tsp. salt
- 1 tsp. baking powder
- 1 tsp. ground cinnamon

FILLING
- 1 Tbsp. cornstarch
- 1 cup whole milk
- ½ cup shortening
- ¼ cup butter, softened
- 2¾ cups confectioners' sugar
- ½ tsp. vanilla extract, optional
   Whole cloves, optional

1. Preheat oven to 350°. In a large bowl, beat sugar, oil, pumpkin and eggs until well blended. Combine flour, baking soda, salt, baking powder and cinnamon; gradually beat into pumpkin mixture until well blended.
2. Fill paper-lined muffin cups two-thirds full. Bake until a toothpick inserted in center comes out clean, 18-22 minutes. Cool for 10 minutes before removing from pans to wire racks to cool completely.
3. For filling, combine cornstarch and milk in a small saucepan until smooth. Bring to a boil, stirring constantly. Remove from heat; cool to room temperature.
4. In a large bowl, cream shortening, butter and confectioners' sugar until light and fluffy. Beat in vanilla if desired. Gradually add cornstarch mixture, beating until smooth, 3-5 minutes.
5. Using a sharp knife, cut a 1-in. circle 1 in. deep in the top of each cupcake. Carefully remove tops and set aside. Spoon or pipe filling into cupcakes. Replace tops. If desired, add a clove pumpkin stem to the tops.
1 cupcake: 397 cal., 19g fat (4g sat. fat), 49mg chol., 342mg sod., 54g carb. (42g sugars, 1g fiber), 4g pro.

MAPLE & CREAM APPLE PIE

The cream in this pie makes it so rich and delicious. If you're looking for something a little out of the ordinary, this is it.
—Glenda Ardoin, Hessmer, LA

- -

Prep: 40 min. • **Bake:** 40 min. + cooling
Makes: 8 servings

- 1 cup plus ¼ tsp. sugar, divided
- 3 Tbsp. cornstarch
- ½ tsp. salt
- 6 cups thinly sliced peeled Granny Smith apples
- 6 Tbsp. maple syrup
- ¼ cup heavy whipping cream
   Dough for double-crust pie
- ½ tsp. 2% milk

1. Preheat oven to 400°. For filling, in a large bowl, combine 1 cup sugar, cornstarch and salt. Add the apples; toss gently to coat. Combine maple syrup and cream; pour over apple mixture.
2. On a lightly floured surface, roll half the dough to a ⅛-in.-thick circle; transfer to a 9-in. pie plate. Trim crust to ½ in. beyond rim of plate; flute edge. Add filling. Roll remaining dough to ⅛ in. thick. Cut out crust with a 1½-in. leaf-shaped cookie cutter. With a sharp knife, lightly score cutouts to resemble veins on leaves. Place cutouts over filling. Brush cutouts with milk; sprinkle with remaining ¼ tsp sugar.
3. Cover edge loosely with foil. Bake for 20 minutes. Uncover; bake 20-25 minutes until the crust is golden brown and filling is bubbly. Cool completely on a wire rack. Refrigerate leftovers.
1 piece: 557 cal., 26g fat (16g sat. fat), 69mg chol., 462mg sod., 79g carb. (44g sugars, 2g fiber), 5g pro.
Dough for double-crust pie: Combine 2½ cups all-purpose flour and ½ tsp. salt; cut in 1 cup of cold butter until crumbly. Gradually add ⅓-⅔ cup ice water, tossing with a fork until dough holds together when pressed. Divide dough in half. Shape each into a disk; wrap and refrigerate 1 hour.

MAPLE & CREAM
APPLE PIE

MOIST LAZY DAISY CAKE

We always called this Mama's never-fail recipe. I guess the same holds true for me since I've won contests with this cake. The tasty dessert always brings back fond memories of Mama.
—Carrie Bartlett, Gallatin, TN

- -

Prep: 20 min. • **Bake:** 25 min.
Makes: 9 servings

- 2 large eggs, room temperature
- 1 cup sugar
- 1 tsp. vanilla extract
- 1 cup cake flour
- 1 tsp. baking powder
- ¼ tsp. salt
- ½ cup 2% milk
- 2 Tbsp. butter

FROSTING

- ¾ cup packed brown sugar
- ½ cup butter, melted
- 2 Tbsp. half-and-half cream
- 1 cup sweetened shredded coconut

1. Preheat oven to 350°. In a large bowl, beat eggs, sugar and vanilla on high until thick and lemon-colored, about 4 minutes. Combine flour, baking powder and salt; add to egg mixture. Beat on low just until combined. Heat milk and butter in a small saucepan until butter melts. Add to batter; beat thoroughly (the batter will be thin). Pour batter into a greased 9-in. square baking pan.
2. Bake 20-25 minutes or until a toothpick inserted in center comes out clean. Cool slightly. For frosting, blend all ingredients well; spread over warm cake. Broil about 4 in. from the heat for 3-4 minutes or until the top is lightly browned.
1 piece: 405 cal., 18g fat (12g sat. fat), 78mg chol., 277mg sod., 58g carb. (46g sugars, 1g fiber), 4g pro.

ITALIAN CREAM CHEESE CAKE

ITALIAN CREAM CHEESE CAKE

Buttermilk makes every bite of this awesome cake moist and flavorful. I rely on this recipe year-round.
—Joyce Lutz, Centerview, MO

- -

Prep: 40 min. • **Bake:** 20 min. + cooling
Makes: 16 servings

- ½ cup butter, softened
- ½ cup shortening
- 2 cups sugar
- 5 large eggs, separated, room temperature
- 1 tsp. vanilla extract
- 2 cups all-purpose flour
- 1 tsp. baking soda
- 1 cup buttermilk
- 1½ cups sweetened shredded coconut
- 1 cup chopped pecans

CREAM CHEESE FROSTING

- 11 oz. cream cheese, softened
- ¾ cup butter, softened
- 6 cups confectioners' sugar
- 1½ tsp. vanilla extract
- ¾ cup chopped pecans

1. Preheat oven to 350°. Grease and flour three 9-in. round baking pans. In a large bowl, cream butter, shortening and sugar until light and fluffy, 5-7 minutes. Beat in egg yolks and vanilla. Combine flour and baking soda; add to creamed mixture alternately with buttermilk. Beat until just combined. Stir in coconut and pecans.
2. In another bowl, beat egg whites with clean beaters until stiff but not dry. Fold a fourth of the egg whites into batter, then fold in remaining whites. Pour into prepared pans.
3. Bake until a toothpick inserted in the center comes out clean, 20-25 minutes. Cool 10 minutes before removing from pans to wire racks to cool completely.
4. For frosting, beat the cream cheese and butter until smooth. Beat in confectioners' sugar and vanilla until fluffy. Stir in pecans. Spread frosting between layers and over top and sides of cake. Refrigerate.
1 piece: 736 cal., 41g fat (19g sat. fat), 117mg chol., 330mg sod., 90g carb. (75g sugars, 2g fiber), 7g pro

TEST KITCHEN TIP

Unless otherwise specified, our recipes are tested with lightly salted butter. Unsalted, or sweet, butter is used to achieve a buttery flavor, such as in shortbread cookies or buttercream frosting. In these recipes, added salt would detract from the buttery taste desired.

GANACHE-TOPPED PUMPKIN TART

I love the flavor combination of spiced pumpkin and chocolate, which inspired me to create this tart. Sometimes I like to sprinkle chopped crystallized ginger over the chocolate ganache for extra flavor and texture.
—Bernice Janowski, Stevens Point, WI

Prep: 20 min. + chilling
Bake: 55 min. + cooling • **Makes:** 8 servings

- 1 cup all-purpose flour
- ¾ cup sugar
- ½ cup baking cocoa
- 1 tsp. pumpkin pie spice
- ½ tsp. salt
- ½ cup butter, melted

FILLING

- 1 can (15 oz.) pumpkin
- 3 large eggs
- ¾ cup packed dark brown sugar
- 2 tsp. grated orange zest
- 2 tsp. pumpkin pie spice
- ¼ tsp. salt
- ½ cup heavy whipping cream

GANACHE

- ¾ cup semisweet chocolate chips
- ½ cup heavy whipping cream
  Crystallized ginger, chopped, optional

1. Preheat the oven to 425°. In a large bowl, combine flour, sugar, baking cocoa, pie spice and salt. Stir in butter until crumbly. Press onto bottom and up side of a 9-in. tart pan with removable bottom; place on a baking sheet. Bake 10 minutes; cool on a wire rack.
2. Meanwhile, in another large bowl, whisk pumpkin, eggs, brown sugar, orange zest, pie spice and salt. Slowly whisk in cream. Pour into crust. Bake 15 minutes. Reduce oven temperature to 350°. Bake until filling is set, 40-45 minutes. Cool on a wire rack.
3. For ganache, place chocolate chips in a small bowl. In a small saucepan, bring cream just to a boil. Pour over chocolate; let stand 10 minutes. Stir with a whisk until smooth. Spread over tart; chill until set. If desired, garnish with crystallized ginger.
1 piece: 551 cal., 30g fat (18g sat. fat), 134mg chol., 358mg sod., 70g carb. (50g sugars, 4g fiber), 7g pro.

GANACHE-TOPPED PUMPKIN TART

BANANAS & CREAM POUND CAKE

This banana pound cake got me a date with my future husband. At a church event, he loved it so much, he asked for another piece. The rest is history!
—Courtney Meckley, Cartersville, GA

Prep: 20 min. • **Bake:** 40 min. + chilling
Makes: 15 servings

- ½ cup butter, softened
- 1½ cups sugar
- 3 large eggs, room temperature
- 1 tsp. vanilla extract
- 1½ cups all-purpose flour
- ¼ tsp. salt
- ⅛ tsp. baking soda
- ½ cup buttermilk

LAYERS

- 2 cups 2% milk
- 1 pkg. (3.4 oz.) instant French vanilla pudding mix
- 1 pkg. (8 oz.) cream cheese, softened
- ½ cup sweetened condensed milk
- 1 pkg. (12 oz.) frozen whipped topping, thawed, divided
- 5 medium ripe bananas

1. Preheat oven to 325°. In a large bowl, cream butter and sugar until light and fluffy, 5-7 minutes. Add eggs, 1 at a time, beating well after each addition. Beat in vanilla. In another bowl, mix the flour, salt and baking soda; add to the creamed mixture alternately with buttermilk, beating well after each addition.
2. Transfer to a greased and floured 9x5-in. loaf pan. Bake until a toothpick inserted in center comes out clean, 40-45 minutes. Cool in pan 10 minutes before removing to a wire rack to cool completely.
3. In a small bowl, whisk milk and pudding mix for 2 minutes. Let stand for 2 minutes. In a large bowl, beat the cream cheese and condensed milk until smooth; fold in the pudding. Fold in 3½ cups whipped topping.
4. Cut the cake into 8 pieces; arrange on the bottom of an ungreased 13x9-in. dish, trimming to fit as necessary. Slice bananas; arrange over cake. Spread pudding mixture over top. Refrigerate, covered, for 3 hours. Serve with remaining whipped topping and, if desired, additional bananas.
1 piece: 419 cal., 18g fat (12g sat. fat), 75mg chol., 295mg sod., 57g carb. (43g sugars, 1g fiber), 6g pro.

APPLE SPICE CAKE WITH BROWN SUGAR FROSTING

I am a healthy eater most of the time, but this cake is worth the splurge! Every year, I treasure the opportunity to make my own birthday cake, and I choose this. You can add a cup of raisins to the batter before baking if you'd like.
—Jennifer Owen, Louisville, KY

- -

Prep: 30 min. • **Bake:** 35 min. + cooling
Makes: 16 servings

- 4 medium Honeycrisp apples, peeled and cut into 1-in. pieces (about 1½ lbs.)
- 2 cups sugar
- ½ cup canola oil
- 2 large eggs, room temperature
- 2 tsp. vanilla extract
- 2 cups all-purpose flour
- 1 Tbsp. pumpkin pie spice
- 2 tsp. baking powder
- 1 tsp. salt
- ½ cup buttermilk
- 1½ cups chopped walnuts, toasted

FROSTING
- 1 pkg. (8 oz.) cream cheese, softened
- ½ cup butter, softened
- 1 cup confectioners' sugar
- 1 cup packed brown sugar
- 1½ tsp. vanilla extract
- 1 tsp. pumpkin pie spice
- 1½ cups chopped walnuts, toasted

1. Preheat oven to 350°. Line bottoms of 2 greased 9-in. round baking pans with parchment; grease parchment.
2. Place apples in a food processor; pulse until finely chopped. In a large bowl, beat sugar, oil, eggs and vanilla until well blended. In another bowl, whisk flour, pie spice, baking powder and salt; gradually beat into sugar mixture alternately with buttermilk. Stir in apples and walnuts.
3. Transfer to prepared pans. Bake until a toothpick inserted in the center comes out clean, 35-40 minutes. Cool in pans 10 minutes before removing to wire racks; remove paper. Cool completely.
4. In a large bowl, beat cream cheese, butter, sugars, vanilla and pie spice until smooth. Spread frosting between layers and over top and sides of cake. Gently press walnuts into frosting on top of cake. Refrigerate leftovers.
1 piece: 574 cal., 33g fat (9g sat. fat), 53mg chol., 326mg sod., 67g carb. (51g sugars, 2g fiber), 7g pro.

HONEY PIE

A hint of honey flavors this old-fashioned custard pie that comes together quickly with simple ingredients. Don't be afraid of blind-baking the crust, it's easy to do.
—*Taste of Home* Test Kitchen

- -

Prep: 20 min. + chilling
Bake: 40 min. + chilling
Makes: 8 servings

-    Dough for single-crust pie
- 4 large eggs
- 2½ cups whole milk
- ½ cup packed brown sugar
- ½ cup honey
- 1 tsp. ground nutmeg
- 1 tsp. vanilla extract
- 1 tsp. almond extract
- ½ tsp. salt
-    Optional: Whipped cream and flaky sea salt

1. On a lightly floured surface, roll the dough to a ⅛-in.-thick circle; transfer to a 9-in. pie plate. Trim to ½ in. beyond rim of plate; flute the edge. Refrigerate 30 minutes. Preheat oven to 400°.
2. Line the unpricked crust with a double thickness of foil. Fill with pie weights, dried beans or uncooked rice. Bake on a lower oven rack until edges are golden brown, 15-20 minutes. Remove foil and weights; bake until the bottom is golden brown, 3-6 minutes longer. Cool on a wire rack.
3. In a large bowl, whisk eggs. Whisk in next 7 ingredients until blended. Pour into crust. Cover edge with foil. Bake at 400° until a knife inserted in the center comes out clean, 40-50 minutes. Cool on a wire rack for 1 hour. Refrigerate for at least 3 hours before serving. Top each serving with optional toppings as desired. Refrigerate leftovers.
1 piece: 374 cal., 17g fat (10g sat. fat), 131mg chol., 375mg sod., 50g carb. (35g sugars, 1g fiber), 8g pro.
Dough for single-crust pie: Combine 1¼ cups all-purpose flour and ¼ tsp. salt; cut in ½ cup cold butter until crumbly. Gradually add 3-5 Tbsp. ice water, tossing with a fork until dough holds together when pressed. Wrap and refrigerate 1 hour.

APPLE SPICE CAKE WITH BROWN SUGAR FROSTING

CARROT CUPCAKES

To try to get my family to eat more vegetables, I often hide nutritional foods inside sweet treats. Now we can have our cake and our vegetables, too!
—Doreen Kelly, Rosyln, PA

Prep: 15 min. • **Bake:** 20 min.
Makes: 2 dozen

- 4 large eggs, room temperature
- 2 cups sugar
- 1 cup canola oil
- 2 cups all-purpose flour
- 2 tsp. ground cinnamon
- 1 tsp. baking soda
- 1 tsp. baking powder
- 1 tsp. ground allspice
- ½ tsp. salt
- 3 cups grated carrots

CHUNKY FROSTING
- 1 pkg. (8 oz.) cream cheese, softened
- ¼ cup butter, softened
- 2 cups confectioners' sugar
- ½ cup sweetened shredded coconut
- ½ cup chopped pecans
- ½ cup chopped raisins

1. Preheat oven to 325°. In a large bowl, beat eggs, sugar and oil. Combine the flour, cinnamon, baking soda, baking powder, allspice and salt; gradually add to egg mixture. Stir in carrots.

2. Fill greased or paper-lined muffin cups two-thirds full. Bake until a toothpick inserted in the center comes out clean, 20-25 minutes. Cool for 5 minutes before removing from pans to wire racks.

3. For frosting, in a large bowl, beat cream cheese and butter until fluffy. Gradually beat in confectioners' sugar until smooth. Stir in the coconut, pecans and raisins. Frost cupcakes. Store in the refrigerator.

1 serving: 326 cal., 18g fat (5g sat. fat), 51mg chol., 187mg sod., 40g carb. (30g sugars, 1g fiber), 3g pro.

TEST KITCHEN TIP

To shred carrots like Grandma, break out the classic box grater! First peel the carrots, then shred away on the grater. The side with the largest holes is the easiest to use and makes perfect-sized shreds for these cupcakes.

CARROT CUPCAKES

MISSISSIPPI
MUD CAKE

MISSISSIPPI MUD CAKE

This cake features a fudgy brownie-like base topped with marshmallow creme and a nutty frosting. Serve big slices with glasses of cold milk or steaming mugs of coffee.
—Tammi Simpson, Greensburg, KY

Prep: 20 min. • **Bake:** 35 min. + cooling
Makes: 20 servings

- 1 cup butter, softened
- 2 cups sugar
- 4 large eggs, room temperature
- 1½ cups self-rising flour
- ½ cup baking cocoa
- 1 cup chopped pecans
- 1 jar (7 oz.) marshmallow creme

FROSTING
- ½ cup butter, softened
- 3¾ cups confectioners' sugar
- 3 Tbsp. baking cocoa
- 1 Tbsp. vanilla extract
- 4 to 5 Tbsp. 2% milk
- 1 cup chopped pecans

1. In a large bowl, cream the butter and sugar until light and fluffy, 5-7 minutes. Add eggs, 1 at a time, beating well after each addition. Combine flour and cocoa; gradually add to creamed mixture until blended. Fold in the pecans.
2. Transfer to a greased 13x9-in. baking pan. Bake at 350° for 35-40 minutes or until a toothpick inserted in center comes out clean. Cool for 3 minutes (cake will fall in the center). Spoon the marshmallow creme over cake; carefully spread to cover top. Cool completely.
3. For frosting, in a small bowl, cream butter and confectioners' sugar until light and fluffy. Beat in the cocoa, vanilla and enough milk to achieve frosting consistency. Fold in the pecans. Spread over the marshmallow creme layer. Store in the refrigerator.
Note: As a substitute for 1½ cups self-rising flour, place 2¼ tsp. baking powder and ¾ tsp. salt in a measuring cup. Add all-purpose flour to measure 1 cup. Combine with an additional ½ cup all-purpose flour.
1 piece: 457 cal., 24g fat (10g sat. fat), 80mg chol., 270mg sod., 61g carb. (48g sugars, 2g fiber), 4g pro.

APPLE PIE CUPCAKES WITH CINNAMON BUTTERCREAM

APPLE PIE CUPCAKES WITH CINNAMON BUTTERCREAM

These cupcakes are always a hit! They are so easy to make, and the flavor just screams fall—of course, they're just as delicious any other time of year, too.
—Jennifer Stowell, Deep River, IA

Prep: 20 min. • **Bake:** 20 min. + cooling
Makes: 2 dozen

- 1 pkg. yellow cake mix (regular size)
- 2 Tbsp. butter
- 4 medium tart apples, peeled and finely chopped (about 4 cups)
- ¾ cup packed brown sugar
- 1 Tbsp. cornstarch
- 1 Tbsp. water

FROSTING
- 1 cup butter, softened
- 3 cups confectioners' sugar
- 2 Tbsp. heavy whipping cream
- 1 tsp. vanilla extract
- 1½ tsp. ground cinnamon
  Thinly sliced apples, optional

1. Prepare and bake cake mix according to package directions for cupcakes.
2. In a large skillet, heat butter over medium heat. Add apples and brown sugar; cook and stir until apples are tender, 10-12 minutes. In a small bowl, mix cornstarch and water until smooth; stir into pan. Bring to a boil; cook and stir until thickened, 1-2 minutes. Remove from heat; cool completely.
3. Using a paring knife, cut a 1-in.-wide cone-shaped piece from the top of each cupcake; discard removed portion. Fill cavity with apple mixture.
4. In a bowl, combine the 5 frosting ingredients; beat until smooth. Frost the cupcakes. If desired, top with apple slices to serve.
1 cupcake: 300 cal., 15g fat (7g sat. fat), 48mg chol., 221mg sod., 41g carb. (32g sugars, 1g fiber), 1g pro.

DID YOU KNOW?
Dark brown sugar contains more molasses than light or golden brown sugar. The types are generally interchangeable in recipes. But if you prefer a bolder flavor, choose dark brown sugar.

PINEAPPLE UPSIDE-DOWN MUFFIN CAKES

A friend submitted this recipe to a cookbook our school district was compiling. The first time I made the cakes, my whole family declared the recipe a winner. Delicious and healthy to boot, they remain a favorite to this day.
—Joan Hallford, North Richland Hills, TX

Prep: 25 min. • **Bake:** 15 min.
Makes: 1 dozen

- ⅓ cup packed brown sugar or 3 Tbsp. brown sugar substitute blend
- 2 Tbsp. butter, melted
- 3 canned pineapple slices

CAKES

- ⅓ cup butter, softened
- ½ cup sugar
- 1 large egg, room temperature
- ½ tsp. vanilla extract
- 1 cup all-purpose flour
- 1 tsp. baking powder
- ¼ tsp. baking soda
- ¼ tsp. salt
- ½ cup fat-free lemon or vanilla Greek yogurt
- ¼ cup fat-free milk

1. Preheat oven to 350°. Coat 12 muffin cups with cooking spray. Mix brown sugar and melted butter; divide among prepared cups. Quarter each pineapple slice; place 1 piece in each cup.

2. For cakes, cream butter and sugar until light and fluffy, 5-7 minutes; beat in egg and vanilla. In another bowl, whisk together flour, baking powder, baking soda and salt; add to creamed mixture alternately with yogurt and milk, beating well after each addition.

3. Fill prepared cups two-thirds full. Bake until a toothpick inserted in the center comes out clean, 12-15 minutes. Cool in pan 2 minutes; invert onto a serving plate. Serve warm or at room temperature.

1 muffin cake: 177 cal., 8g fat (5g sat. fat), 34mg chol., 178mg sod., 25g carb. (17g sugars, 0 fiber), 3g pro. **Diabetic exchanges:** 1½ starch, 1½ fat.

PUMPKIN TORTE

This beautiful layered cake has a creamy pumpkin-spice filling. It is easy and always turns out so well. The nuts and caramel topping add a nice finishing touch.
—Trixie Fisher, Piqua, OH

Prep: 30 min.
Bake: 25 min. + cooling
Makes: 12 servings

- 1 pkg. yellow cake mix (regular size)
- 1 can (15 oz.) pumpkin, divided
- 4 large eggs, room temperature
- ½ cup 2% milk
- ⅓ cup canola oil
- 1½ tsp. pumpkin pie spice, divided
- 1 pkg. (8 oz.) cream cheese, softened
- 1 cup confectioners' sugar
- 1 carton (16 oz.) frozen whipped topping, thawed
- ¼ cup caramel ice cream topping Pecan halves, toasted

1. Preheat oven to 350°. Line the bottoms of 2 greased 9-in. round baking pans with parchment; grease paper.

2. Combine cake mix, 1 cup pumpkin, eggs, milk, oil and 1 tsp. pie spice; beat on low speed for 30 seconds. Beat on medium 2 minutes. Transfer to prepared pans.

3. Bake until a toothpick inserted in center comes out clean, 25-30 minutes. Cool for 10 minutes before removing from pans to wire racks; cool completely.

4. Beat cream cheese until light and fluffy. Beat in confectioners' sugar and remaining pumpkin and pie spice until smooth. Fold in whipped topping.

5. Using a long serrated knife, cut each cake horizontally in half. Place 1 cake layer on a serving plate; spread with a fourth of the filling. Repeat 3 times. Drizzle with caramel topping; sprinkle with the pecans. Store in the refrigerator.

1 piece: 476 cal., 24g fat (12g sat. fat), 82mg chol., 367mg sod., 58g carb. (41g sugars, 1g fiber), 6g pro.

PUMPKIN TORTE

CHOCOLATE SILK PIE

SPICED PLUM PIE

If you're craving comfort food, give this pie a try. Served warm and a la mode, it simply can't be beat.
—Lucille Mead, Ilion, NY

Prep: 20 min. • **Bake:** 45 min. + cooling
Makes: 8 servings

Dough for double-crust pie
4½ **cups sliced fresh plums**
⅔ **cup sugar**
¼ **cup all-purpose flour**
1 **tsp. ground cinnamon**
¼ **tsp. salt**
¼ **tsp. ground nutmeg**
1 **large egg, room temperature, lightly beaten**
½ **cup orange juice**
1 **tsp. grated orange zest**
2 **Tbsp. butter**
 Vanilla ice cream, optional

1. Preheat oven to 400°. On a lightly floured surface, roll half the dough to ⅛-in.-thick circle; transfer to a 9-in. pie plate or cast-iron skillet. Trim even with rim. Arrange plums in crust. In a small bowl, combine sugar, flour, cinnamon, salt and nutmeg. Stir in the egg, orange juice and zest. Pour over plums; dot with butter.

2. Roll out remaining dough to a ⅛-in.-thick circle. Place over filling. Trim, seal and flute edge. Cut slits in top.

3. Bake until the crust is golden brown and filling is bubbly (cover the edge with foil during the last 15 minutes if needed to prevent overbrowning), 45-50 minutes. Remove foil. Cool on a wire rack 10 minutes before cutting. If desired, serve warm with ice cream.

1 piece: 412 cal., 18g fat (8g sat. fat), 44mg chol., 303mg sod., 60g carb. (30g sugars, 2g fiber), 4g pro.

Dough for double-crust pie: Combine 2½ cups all-purpose flour and ½ tsp. salt; cut in 1 cup cold butter until crumbly. Gradually add ⅓-⅔ cup ice water, tossing with a fork until the dough holds together when pressed. Divide dough in half. Shape each into a disk; wrap and refrigerate 1 hour.

CHOCOLATE SILK PIE

This creamy, quick chocolate pie not only melts in your mouth, it also melts any and all resistance to dessert!
—Mary Relyea, Canastota, NY

Prep: 40 min. + chilling
Cook: 10 min. + cooling
Makes: 8 servings

 Dough for single-crust pie
1 **jar (7 oz.) marshmallow creme**
1 **cup semisweet chocolate chips**
¼ **cup butter, cubed**
2 **oz. unsweetened chocolate**
2 **Tbsp. strong brewed coffee**
1 **cup heavy whipping cream, whipped**
TOPPING
1 **cup heavy whipping cream**
2 **Tbsp. confectioners' sugar**
 Chocolate curls, optional

1. On a lightly floured surface, roll dough to ⅛-in.-thick circle; transfer to a 9-in. pie plate. Trim to ½ in. beyond rim of plate; flute edge. Refrigerate 30 minutes. Preheat oven to 425°.

2. Line the crust with a double thickness of foil. Fill with pie weights, dried beans or uncooked rice. Bake on a lower oven rack until edges are golden brown, 20-25 minutes. Remove foil and weights; bake until bottom is golden brown, 3-6 minutes longer. Cool on a wire rack.

3. Meanwhile, in a heavy saucepan, combine the marshmallow creme, chocolate chips, butter, unsweetened chocolate and coffee; cook and stir over low heat until chocolate is melted and mixture is smooth. Cool. Fold in whipped cream; pour into crust.

4. For topping, in a large bowl, beat cream until it begins to thicken. Add confectioners' sugar; beat until stiff peaks form. Spread over the filling. Refrigerate at least 3 hours before serving. Garnish with chocolate curls if desired.

1 piece: 666 cal., 49g fat (31g sat. fat), 113mg chol., 240mg sod., 49g carb. (31g sugars, 3g fiber), 6g pro.

Dough for single-crust pie: Combine 1¼ cups all-purpose flour and ¼ tsp. salt; cut in ½ cup cold butter until crumbly. Gradually add 3-5 Tbsp. ice water, tossing with a fork until the dough holds together when pressed. Shape into a disk; wrap and refrigerate 1 hour.

"French silk pie is my all-time favorite dessert! I love this recipe because it's so easy. Sometimes I'll add a drop of mint extract to the filling and whipped cream, then crumble chopped Andes candies on top."

—AMY GLANDER, EDITOR

PERSONAL PEAR POTPIES

Talk about cutie pies! These mini treats baked in ramekins are yummy and easy to prepare using frozen puff pastry. Top each warm dessert with a scoop of vanilla ice cream.

—Bee Engelhart, Bloomfield Township, MI

- -

Prep: 30 min. • **Bake:** 25 min.
Makes: 4 servings

2	Tbsp. butter, divided
2	Tbsp. sugar
1	Tbsp. cornflake crumbs
1	Tbsp. brown sugar
¼	tsp. ground ginger
2	cups finely chopped peeled Anjou pears
2	cups finely chopped peeled Bartlett pears
1	Tbsp. orange juice
½	sheet frozen puff pastry, thawed
1	large egg, lightly beaten Vanilla ice cream

1. Preheat oven to 400°. Grease bottoms and sides of four 8-oz. ramekins with 1 Tbsp. butter (do not butter rims). Place on a baking sheet.
2. In a small bowl, mix sugar, cornflake crumbs, brown sugar and ginger. In a large bowl, toss pears with orange juice. Add the crumb mixture and toss to combine. Divide mixture among the ramekins; dot with the remaining butter.
3. Unfold the pastry; cut into ½-in. strips. Arrange over ramekins in a lattice pattern, trimming to fit. Gently press ends onto ramekin rims. Brush lattices with egg.
4. Bake until filling is bubbly and pastry is golden brown, 25-30 minutes. Serve warm with ice cream.
1 potpie: 343 cal., 15g fat (6g sat. fat), 62mg chol., 177mg sod., 50g carb. (24g sugars, 7g fiber), 5g pro.

PERSONAL PEAR POTPIES

DUTCH APPLE CAKE

My husband and I came to Canada from Holland more than 40 years ago. This traditional Dutch recipe is a family favorite and has frequently gone along with me to potluck suppers and other get-togethers.
—Elizabeth Peters, Martintown, ON

- -

Prep: 15 min. + standing
Bake: 1½ hours + cooling
Makes: 12 servings

  3 **medium tart apples, peeled and cut into ¼-in. slices (3 cups)**
  3 **Tbsp. plus 1 cup sugar, divided**
  1 **tsp. ground cinnamon**
  ⅔ **cup butter, softened**
  4 **large eggs, room temperature**
  1 **tsp. vanilla extract**
  2 **cups all-purpose flour**
  ⅛ **tsp. salt**

1. In a large bowl, combine the apples, 3 Tbsp. sugar and cinnamon; let stand for 1 hour.
2. In another bowl, cream the butter and remaining sugar until light and fluffy, 5-7 minutes. Add eggs, 1 at a time, beating well after each addition. Add the vanilla. Combine flour and salt; gradually add to creamed mixture and beat until smooth.
3. Transfer to a greased 9x5-in. loaf pan. Push apple slices vertically into batter, placing them close together.
4. Bake at 300° for 1½-1¾ hours or until a toothpick inserted in the center comes out clean. Cool 10 minutes before removing from pan to a wire rack. Serve warm.
1 piece: 282 cal., 12g fat (7g sat. fat), 97mg chol., 120mg sod., 40g carb. (24g sugars, 1g fiber), 4g pro.

LAVA CHOCOLATE CAKES

True decadence at its best, this rich chocolate cake features a warm, chocolate center that oozes out onto the dessert plate. Whether you enjoy it garnished with a dollop of whipped cream or sprinkled with confectioners' sugar, you'll want to lick the plate clean!
—*Taste of Home* Test Kitchen

- -

Takes: 30 min.
Makes: 4 servings

  4 **tsp. sugar**
  ½ **cup butter, cubed**
  4 **oz. semisweet chocolate, chopped**
  1 **cup confectioners' sugar**
  2 **large eggs, room temperature**
  2 **large egg yolks, room temperature**
1½ **tsp. instant coffee granules**
  ¾ **tsp. vanilla extract**
  6 **Tbsp. all-purpose flour**
  ½ **tsp. salt**
     Optional: Whipped cream or additional confectioners' sugar

1. Grease the bottom and sides of four 6-oz. ramekins; sprinkle each with 1 tsp. sugar. Place ramekins on a baking sheet; set aside.
2. In a medium microwave-safe bowl, melt butter and chocolate; stir until smooth. Stir in confectioners' sugar until smooth. Whisk in the eggs, egg yolks, instant coffee and vanilla. Stir in flour and salt; spoon batter into prepared ramekins.
3. Bake at 400° for about 12 minutes or until a thermometer reads 160° and cake sides are set and centers are soft.
4. Remove ramekins to a wire rack to cool for 5 minutes. Carefully run a small knife around cakes to loosen. Invert warm cakes onto serving plates. Lift ramekins off cakes. Serve warm with whipped cream or sprinkle with additional confectioners' sugar if desired.
1 cake: 583 cal., 37g fat (21g sat. fat), 268mg chol., 496mg sod., 60g carb. (47g sugars, 2g fiber), 8g pro.

"I have my ingredients portioned out and ready to whip together as soon as we finish dinner. The bake time is short, so the timing works out perfectly."

—CATHERINE WARD, PREP KITCHEN MANAGER

LAVA CHOCOLATE CAKES

MINIATURE ALMOND TARTS

LINGONBERRY-CARDAMOM CAKE

Our family is Scandinavian, and we love the flavors of almonds, cardamom and lingonberries in desserts. If lingonberry jam is difficult to obtain, you can use pureed cranberry sauce with a little lemon juice to get a similar sweet-tart flavor. Whipped cream is a perfect topping.

—Barbara Kvale, Cologne, MN

Prep: 30 min. • **Bake:** 70 min. + chilling
Makes: 16 servings

- 1 cup sliced almonds, divided
- 1 pkg. white cake mix (regular size)
- 1½ tsp. ground cardamom
- ¾ cup cold stick margarine
- 1¼ cups sour cream
- 2 large eggs, room temperature, divided use
- 2 tsp. almond extract, divided
- 2 pkg. (8 oz. each) cream cheese, softened
  Sugar substitute equivalent to ⅓ cup sugar
- 1¼ cups lingonberry jam
  Whipped cream, optional

1. Preheat oven to 350°. Sprinkle ½ cup almonds onto bottom of a greased 10-in. springform pan. In a large bowl, combine cake mix and cardamom; cut in margarine until crumbly. Reserve 1 cup mixture for topping. To remaining mixture, beat in the sour cream, 1 egg and 1 tsp. almond extract. Spread over almonds.

2. In another large bowl, beat cream cheese, sugar substitute and remaining 1 tsp. almond extract until smooth. Gently beat in the remaining egg. Alternately drop the cream cheese mixture and jam over cake mix. Sprinkle with the reserved topping. Bake for 40 minutes.

3. Sprinkle with remaining ½ cup almonds. Bake until the edges are golden brown and center is almost set, 30-40 minutes longer. Cool on a wire rack 10 minutes. Loosen sides from pan with a knife. Cool 1 hour longer. Refrigerate until chilled, at least 4 hours, covering when completely cooled. Remove rim from pan. Serve with whipped cream, if desired. Refrigerate leftovers.

1 piece: 404 cal., 24g fat (10g sat. fat), 56mg chol., 398mg sod., 44g carb. (29g sugars, 1g fiber), 6g pro.

MINIATURE ALMOND TARTS

My family requests these adorable little tarts each Christmas. I enjoy making them since the almond paste in the filling reflects our Dutch heritage, plus they're popular at special gatherings.

—Karen Van Den Berge, Holland, MI

Prep: 35 min. + chilling
Bake: 25 min. + cooling
Makes: 4 dozen

- 1 cup butter, softened
- 6 oz. cream cheese, softened
- 2 cups all-purpose flour

FILLING
- 6 oz. almond paste, crumbled
- 2 large eggs, lightly beaten
- ½ cup sugar

FROSTING
- 1½ cups confectioners' sugar
- 3 Tbsp. butter, softened
- 4 to 5 tsp. 2% milk
- 48 maraschino cherry halves

1. In a large bowl, cream butter and cream cheese until smooth. Gradually add flour until well blended. Refrigerate for 1 hour.

2. Shape into 1-in. balls. Place in ungreased miniature muffin cups; press onto bottom and up the sides to form a shell.

3. For filling, in a small bowl, beat almond paste, eggs and sugar until blended. Fill each shell with about 1½ tsp. filling.

4. Bake at 325° for 25-30 minutes or until edges are golden brown. Cool 10 minutes before removing to wire racks to cool completely.

5. For frosting, combine the confectioners' sugar, butter and enough milk to achieve desired consistency. Pipe or spread over tarts. Top each with a cherry half.

1 tart: 124 cal., 7g fat (4g sat. fat), 23mg chol., 51mg sod., 15g carb. (10g sugars, 0 fiber), 1g pro.

LINGONBERRY-
CARDAMOM CAKE

MOM'S CUSTARD PIE

Just a single bite of this traditional custard pie takes me back to the days when Mom would fix this pie for Dad, Grandfather and me. Mom also regularly prepared pies for large gatherings.
—Barbara Hyatt, Folsom, CA

- -

Prep: 25 min. + chilling
Bake: 40 min. + cooling
Makes: 8 servings

     Dough for single-crust pie
  4 **large eggs**
  ½ **cup sugar**
  ¼ **tsp. salt**
  1 **tsp. vanilla extract**
2½ **cups 2% milk**
  ¼ **tsp. ground nutmeg**

1. On a lightly floured surface, roll dough to a ⅛-in.-thick circle; transfer to a 9-in. pie plate. Trim crust to ½ in. beyond rim of plate; flute edge. Refrigerate 30 minutes. Preheat oven to 425°. Line unpricked crust with a double thickness of foil. Fill with pie weights, dried beans or uncooked rice. Bake on a lower oven rack until edge is light golden brown, 15-20 minutes. Remove the foil and weights; bake until bottom is golden brown, 3-6 minutes longer. Cool on a wire rack. Reduce oven setting to 350°.

2. Separate 1 egg; set the white aside in a large bowl and let stand for 15 minutes. In a small bowl, beat the yolk and remaining eggs just until combined. Blend in the sugar, salt and vanilla. Stir in milk. Beat reserved egg white until stiff peaks form; fold into egg mixture.

3. Carefully pour into crust. Cover edge of pie with foil. Bake for 25 minutes. Remove foil; bake until a knife inserted in the center comes out clean, 15-20 minutes longer. Cool on a wire rack. Sprinkle with nutmeg. Store in the refrigerator.

1 piece: 254 cal., 12g fat (5g sat. fat), 122mg chol., 243mg sod., 29g carb. (17g sugars, 0 fiber), 7g pro.

Dough for single-crust pie: Combine 1¼ cups all-purpose flour and ¼ tsp. salt; cut in ½ cup cold butter until crumbly. Gradually add 3-5 Tbsp. ice water, tossing with a fork until dough holds together when pressed. Shape into a disk; wrap and refrigerate 1 hour.

MAPLE CREAM MERINGUE PIE

MAPLE CREAM MERINGUE PIE

This dessert won first place in the pie category at the annual Vermont Maple Festival. It's simple to make and it uses more maple syrup than most other maple cream pies.
—Nicole Hardy, St. Albans, VT

- -

Prep: 35 min. • **Bake:** 15 min. + chilling
Makes: 8 servings

  1 **sheet refrigerated pie crust**
  2 **Tbsp. cornstarch**
  ¼ **cup water**
  1 **cup maple syrup**
  1 **cup heavy whipping cream**
  2 **large egg yolks, lightly beaten**
  3 **Tbsp. butter**
  3 **large egg whites**
  ½ **tsp. vanilla extract**
  ¼ **tsp. cream of tartar**
  6 **Tbsp. sugar**

1. Preheat oven to 350°. On a lightly floured surface, roll crust to fit a 9-in. pie plate. Trim and flute edge. Line unpricked crust with a double thickness of foil. Fill with pie weights. Bake on a lower oven rack until golden brown, 15-20 minutes. Remove the foil and weights; bake until bottom is golden brown, 3-6 minutes longer. Cool on a wire rack.

2. In a small saucepan, combine cornstarch and water until smooth. Stir in syrup and cream. Cook and stir over medium-high heat until thickened and bubbly, 2-3 minutes. Reduce the heat to medium; cook, stirring constantly, 2 minutes longer. Remove from the heat.

3. Stir a small amount of hot filling into egg yolks; return all to pan, stirring constantly. Bring to a gentle boil; cook and stir 2 minutes longer. Remove from the heat. Gently stir in butter. Pour into crust.

4. In a large bowl, beat egg whites, vanilla and cream of tartar on medium speed until soft peaks form. Gradually beat in sugar, 1 Tbsp. at a time, on high until stiff glossy peaks form and sugar is dissolved. Spread evenly over hot filling, sealing edges to crust.

5. Bake until the meringue is golden brown, 12-15 minutes. Cool on a wire rack for 1 hour. Refrigerate at least 3 hours before serving. Store leftovers in the refrigerator.

1 piece: 389 cal., 20g fat (11g sat. fat), 108mg chol., 138mg sod., 48g carb. (34g sugars, 0 fiber), 4g pro.

MINT-FROSTED CHOCOLATE CAKE

I often make a peanut butter version of this cake but wanted to switch things up by introducing a new flavor. I tinkered with the recipe and decided mint was my new go-to ingredient. My son came up with the idea for the frosting. The rest is delicious history! Freezing the layers makes them easier to handle.

—Melanie Cooksey, Monroe, GA

- -

Prep: 25 min. + chilling
Bake: 30 min. + cooling
Makes: 16 servings

- 2 large eggs, room temperature
- 1½ cups water
- 1 cup canola oil
- 1 cup sour cream
- 2 Tbsp. white vinegar
- 1 tsp. vanilla extract
- 2½ cups sugar
- 2 cups all-purpose flour
- ¾ cup baking cocoa
- 2 tsp. baking soda
- 1 tsp. salt

MINT FROSTING

- 1 pkg. (8 oz.) cream cheese, softened
- ½ cup butter, softened
- 5 cups confectioners' sugar
- ¾ tsp. mint extract
- 2 to 3 drops green food coloring
- 24 mint Andes candies, chopped

CHOCOLATE GLAZE

- 8 oz. semisweet chocolate, coarsely chopped
- ½ cup half-and-half cream
- 2 Tbsp. light corn syrup
  Additional mint Andes candies, chopped, optional

1. Preheat oven to 350°. Line the bottoms of 3 greased 8-in. round baking pans with parchment; grease paper.

2. In a large bowl, beat the eggs, water, oil, sour cream, vinegar, and vanilla until well blended. In another bowl, whisk sugar, flour, cocoa, baking soda and salt; gradually beat into egg mixture.

3. Transfer to prepared pans. Bake until a toothpick inserted in the center comes out clean, 30-35 minutes. Cool in pans 10 minutes before removing to wire racks; remove parchment. Cool completely.

4. In a large bowl, beat cream cheese and butter until blended. Gradually beat in confectioners' sugar until smooth. Beat in mint extract and food coloring.

5. Place 1 cake layer on a serving plate; spread with ⅔ cup mint frosting. Sprinkle with half the mints. Repeat layers. Top with remaining cake layer. Frost top and sides of cake with remaining frosting. Refrigerate until set.

6. Place chocolate in a small bowl. In a small saucepan, bring the cream just to a boil. Pour over chocolate; let stand 5 minutes. Stir with a whisk until smooth. Stir in corn syrup. Cool slightly, stirring occasionally. Pour over the cake and quickly spread to edges. If desired, top with additional mints. Refrigerate until serving.

1 piece: 737 cal., 37g fat (15g sat. fat), 67mg chol., 419mg sod., 99g carb. (81g sugars, 2g fiber), 6g pro.

MINT-FROSTED
CHOCOLATE CAKE

ASK SARAH

HOW DO I GET EVEN CAKE LAYERS?

If your cake layers are domed after baking, shave any bumps with a bread knife until the surfaces are even.

LINZER TART

This lovely versatile tart shows up regularly at family gatherings. I can customize it for any holiday occasion by using different-shaped cookie cutouts or different fruit fillings. And even my picky children can't help but eat it up!
—Karen Ehatt, Chester, MD

Prep: 25 min. + freezing
Bake: 20 min. + cooling
Makes: 12 servings

- ½ cup butter, softened
- ¾ cup sugar
- 1 large egg, room temperature
- ½ tsp. grated lemon zest
- ½ cup slivered almonds, toasted
- 1½ cups all-purpose flour
- 1 tsp. ground cinnamon
- ¼ tsp. salt
- 1 jar (18 oz.) raspberry preserves
  Confectioners' sugar, optional

1. In a large bowl, cream butter and sugar until light and fluffy, 5-7 minutes. Add egg and lemon zest; mix well. Place almonds in a blender, cover and process until ground. Combine the almonds, flour, cinnamon and salt; gradually add to creamed mixture until well blended. Remove ⅓ cup dough. Roll between 2 sheets of waxed paper to ⅛-in. thickness. Freeze 8-10 minutes or until firm.
2. Press remaining dough evenly onto the bottom and up the sides of an ungreased 11-in. fluted tart pan with removable bottom. Spread raspberry preserves over crust. Remove the remaining dough from freezer; using small cookie cutters, cut out desired shapes. Place over preserves.
3. Bake at 375° for 20-25 minutes or until crust is golden brown and filling is bubbly. Cool for 10 minutes. Loosen sides of pan. Cool completely on a wire rack. Remove sides of pan. If desired, sprinkle top with confectioners' sugar.

1 piece: 311 cal., 10g fat (5g sat. fat), 38mg chol., 132mg sod., 53g carb. (38g sugars, 1g fiber), 3g pro.

PEANUT BUTTER SHEET CAKE

I received the recipe from a minister's wife, and my family loves it.
—Brenda Jackson, Garden City, KS

Prep: 15 min. • **Bake:** 20 min.
Makes: 24 servings

- 2 cups all-purpose flour
- 2 cups sugar
- 1 tsp. baking soda
- ½ tsp. salt
- 1 cup water
- ¾ cup butter, cubed
- ½ cup chunky peanut butter
- ¼ cup canola oil
- 2 large eggs, room temperature
- ½ cup buttermilk
- 1 tsp. vanilla extract

GLAZE
- ⅔ cup sugar
- ⅓ cup evaporated milk
- 1 Tbsp. butter
- ⅓ cup chunky peanut butter
- ⅓ cup miniature marshmallows
- ½ tsp. vanilla extract

1. Preheat oven to 350°. Grease a 15x10x1-in. baking pan.
2. In a large bowl, whisk flour, sugar, baking soda and salt. In a small saucepan, combine water and butter; bring just to a boil. Stir in peanut butter and oil until blended. Stir into flour mixture. In a small bowl, whisk eggs, buttermilk and vanilla until blended; add to flour mixture, whisking constantly.
3. Transfer to prepared pan. Bake until a toothpick inserted in center comes out clean, 20-25 minutes.
4. Meanwhile, for the glaze, combine sugar, milk and butter in a saucepan. Bring to a boil, stirring constantly; cook and stir 2 minutes. Remove from heat; stir in peanut butter, marshmallows and vanilla until blended. Spoon over warm cake, spreading evenly. Cool on a wire rack.

1 piece: 266 cal., 14g fat (5g sat. fat), 36mg chol., 222mg sod., 33g carb. (23g sugars, 1g fiber), 4g pro.

LINZER TART

TEXAS SHEET CAKE

This chocolaty delight was one of my favorites growing up. The cake is so moist and the icing so sweet that everyone who samples it wants a copy of the recipe.
—Susan Ormond, Jamestown, NC

Prep: 20 min. • **Bake:** 20 min. + cooling
Makes: 15 servings

- 1 cup butter, cubed
- 1 cup water
- ¼ cup baking cocoa
- 2 cups all-purpose flour
- 2 cups sugar
- 1 tsp. baking soda
- ½ tsp. salt
- ½ cup sour cream

ICING
- ½ cup butter, cubed
- ¼ cup plus 2 Tbsp. 2% milk
- 3 Tbsp. baking cocoa
- 3¾ cups confectioners' sugar
- 1 tsp. vanilla extract

1. In a large saucepan, bring the butter, water and cocoa to a boil. Remove from the heat. Combine the flour, sugar, baking soda and salt; add to cocoa mixture. Stir in the sour cream until smooth.

2. Pour into a greased 15x10x1-in. baking pan. Bake at 350° for 20-25 minutes or until a toothpick inserted in the center comes out clean.

3. In a small saucepan, melt butter; add the milk and cocoa. Bring to a boil. Remove from the heat. Whisk in confectioners' sugar and vanilla until smooth. Pour over warm cake. Cool completely on a wire rack.

Note: This recipe does not use eggs.

1 piece: 418 cal., 14g fat (9g sat. fat), 35mg chol., 266mg sod., 72g carb. (57g sugars, 1g fiber), 3g pro.

> "I love the smooth chocolate taste of this cake. It's rich without being over the top. Plus, it is easy to make and takes only about an hour from start to finish."
>
> —STEPHANIE MARCHESE, EXECUTIVE DIRECTOR, VISUAL PRODUCTION

TEXAS SHEET CAKE

EGGNOG PUMPKIN PIE

This pie from my mom is the absolute best pumpkin pie I have ever tasted. Eggnog is the special ingredient in the creamy custard filling.
—Terri Gonzalez, Roswell, NM

- -

Prep: 10 min. • **Bake:** 1 hour + cooling
Makes: 8 servings

    1   sheet refrigerated pie crust
    1   can (15 oz.) pumpkin
 1¼   cups eggnog
  ⅔   cup sugar
    3   large eggs
 1½   tsp. pumpkin pie spice
  ¼   tsp. salt
        Whipped cream, optional

1. Preheat oven to 375°. On a lightly floured surface, roll dough to a ⅛-in.-thick circle; transfer to a 9-in. pie plate. Trim crust to ½ in. beyond rim of plate; flute edge. In a large bowl, combine pumpkin, eggnog, sugar, eggs, pumpkin pie spice and salt. Pour into crust.
2. Bake until a knife inserted in center comes out clean, 60-65 minutes. Cool on a wire rack. Refrigerate until serving. If desired, top with whipped cream.
Note: Recipe was tested with commercially prepared eggnog.
1 piece: 317 cal., 15g fat (9g sat. fat), 123mg chol., 280mg sod., 40g carb. (22g sugars, 2g fiber), 7g pro.

BROWNIE KISS CUPCAKES

It's fun to prepare individual brownie cupcakes with a chocolaty surprise inside. My goddaughter asked me to make them for her birthday to share at school. She requested 32. I later found out she needed only 27 for her class...wonder where the other five went!
—Pamela Lute, Mercersburg, PA

- -

Takes: 30 min. • **Makes:** 9 servings

  ⅓   cup butter, softened
    1   cup sugar
    2   large eggs, room temperature
    1   tsp. vanilla extract
  ¾   cup all-purpose flour
  ½   cup baking cocoa
  ¼   tsp. baking powder
  ¼   tsp. salt
    9   milk chocolate kisses

1. Preheat oven to 350°. In a large bowl, cream butter and sugar until light and fluffy, 5-7 minutes. Beat in the eggs and vanilla. Combine the flour, cocoa, baking powder and salt; gradually add to the creamed mixture and mix well.
2. Fill paper- or foil-lined muffin cups two-thirds full. Place a chocolate kiss, tip end down, in the center of each.
3. Bake until top of brownie springs back when lightly touched, 20-25 minutes.
1 serving: 239 cal., 10g fat (5g sat. fat), 66mg chol., 163mg sod., 36g carb. (24g sugars, 1g fiber), 4g pro.

CREAMY COCONUT PEPPERMINT PIE

Garnished with toasted coconut and more peppermint candy, this creamy dessert welcomes the holidays. Look for premade shortbread crusts in the baking aisle of the grocery store.
—Cheryl Perry, Hertford, NC

- -

Prep: 15 min. + chilling • **Makes:** 8 servings

    1   envelope unflavored gelatin
  ½   cup coconut milk
 2½   cups peppermint ice cream, melted
  ¼   cup crushed peppermint candies, divided
  ¼   tsp. coconut extract
    1   cup flaked coconut, toasted, divided
    1   shortbread crust (9 in.)

1. In a large microwave-safe bowl, sprinkle the gelatin over coconut milk; let stand for 1 minute. Microwave on high 30-40 seconds. Stir until the gelatin is completely dissolved, 1 minute.
2. Stir ice cream, 2 Tbsp. crushed candies and extract into gelatin mixture; fold in ½ cup coconut. Pour into crust. Sprinkle with remaining coconut. Refrigerate at least 2 hours before serving.
3. Just before serving, top with remaining crushed candies.
1 piece: 281 cal., 15g fat (10g sat. fat), 18mg chol., 165mg sod., 33g carb. (22g sugars, 1g fiber), 4g pro.

TART CRANBERRY CAKE

You can't beat this recipe to showcase true fall flavor. The ruby cranberries stay bright and beautiful, and their tartness is irresistible. I've made this cake many times to share.
—Marilyn Paradis, Woodburn, OR

- -

Prep: 15 min. • **Bake:** 45 min.
Makes: 20 servings

- 3 large eggs, room temperature
- 2 cups sugar
- ¾ cup butter, softened
- 1 tsp. almond extract
- 2 cups all-purpose flour
- 2½ cups fresh or frozen cranberries, thawed
- ⅔ cup chopped pecans
  Optional: Whipped cream and cranberries

1. Preheat oven to 350°. In a large bowl, beat eggs and sugar until slightly thickened and lemon-colored, about 5 minutes. Add butter and extract; beat 2 minutes. Gradually stir in flour just until combined. Stir in the cranberries and pecans. Spread in a greased 13x9-in. baking dish.
2. Bake until a toothpick inserted in center comes out clean, 45-50 minutes. If desired, garnish each serving with whipped cream and a cranberry.
1 piece: 227 cal., 10g fat (5g sat. fat), 46mg chol., 66mg sod., 32g carb. (21g sugars, 1g fiber), 3g pro.

APRICOT-ALMOND TARTLETS

These delicate, buttery tarts melt in your mouth. With their jeweled apricot tops, they make a pretty presentation on your holiday cookie tray.
—Julie Dunsworth, Oviedo, FL

- -

Prep: 25 min. • **Bake:** 20 min. + cooling
Makes: 2 dozen

- 1 cup all-purpose flour
- 3 Tbsp. confectioners' sugar
- ⅓ cup cold butter
- 1 large egg yolk
- 1 to 2 Tbsp. water
FILLING
- ½ cup almond paste
- ¼ cup butter, softened
- 1 large egg white
- ¼ tsp. almond extract
- ½ cup apricot preserves

1. In a large bowl, combine the flour and confectioners' sugar; cut in butter until mixture resembles coarse crumbs. Add egg yolk and water; stir until dough forms a ball. Roll into twenty-four 1-in. balls. Press onto bottoms and up sides of greased miniature muffin cups.
2. In a small bowl, beat almond paste and butter until blended; beat in egg white and almond extract. Spoon into tart shells, about 2 tsp. in each.
3. Bake at 350° for 20-25 minutes or until golden brown. Cool for 5 minutes before removing from pans to wire racks. Top with apricot preserves.
1 tartlet: 103 cal., 6g fat (3g sat. fat), 20mg chol., 37mg sod., 12g carb. (5g sugars, 0 fiber), 1g pro.

DREAMY S'MORE PIE

I love desserts and was looking for a way to use hazelnut spread when I came up with this recipe. I wanted something that could be prepped quickly, too. This certainly delivered on both counts.
—Karen Bowlden, Boise, ID

- -

Prep: 10 min. + chilling • **Makes:** 8 servings

- 1 pkg. (8 oz.) cream cheese, softened
- 1¼ cups heavy whipping cream
- 1 jar (13 oz.) Nutella
- 1 graham cracker crust (9 in.)
- 3 cups miniature marshmallows

1. In a large bowl, beat cream cheese and cream until thickened. Add Nutella; beat just until combined. Spoon into crust. Cover and refrigerate for at least 3 hours.
2. Just before serving, top pie with the marshmallows; press gently into filling. If desired, heat marshmallows with a kitchen torch until lightly browned, 30-45 seconds.
1 piece: 621 cal., 42g fat (18g sat. fat), 83mg chol., 247mg sod., 59g carb. (46g sugars, 2g fiber), 7g pro.

> "When you're craving the taste of s'mores, this pie recipe provides an easy fix. It combines all the classic flavors without the fireside hassle."
>
> —SAMMI DIVITO, ASSISTANT EDITOR

SOUTHERN
BANANA PUDDING,
PAGE 227

Desserts

There's always room for dessert! In this chapter, you're sure to find a heavenly sweet treat to make any meal ending extra special.

PUMPKIN CHEESECAKE EMPANADAS

These cute pumpkin empanadas make the perfect treat—and we love that they are baked and not fried!
—*Taste of Home* Test Kitchen

- -

Prep: 25 min. • **Bake:** 15 min.
Makes: 3 dozen

- 1 large egg white
- ½ tsp. vanilla extract
- 1½ tsp. packed brown sugar
- 1½ tsp. aniseed
- ¾ tsp. ground cinnamon
- ¼ tsp. ground nutmeg

EMPANADAS

- 3 oz. cream cheese, softened
- ¼ cup canned pumpkin pie mix
- 1 large egg yolk, room temperature, lightly beaten
- 1 Tbsp. finely chopped pecans, toasted
- 2 sheets refrigerated pie crust

1. Preheat oven to 400°. In a small bowl, whisk egg white and vanilla; set aside. In another small bowl, combine brown sugar, aniseed, cinnamon and nutmeg; set aside.
2. In a bowl, beat cream cheese and pie mix until smooth. Add egg yolk; beat on low speed just until blended. Stir in pecans.
3. On a lightly floured surface, roll each crust to ¼-in. thickness. Cut with a floured 3-in. round biscuit cutter. Place circles 2 in. apart on parchment-lined baking sheets. Place 1 tsp. filling on 1 side of each circle. Brush edges of crust with the egg white mixture; fold circles in half. With a fork, press edges to seal. Brush with egg white mixture and sprinkle with spice mixture. Bake until golden brown, 15-20 minutes.

Freeze option: Cover and freeze unbaked empanadas on parchment-lined baking sheets until firm. Transfer to a freezer container; return to the freezer. To use, bake empanadas as directed.

Note: To toast nuts, bake in a shallow pan in a 350° oven for 5-10 minutes or cook in a skillet over low heat until lightly browned, stirring occasionally.

1 empanada: 69 cal., 4g fat (2g sat. fat), 10mg chol., 56mg sod., 7g carb. (1g sugars, 0 fiber), 1g pro.

MAPLE-APPLE CLAFOUTIS

This fruit pudding could not be easier to make! A traditional comfort food in France, clafoutis is often made with cherries. I use apples and maple syrup to give it a real Midwestern flair.
—Bridget Klusman, Otsego, MI

- -

Prep: 20 min. • **Bake:** 40 min.
Makes: 8 servings

- 4 medium tart apples, thinly sliced
- 2 Tbsp. lemon juice
- 4 large eggs
- 1¼ cups 2% milk
- ½ cup maple syrup
- 1 tsp. vanilla extract
- ½ cup all-purpose flour
- ½ tsp. ground cinnamon
  Dash salt
  Additional maple syrup, optional

1. Preheat oven to 375°. Toss apples with lemon juice; place in a greased 2-qt. baking dish. In a large bowl, whisk eggs, milk, syrup and vanilla until combined. In another bowl, combine flour, cinnamon and salt; add to egg mixture. Pour batter over apples.
2. Bake until puffed and lightly browned, 40-50 minutes. Serve warm, or cool on a wire rack. If desired, serve with additional maple syrup.

1 piece: 177 cal., 3g fat (1g sat. fat), 96mg chol., 75mg sod., 32g carb. (22g sugars, 2g fiber), 5g pro. **Diabetic exchanges:** 1½ starch, ½ fruit, ½ fat.

TEST KITCHEN TIP

When this is pulled right out of the oven, it is a showstopping masterpiece, all puffed up and golden brown. However, as it sits, it will deflate a little bit. So if you're looking to impress folks, serve it hot out of the oven.

PUMPKIN
CHEESECAKE
EMPANADAS

SALTED PEANUT SQUARES

Want to give something a little out of the ordinary to loved ones? This recipe makes nearly 10 dozen chewy, nutty, sweet-and-salty bars.
—Barb Timm, Lakeville, MN

- -

Prep: 20 min. + chilling • **Makes:** 9¾ dozen

3½ cups dry-roasted peanuts, divided
1   pkg. (10 oz.) peanut butter chips
2   Tbsp. butter
1   can (14 oz.) sweetened condensed milk
1   jar (7 oz.) marshmallow creme
36 miniature Snickers candy bars, chopped

1. Sprinkle half the peanuts into a greased 13x9-in. baking pan. In a large microwave-safe bowl, heat the chips and butter at 50% power for 1 minute; stir. Microwave in 20-second intervals until melted; stir until smooth. Stir in sweetened condensed milk; cook, uncovered, on high for 1 minute.
2. Stir in marshmallow creme and chopped candy bars. Spread in the prepared pan. Sprinkle with remaining peanuts. Cover with parchment; press down lightly.
3. Refrigerate until set. Cut into 1-in. squares. Store in an airtight container.
1 piece: 64 cal., 3g fat (1g sat. fat), 2mg chol., 47mg sod., 7g carb. (5g sugars, 0 fiber), 2g pro.

DID YOU KNOW?

Condensed milk is made by removing water from milk and adding lots of sugar. The end result is super thick and sweet. With all this added sugar, condensed milk can last for years in the pantry without going bad.

GINGERBREAD PUMPKIN TRIFLE

GINGERBREAD PUMPKIN TRIFLE

I like to spice up special dinners with this towering dessert featuring two popular fall flavors. A deliciously fun alternative to pumpkin pie, it's always my favorite potluck contribution.
—Deborah Hahn, Belle, MO

- -

Prep: 1 hour + chilling • **Makes:** 16 servings

½   cup shortening
⅓   cup sugar
1   cup molasses
1   large egg, room temperature
2⅓ cups all-purpose flour
1   tsp. baking soda
1   tsp. ground ginger
1   tsp. ground cinnamon
¾   tsp. salt
¾   cup hot water
FILLING/TOPPING
2   cups cold 2% milk
1   pkg. (3.4 oz.) instant vanilla pudding mix
1   can (15 oz.) pumpkin
½   cup packed brown sugar
1   tsp. vanilla extract
½   tsp. ground cinnamon
2   cups heavy whipping cream
⅓   cup sugar
1   tsp. rum extract

1. In a large bowl, cream shortening and sugar until light and fluffy, 5-7 minutes. Beat in molasses and egg. Combine the flour, baking soda, ginger, cinnamon and salt; add to creamed mixture alternately with water, beating well after each addition.
2. Pour into a greased 13x9-in. baking pan. Bake at 350° for 25-30 minutes or until a toothpick inserted in the center comes out clean. Cool on a wire rack. Cut gingerbread into ½-in. to 1-in. cubes.
3. In a large bowl, whisk milk and pudding mix for 2 minutes. Let stand for 2 minutes or until soft-set. Combine pumpkin, brown sugar, vanilla and cinnamon; stir into the pudding. In another bowl, beat cream until it begins to thicken. Add sugar and extract; beat until stiff peaks form.
4. Set aside ¼ cup gingerbread cubes. In a 4-qt. trifle bowl or glass serving bowl, layer a third of the remaining gingerbread cubes; top with a third of the pumpkin mixture and the whipped cream. Repeat the layers twice. Crumble reserved gingerbread; sprinkle over top. Cover and refrigerate for at least 1 hour before serving.
1 cup: 400 cal., 19g fat (9g sat. fat), 57mg chol., 314mg sod., 55g carb. (34g sugars, 2g fiber), 4g pro.

ROASTED GRAPE & SWEET CHEESE PHYLLO GALETTE

Faced with an abundant grape crop, I had to come up with some creative ways to use them. This became one of my quick and easy ways to make an impressive-looking dessert. It's fun to work with phyllo dough, and it bakes up golden and flaky. You can use berries for this, too.
—Kallee Krong-Mccreery, Escondido, CA

- -

Prep: 25 min. • **Bake:** 35 min. + cooling
Makes: 10 servings

- 1 pkg. (8 oz.) cream cheese, softened
- 2 Tbsp. orange marmalade
- 1 tsp. sugar
- 8 sheets phyllo dough (14x9-in. size)
- 4 Tbsp. butter, melted
- 1 cup seedless grapes
- 1 Tbsp. honey
- 2 tsp. coarse sugar

1. Preheat oven to 350°. In a large bowl, beat cream cheese, marmalade and sugar until smooth; set aside.

2. Place 1 sheet of phyllo on a parchment-lined baking sheet; brush with butter. Layer with remaining phyllo sheets, brushing each layer. (Keep remaining phyllo covered with a damp towel to prevent it from drying out.) Spread cream cheese mixture over phyllo to within 2 in. of edges. Arrange grapes over cream cheese.

3. Fold edges of phyllo over filling, leaving center uncovered. Brush folded phyllo with any remaining butter; drizzle with honey and sprinkle with coarse sugar. Bake until phyllo is golden brown, 35-40 minutes. Transfer to a wire rack to cool completely. Refrigerate the leftovers.

1 piece: 177 cal., 13g fat (8g sat. fat), 35mg chol., 148mg sod., 15g carb. (9g sugars, 0 fiber), 2g pro.

> "I have always loved phyllo pastries like this with cream cheese filling. The roasted grapes are perfect pops of sweetness!"
>
> —SARAH FARMER, EXECUTIVE CULINARY DIRECTOR

EASY APPLE DUMPLINGS

Mother often prepared this special treat for us to eat when we came home from school. I remember so vividly, upon opening the door to the house, the magnificent aroma!
—Marjorie Thompson, West Sacramento, CA

- -

Prep: 30 min. • **Bake:** 45 min.
Makes: 6 servings

- 1½ cups sugar, divided
- 1 cup water
- 4 Tbsp. butter, divided
- ½ tsp. ground cinnamon, divided
  Dough for double-crust pie
- 6 small to medium apples, peeled and cored

1. Preheat oven to 375°. For the syrup, place 1 cup sugar, water, 3 Tbsp. butter and ¼ tsp. cinnamon in a saucepan; bring to a boil. Boil 3 minutes; remove from heat.

2. Mix the remaining ½ cup sugar and ¼ tsp. cinnamon. On a lightly floured surface, roll the dough to a 21x14-in. rectangle; cut into 6 squares. Place an apple on each square. Fill center of each with 4 tsp. sugar mixture and ½ tsp. butter. Moisten edges of crust with water; bring up corners over apples, pinching the edges to seal. Place in an ungreased 13x9-in. baking dish.

3. Pour syrup around the apples. Bake until golden brown and apples are tender, about 45 minutes. Serve warm.

1 serving: 773 cal., 39g fat (24g sat. fat), 101mg chol., 475mg sod., 104g carb. (62g sugars, 4g fiber), 6g pro.

Dough for double-crust pie: Combine 2½ cups all-purpose flour and ½ tsp. salt; cut in 1 cup cold butter until crumbly. Gradually add ⅓-⅔ cup ice water, tossing with a fork until dough holds together when pressed. Shape into a 1-in.-thick square; cover and refrigerate 1 hour or overnight.

ROASTED GRAPE & SWEET CHEESE PHYLLO GALETTE

BLUEBERRY ZUCCHINI SQUARES

1. Preheat the oven to 350°. Grease a 15x10x1-in. baking pan.

2. In a small bowl, combine the zucchini, buttermilk, lemon zest and lemon juice; toss to combine. In a large bowl, cream the butter and sugar until light and fluffy, 5-7 minutes. Beat in eggs, 1 at a time. In another bowl, whisk 3¼ cups flour, baking soda and salt; gradually add to creamed mixture alternately with zucchini mixture, mixing well after each addition. Toss the blueberries with remaining flour; fold into batter.

3. Transfer the batter to prepared pan, spreading evenly (pan will be full). Bake 30-35 minutes or until light golden brown and a toothpick inserted in center comes out clean. Cool completely in the pan on a wire rack.

4. In a small bowl, mix glaze ingredients until smooth; spread over top. Let stand until set.

Note: If using frozen blueberries, use without thawing to avoid discoloring the batter.

1 piece: 270 cal., 8g fat (5g sat. fat), 36mg chol., 197mg sod., 47g carb. (33g sugars, 1g fiber), 3g pro.

"My mom grows zucchini, and I always stock up on fresh blueberries at the farmers market, so these squares are the perfect way to put the produce to good use."

—AMY GLANDER, EDITOR

BLUEBERRY ZUCCHINI SQUARES

I saw a bar recipe using apple and lemon zest on a muffin mix. I tried it from scratch with shredded zucchini and fresh blueberries instead. It's a nifty combo.
—Shelly Bevington, Hermiston, OR

- -

Prep: 30 min. • **Bake:** 30 min. + cooling
Makes: 2 dozen

- 2 cups shredded zucchini (do not pack)
- ½ cup buttermilk
- 1 Tbsp. grated lemon zest
- 3 Tbsp. lemon juice
- 1 cup butter, softened
- 2½ cups sugar
- 2 large eggs, room temperature
- 3¼ cups plus 2 Tbsp. all-purpose flour, divided
- 1 tsp. baking soda
- ½ tsp. salt
- 2 cups fresh or frozen blueberries

GLAZE
- 2 cups confectioners' sugar
- ¼ cup buttermilk
- 1 Tbsp. grated lemon zest
- 2 tsp. lemon juice
- ⅛ tsp. salt

CHOCOLATE BANANA BUNDLES

Banana with chocolate is such an irresistible combo that I make this quick dessert often. You can also top these tasty bundles with the butter and brown sugar mixture left over from coating the bananas, or sprinkle on a dash of sea salt.

—Thomas Faglon, Somerset, NJ

- -

Takes: 30 min. • **Makes:** 4 servings

2 **Tbsp. butter**
¼ **cup packed brown sugar**
2 **medium ripe bananas,**
   halved lengthwise
1 **sheet frozen puff pastry, thawed**
4 **oz. semisweet chocolate, melted**
   Vanilla ice cream, optional

1. Preheat oven to 400°. In a large cast-iron or other heavy skillet, melt butter over medium heat. Stir in brown sugar until blended. Add bananas; stir to coat. Remove from heat; set aside.
2. Unfold puff pastry; cut into 4 rectangles. Place a halved banana in center of each square. Overlap 2 opposite corners of pastry over banana; pinch tightly to seal. Place on parchment-lined baking sheets.
3. Bake until golden brown, 20-25 minutes. Drizzle with chocolate. Serve warm, with ice cream if desired.
1 serving: 596 cal., 31g fat (12g sat. fat), 15mg chol., 249mg sod., 78g carb. (35g sugars, 8g fiber), 7g pro.
Caramel Banana Bundles: Omit chocolate. Drizzle with caramel ice cream topping.

CHOCOLATE BANANA
BUNDLES

SOUTHERN
BANANA PUDDING

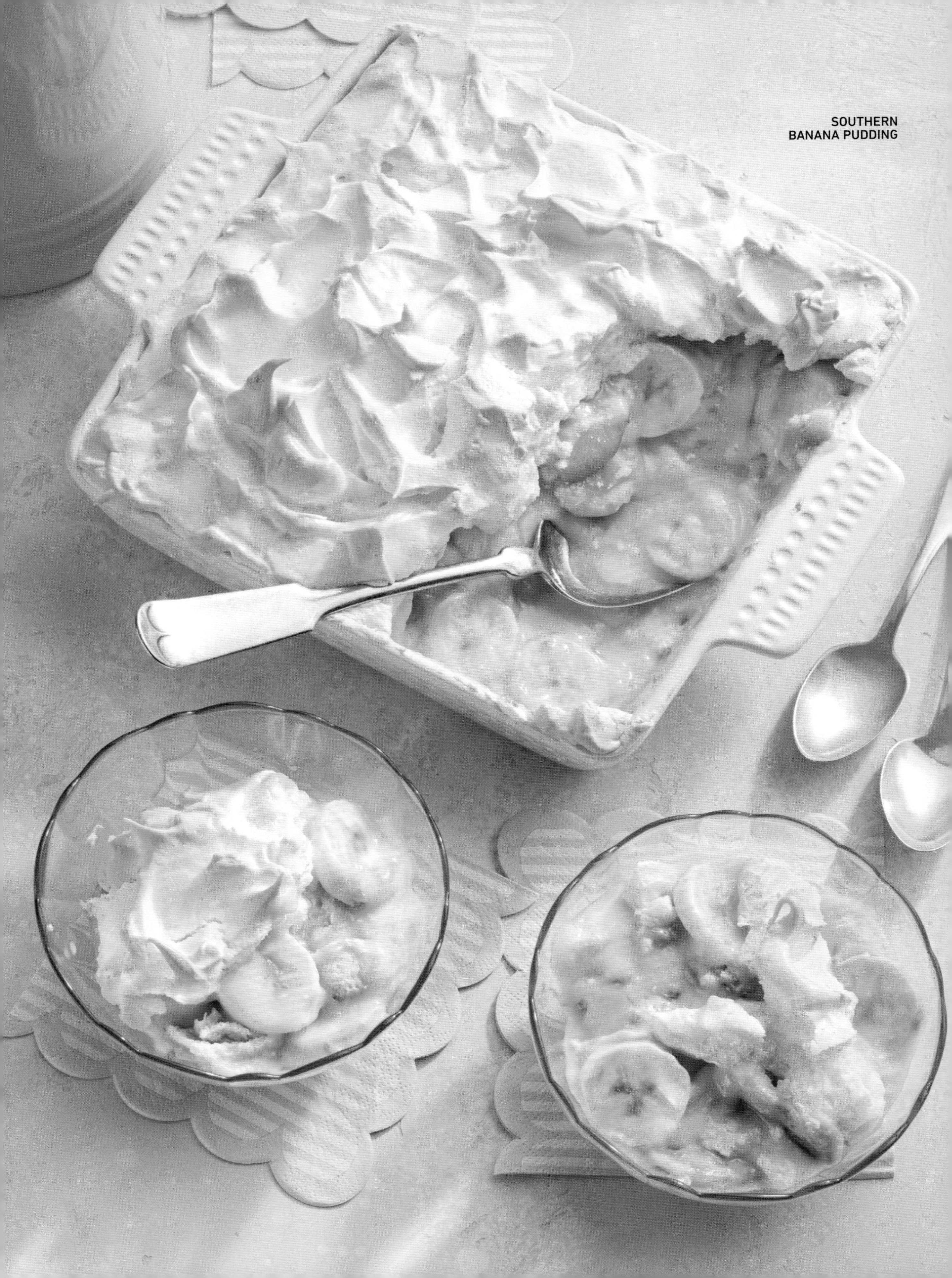

SOUTHERN BANANA PUDDING

This old southern recipe features a comforting custard layered with sliced bananas and vanilla wafers, then it is topped with meringue. I serve it year-round.
—Jan Campbell, Hattiesburg, MS

Prep: 30 min. • **Bake:** 15 min. + chilling
Makes: 8 servings

- ¾ cup sugar
- ⅓ cup all-purpose flour
- 2 cups 2% milk
- 2 large egg yolks, lightly beaten
- 1 Tbsp. butter
- 1 tsp. vanilla extract
- 36 vanilla wafers
- 3 medium ripe bananas, cut into ¼-in. slices

MERINGUE
- 2 large egg whites, room temperature
- 1 tsp. vanilla extract
- ⅛ tsp. cream of tartar
- 3 Tbsp. sugar

1. Preheat oven to 350°. In a large saucepan, combine sugar and flour. Stir in milk until smooth. Cook and stir over medium-high heat until thickened and bubbly. Reduce heat; cook and stir 2 minutes longer.
2. Remove from the heat. Stir a small amount of hot milk mixture into egg yolks; return all to pan, stirring constantly. Bring to a gentle boil; cook and stir 2 minutes longer. Remove from heat; gently stir in butter and vanilla.
3. In an ungreased 8-in. square baking dish, layer a third of the vanilla wafers, bananas and filling. Repeat layers twice.
4. For meringue, beat egg whites, vanilla and cream of tartar on medium speed until soft peaks form. Gradually beat in sugar, 1 Tbsp. at a time, on high until stiff peaks form. Spread evenly over the hot filling, sealing edges to sides of dish. Bake until meringue is golden, 12-15 minutes. Cool on a wire rack 1 hour. Refrigerate at least 3 hours before serving.
1 serving: 293 cal., 7g fat (3g sat. fat), 58mg chol., 121mg sod., 53g carb. (38g sugars, 2g fiber), 5g pro.

CHOCOLATE-COVERED CHEESECAKE SQUARES

CHOCOLATE-COVERED CHEESECAKE SQUARES

Satisfy your cheesecake craving with these bite-sized delights! The party favorites are perfect for the holidays.
—Esther Neustaeter, La Crete, AB

Prep: 1½ hours + freezing
Makes: 49 squares

- 1 cup graham cracker crumbs
- ¼ cup finely chopped pecans
- ¼ cup butter, melted

FILLING
- 2 pkg. (8 oz. each) cream cheese, softened
- ½ cup sugar
- ¼ cup sour cream
- 2 large eggs, room temperature, lightly beaten
- ½ tsp. vanilla extract

COATING
- 24 oz. semisweet chocolate, chopped
- 3 Tbsp. shortening

1. Line a 9-in. square baking pan with foil and grease the foil. In a small bowl, combine the graham cracker crumbs, pecans and butter. Press into prepared pan; set aside.
2. In a large bowl, beat the cream cheese, sugar and sour cream until smooth. Add eggs and vanilla; beat on low speed just until combined. Pour over crust. Bake at 325° for 35-40 minutes or until center is almost set. Cool on a wire rack. Let freeze overnight.
3. In a microwave, melt the chocolate and shortening; stir until smooth. Cool slightly.
4. Using foil, lift cheesecake out of pan. Gently peel off foil; cut cheesecake into 1¼-in. squares. Work with a few pieces at a time for dipping; keep remaining squares refrigerated until ready to dip.
5. Using a toothpick, completely dip squares, 1 at a time, into melted chocolate; allow excess to drip off. Place on waxed paper-lined baking sheets. Spoon the additional chocolate over tops if necessary to coat. (Reheat chocolate if needed to finish dipping.) Let stand for 20 minutes or until set. Store in an airtight container in the refrigerator or freezer.
1 piece: 141 cal., 10g fat (6g sat. fat), 22mg chol., 48mg sod., 12g carb. (10g sugars, 1g fiber), 2g pro.

BILTMORE'S BREAD PUDDING

Here's one of our estate's classic dessert recipes. A golden caramel sauce enhances the rich bread pudding.
—Biltmore Estate, Asheville, NC

- -

Prep: 30 min. • **Bake:** 40 min.
Makes: 12 servings

- 8 cups cubed day-old bread
- 9 large eggs
- 2¼ cups 2% milk
- 1¾ cups heavy whipping cream
- 1 cup sugar
- ¾ cup butter, melted
- 3 tsp. vanilla extract
- 1½ tsp. ground cinnamon
- **CARAMEL SAUCE**
- 1 cup sugar
- ¼ cup water
- 1 Tbsp. lemon juice
- 2 Tbsp. butter
- 1 cup heavy whipping cream

1. Place bread cubes in a greased 13x9-in. baking dish. In a large bowl, whisk eggs, milk, cream, sugar, butter, vanilla and cinnamon. Pour evenly over bread.
2. Bake, uncovered, at 350° until a knife inserted in center comes out clean, 40-45 minutes. Let stand 5 minutes before cutting.
3. Meanwhile, in a small saucepan, bring the sugar, water and lemon juice to a boil. Reduce heat to medium; cook until sugar is dissolved and mixture turns a golden amber color. Stir in butter until melted. Gradually stir in the cream. Serve with bread pudding.
1 piece with about 2 Tbsp. sauce: 581 cal., 39g fat (23g sat. fat), 273mg chol., 345mg sod., 49g carb. (37g sugars, 1g fiber), 9g pro.

GET-WELL CUSTARD

Whenever a friend or relative was ailing, my mother-in-law would bake some fresh custard and take it along when she visited. Because she took folks this special treat so often, our family began calling it get-well custard!
—Ruth Van Dyke, Traverse City, MI

- -

Prep: 15 min. • **Bake:** 55 min. + chilling
Makes: 10 servings

- 4 cups whole milk
- 4 large eggs
- ½ cup sugar
- ¼ tsp. salt
- 1 tsp. vanilla extract
- Ground nutmeg

1. Preheat oven to 350°. In a small saucepan, heat milk until bubbles form around sides of pan; remove from heat. In a large bowl, whisk the eggs, sugar and salt until blended but not foamy. Slowly stir in hot milk. Stir in vanilla.
2. Pour egg mixture through a strainer into a 1½-qt. round baking dish; sprinkle with nutmeg. Place round baking dish in a larger baking pan. Place pan on oven rack; add very hot water to pan to within ½ in. of the top of round baking dish. Bake until a knife inserted near the center comes out clean, 55-60 minutes. Centers will be soft and jiggle even after chilling. Remove baking dish from water bath immediately to a wire rack; cool 30 minutes. Refrigerate until cold.
½ cup: 128 cal., 5g fat (2g sat. fat), 84mg chol., 130mg sod., 15g carb. (15g sugars, 0 fiber), 6g pro.

TEST KITCHEN TIP
Custard is tasty just by itself, but try serving it with a handful of fresh berries. It adds a fun pop of color!

GET-WELL CUSTARD

BAKLAVA

3. Spread with 2 cups of the walnut mixture. Top with 5 layers of phyllo dough, brushing with butter between each sheet. Spread with remaining walnut mixture. Top with 1 layer of phyllo dough; brush with butter. Repeat 14 times. Cut into 2½-in. squares; cut each square in half diagonally. Brush remaining butter over top. Bake at 350° until golden brown, 40-45 minutes.

4. In a saucepan, bring syrup ingredients to a boil. Reduce heat; simmer for 10 minutes. Strain and discard zest; cool to lukewarm. Pour syrup over warm baklava.

1 baklava triangle: 271 cal., 16g fat (5g sat. fat), 21mg chol., 162mg sod., 30g carb. (17g sugars, 1g fiber), 5g pro.

Pistachio Almond Baklava: Omit walnuts. In a food processor, combine 4 cups unsalted pistachios and 3 cups unsalted unblanched almonds; cover and process until finely chopped. Proceed as directed in step 1.

Chocolate Baklava: For the nut mixture, combine 1 pound finely chopped walnuts, 1 package (12 oz.) miniature semisweet chocolate chips, ¾ cup sugar, 1½ tsp. ground cinnamon and 1 tsp. grated lemon zest. Layer and bake as directed.

ASK SARAH

HOW LONG DOES PHYLLO DOUGH STAY FRESH?
Refrigerate unopened phyllo dough up to 3 weeks or freeze up to 3 months. Once opened, use within 3 days.

BAKLAVA

Baklava is a traditional Middle Eastern pastry made with flaky phyllo dough, chopped nuts and sweet honey. This dessert is very rich, so one pan goes a long way.
—Judy Losecco, Buffalo, NY

- -

Prep: 30 min. • **Bake:** 40 min.
Makes: 4 dozen

- 1½ **lbs. finely chopped walnuts**
- ½ **cup sugar**
- ½ **tsp. ground cinnamon**
- ⅛ **tsp. ground cloves**
- 1 **lb. butter, melted, divided**
- 2 **pkg. (16 oz. each, 14x9-in. sheet size) frozen phyllo dough, thawed**

SYRUP
- 2 **cups sugar**
- 2 **cups water**
- 1 **cup honey**
- 1 **Tbsp. grated lemon or orange zest**

1. In a bowl, combine the walnuts, sugar, cinnamon and cloves; set aside. Brush a 15x10x1-in. baking pan with some of the butter. Unroll 1 package phyllo dough; cut stack into a 10½x9-in. rectangle. Repeat with remaining phyllo. Discard the scraps.
2. Line the bottom of prepared pan with 2 sheets of phyllo dough (sheets will overlap slightly). Brush with butter. Repeat layers 14 times. (Keep dough covered with a damp towel until ready to use to prevent sheets from drying out.)

SEMISWEET
CHOCOLATE
MOUSSE

SEMISWEET CHOCOLATE MOUSSE

A friend shared this rich, velvety mousse recipe with me. I love to cook and have tons of recipes, but this one is a favorite. Best of all, it's easy to make.
—Judy Spencer, San Diego, CA

Prep: 20 min. + chilling • **Makes:** 2 servings

- ¼ **cup semisweet chocolate chips**
- 1 **Tbsp. water**
- 1 **large egg yolk, lightly beaten**
- 1½ **tsp. vanilla extract**
- ½ **cup heavy whipping cream**
- 1 **Tbsp. sugar**
   Optional: Whipped cream and raspberries

1. In a small saucepan, melt chocolate chips with water; stir until smooth. Stir a small amount of hot chocolate mixture into egg yolk; return all to the pan, stirring constantly. Cook and stir for 2 minutes or until slightly thickened. Remove from the heat; stir in vanilla. Quickly transfer to a small bowl. Stir occasionally until completely cooled.
2. In a small bowl, beat whipping cream until it begins to thicken. Add sugar; beat until soft peaks form. Fold into the cooled chocolate mixture. Cover and refrigerate for at least 2 hours. If desired, garnish with whipped cream and raspberries.
1 cup: 367 cal., 31g fat (18g sat. fat), 188mg chol., 29mg sod., 21g carb. (20g sugars, 1g fiber), 3g pro.

TEST KITCHEN TIP
If your mousse is not fluffy, it may be because your cream was not adequately whipped when you folded it into the chocolate mixture.

QUICK & EASY TIRAMISU

No one can resist this classic cool and creamy dessert. It is quick to prepare but can be made ahead for added mealtime convenience.
—*Taste of Home* Test Kitchen

Prep: 20 min. + chilling • **Makes:** 6 servings

- 2   **cups cold 2% milk**
- 1   **pkg. (3.4 oz.) instant vanilla pudding mix**
- 1   **cup heavy whipping cream**
- 3   **Tbsp. confectioners' sugar**
- 28 **soft ladyfingers, split**
- 2½ **tsp. instant coffee granules**
- ½   **cup boiling water**
- 1   **Tbsp. baking cocoa**

1. In a large bowl, whisk milk and pudding mix for 2 minutes. Let stand until soft-set, about 2 minutes. In a small bowl, beat cream until it begins to thicken. Add confectioners' sugar; beat until soft peaks form. Fold into pudding; cover and refrigerate.
2. Arrange half the ladyfingers cut side up in an 11x7-in. dish. Dissolve the coffee granules in boiling water; drizzle half over the ladyfingers. Spread with half the pudding mixture. Repeat layers. Sprinkle with cocoa. Refrigerate until serving.
1 piece: 384 cal., 19g fat (11g sat. fat), 123mg chol., 379mg sod., 47g carb. (33g sugars, 1g fiber), 7g pro.

HONEY CINNAMON ROLL-UPS

This cinnamon treat reminds me of baklava, but with only a few easy ingredients, it's a fraction of the work. It's my aunt's recipe, and I think of her when I make it.
—Susan Falk, Sterling Heights, MI

Prep: 35 min. + cooling
Bake: 15 min.
Makes: 24 servings

- 2   **cups ground walnuts, toasted**
- ¼   **cup sugar**
- 2   **tsp. ground cinnamon**
- 12 **sheets frozen phyllo dough, thawed**
- ½   **cup butter, melted**
SYRUP
- ½   **cup honey**
- ½   **cup sugar**
- ½   **cup water**
- 1   **Tbsp. lemon juice**

1. Preheat oven to 350°. Combine the walnuts, sugar and cinnamon.
2. Place 1 sheet of phyllo dough on a 15x12-in. piece of waxed paper; brush with butter. Place a second phyllo sheet on top, brushing it with butter. (Keep remaining phyllo covered with a damp towel to prevent it from drying out.) Sprinkle with ¼ cup walnut mixture. Using waxed paper, roll up tightly jelly-roll style, starting with a long side, removing paper as you roll. Slice roll into 4 smaller rolls; transfer rolls to a greased 13x9-in. baking dish. Repeat with remaining phyllo dough and walnut mixture, by ¼ cupfuls. Bake until light brown, 14-16 minutes. Cool dish on a wire rack.
3. Meanwhile, in a small saucepan, combine all syrup ingredients. Bring to a boil. Reduce heat; simmer 5 minutes. Cool 10 minutes. Drizzle cinnamon rolls with syrup; sprinkle with remaining walnut mixture.
1 cinnamon roll-up: 132 cal., 8g fat (3g sat. fat), 10mg chol., 43mg sod., 15g carb. (12g sugars, 1g fiber), 1g pro.

TEST KITCHEN TIP

To toast nuts, bake in a 350° oven for 5-10 minutes. Or cook in a skillet over low heat, stirring occasionally, until lightly browned and fragrant.

HONEY CINNAMON ROLL-UPS

CHOCOLATE ECLAIRS

CHOCOLATE ECLAIRS

With creamy filling and thick decadent frosting, these eclairs are extra special. Now you can indulge in classic bakery treats without even having to leave the house!
—Jessica Campbell, Viola, WI

- -

Prep: 45 min. • **Bake:** 35 min. + cooling
Makes: 9 servings

- 1 cup water
- ½ cup butter, cubed
- ¼ tsp. salt
- 1 cup all-purpose flour
- 4 large eggs, room temperature

FILLING

- 2½ cups cold whole milk
- 1 pkg. (5.1 oz.) instant vanilla pudding mix
- 1 cup heavy whipping cream
- ¼ cup confectioners' sugar
- 1 tsp. vanilla extract

FROSTING

- 2 oz. semisweet chocolate
- 2 Tbsp. butter
- 1¼ cups confectioners' sugar
- 2 to 3 Tbsp. hot water

1. Preheat oven to 400°. In a large saucepan, bring water, butter and salt to a boil. Add flour all at once and stir until a smooth ball forms. Remove from the heat; let stand for 5 minutes. Add eggs, 1 at a time, beating well after each addition. Continue beating until mixture is smooth and shiny.

2. Using a tablespoon or a pastry tube with a #10 or large round tip, form dough into nine 4x1½-in. strips on a greased baking sheet. Bake for 35-40 minutes or until puffed and golden. Remove to a wire rack. Immediately split eclairs open; remove tops and set aside. Discard soft dough from inside. Cool eclairs.

3. In a large bowl, beat milk and pudding mix according to package directions. In another bowl, whip cream until soft peaks form. Beat in sugar and vanilla; fold into pudding. Fill eclairs (chill any remaining filling for another use).

4. For frosting, in a microwave, melt chocolate and butter; stir until smooth. Stir in sugar and enough hot water to achieve a smooth consistency. Cool slightly. Frost eclairs. Store in refrigerator.

1 serving: 483 cal., 28g fat (17g sat. fat), 174mg chol., 492mg sod., 52g carb. (37g sugars, 1g fiber), 7g pro.

CONTEST-WINNING PUMPKIN CHEESECAKE DESSERT

With its gingersnap crust and maple syrup drizzle, this rich and creamy spiced pumpkin dessert never fails to get rave reviews. It cuts nicely, too.
—Cathy Hall, Lyndhurst, VA

- -

Prep: 25 min. • **Bake:** 40 min. + chilling
Makes: 24 servings

- 1½ cups crushed gingersnaps (about 30 cookies)
- ¼ cup butter, melted
- 5 pkg. (8 oz. each) cream cheese, softened
- 1 cup sugar
- 1 can (15 oz.) pumpkin
- 1 tsp. ground cinnamon
- 1 tsp. vanilla extract
- 5 large eggs, room temperature, lightly beaten
  Ground nutmeg
  Maple syrup
  Sweetened whipped cream, optional

1. In a small bowl, combine gingersnap crumbs and butter. Press onto bottom of a greased 13x9-in. baking dish; set aside.

2. In a large bowl, beat cream cheese and sugar until smooth. Beat in the pumpkin, cinnamon and vanilla. Add eggs; beat on low speed just until combined. Pour over crust; sprinkle with nutmeg.

3. Bake at 350° for 40-45 minutes or until the center is almost set. Cool on a wire rack for 10 minutes. Carefully run a knife around edge of baking dish to loosen; cool 1 hour longer. Refrigerate overnight.

4. Cut into squares; serve with syrup and, if desired, sweetened whipped cream. Refrigerate leftovers.

1 piece: 276 cal., 20g fat (11g sat. fat), 92mg chol., 226mg sod., 20g carb. (13g sugars, 1g fiber), 5g pro.

"I made this for Thanksgiving, and everyone loved it. The maple syrup drizzle is the perfect topping."

—RAEANN THOMPSON, SENIOR ART DIRECTOR

CONTEST-WINNING PUMPKIN
CHEESECAKE DESSERT

LEFTOVER RICE PUDDING

This rice pudding with leftover cooked rice is a delicious classic. We also like to dress it up with English toffee bits, chocolate and toasted coconut.
—Laura German, North Brookfield, MA

Takes: 25 min.
Makes: 4 servings

- 2 **cups cooked long grain rice**
- 2 **cups whole milk**
- 3 **Tbsp. plus 1 tsp. sugar**
- ⅛ **tsp. salt**
- 1 **tsp. vanilla extract**
  Optional: Whipped cream, cinnamon and dried cranberries

In a large saucepan, combine rice, milk, sugar and salt. Cook, uncovered, over medium heat until thickened, stirring often, about 20 minutes. Remove from heat; stir in vanilla. Spoon into serving dishes. Serve warm. If desired, top the pudding with whipped cream, cinnamon and dried cranberries.
⅔ cup: 221 cal., 4g fat (2g sat. fat), 12mg chol., 127mg sod., 39g carb. (17g sugars, 0 fiber), 6g pro.
Toffee Rice Pudding: Combine 3 Tbsp. each English toffee bits, miniature semisweet chocolate and toasted flaked coconut. Place half the rice pudding in 4 individual dessert dishes and top with half the toffee mixture. Repeat layers.

PEAR CRISP

Since my husband is a livestock truck driver, he often starts work early in the morning. A piece of this pear crisp will keep him going until breakfast. Our two boys love to have it for dessert and in their school lunches.
—Joanne Korevaar, Burgessville, ON

Prep: 15 min. • **Bake:** 35 min.
Makes: 12 servings

- 8 **medium ripe pears, peeled and thinly sliced**
- ¼ **cup orange juice**
- ½ **cup sugar**
- 1 **tsp. ground cinnamon**
- ¼ **tsp. ground allspice**
- ¼ **tsp. ground ginger**
TOPPING
- 1 **cup all-purpose flour**
- 1 **cup old-fashioned oats**
- ½ **cup packed brown sugar**
- ½ **tsp. baking powder**
- ½ **cup cold butter, cubed**
  Fresh mint leaves, optional

1. Preheat oven to 350°. Toss pears with orange juice; place in a greased 13x9-in. baking dish. Combine the sugar, cinnamon, allspice and ginger; sprinkle over pears.
2. For topping, in a small bowl, combine the flour, oats, brown sugar and baking powder; cut in the butter until crumbly. Sprinkle over pears.
3. Bake until topping is golden brown and fruit is tender, 35-40 minutes. Serve warm. If desired, garnish with mint.
1 serving: 268 cal., 8g fat (5g sat. fat), 20mg chol., 85mg sod., 49g carb. (29g sugars, 5g fiber), 2g pro.

FROZEN PEPPERMINT DELIGHT

If you're looking for a dessert that's festively fun and easy to make, this is the one for you. Drizzled in hot fudge sauce and loaded with pretty peppermint pieces, this tempting treat will have guests asking for seconds.
—Pam Lancaster, Willis, VA

Prep: 25 min. + freezing • **Makes:** 15 servings

- 1 **pkg. (14.3 oz.) Oreo cookies, crushed**
- ¼ **cup butter, melted**
- 2 **containers (1½ qt. each) peppermint ice cream, slightly softened**
- 1 **carton (12 oz.) frozen whipped topping, thawed**
  Hot fudge ice cream topping, warmed
  Crushed peppermint candy

1. In a large bowl, combine cookie crumbs and butter. Press into an ungreased 13x9-in. dish. Spread ice cream over crust; top with whipped topping. Cover and freeze until solid. May be frozen for up to 2 months.
2. Just before serving, drizzle with hot fudge topping and sprinkle with peppermint candy.
1 piece: 425 cal., 22g fat (11g sat. fat), 24mg chol., 296mg sod., 52g carb. (35g sugars, 2g fiber), 4g pro.

PINEAPPLE CRUNCH

My crunchy pineapple dessert offers quick refreshment. This recipe was given to me years ago by a co-worker. Every time I take it somewhere, it's a favorite.
—Betty Wiersma, Sherwood Park, AB

Prep: 15 min. • **Bake:** 10 min. + cooling
Makes: 9 servings

- 1 cup crushed cornflakes
- 2 Tbsp. sugar
- ⅓ cup butter, melted
- 2 Tbsp. cornstarch
- 2 cans (8 oz. each) crushed pineapple, undrained
- 2 cups vanilla ice cream, softened
- 1 pkg. (3.4 oz.) instant vanilla pudding mix
  Whipped topping, optional

1. Preheat oven to 350°. In a bowl, combine cornflake crumbs, sugar and butter. Press into a greased 9-in. square baking dish. Bake 10 minutes. Cool on a wire rack.
2. In a saucepan, combine cornstarch and pineapple until blended. Bring to a boil; cook and stir 2 minutes or until thickened. Cool.
3. In a bowl, beat the ice cream and pudding mix on low speed 2 minutes or until blended and thickened. Spoon over crust. Top with pineapple mixture. Refrigerate until serving. If desired, serve with whipped topping.
1 piece: 254 cal., 10g fat (6g sat. fat), 31mg chol., 217mg sod., 40g carb. (27g sugars, 1g fiber), 2g pro.

CARAMEL APPLES

Who doesn't love a good gooey caramel apple? Make a double batch because these treats always go fast!
—Karen Ann Bland, Gove, KS

Prep: 10 min. • **Cook:** 40 min.
Makes: 8 apples

- 1 cup butter
- 2 cups packed brown sugar
- 1 cup light corn syrup
- 1 can (14 oz.) sweetened condensed milk
- 1 tsp. vanilla extract
- 8 wooden sticks
- 8 medium tart apples
  Unsalted peanuts, chopped

In a heavy 3-qt. saucepan, combine butter, brown sugar, corn syrup and milk; bring to a boil over medium-high heat. Cook and stir until the mixture reaches 248° (firm-ball stage) on a candy thermometer, 30-40 minutes. Remove from the heat; stir in vanilla. Insert wooden sticks into apples. Dip each apple into hot caramel mixture; turn to coat. Set on waxed paper to cool. If desired, roll the bottom of the dipped apples into chopped peanuts.
½ apple: 388 cal., 14g fat (9g sat. fat), 39mg chol., 145mg sod., 68g carb. (65g sugars, 2g fiber), 2g pro.

WARREN'S OATMEAL JAM SQUARES

At 102, I still love to bake. I make these bars in my toaster oven for my fellow residents at our assisted living home.
—Warren Patrick, Townshend, VT

Prep: 20 min. • **Bake:** 25 min. + cooling
Makes: 16 squares

- 1¼ cups quick-cooking oats
- 1¼ cups all-purpose flour
- ½ cup sugar
- ½ tsp. baking soda
- ¼ tsp. salt
- ¾ cup butter, melted
- 2 tsp. vanilla extract
- 1 jar (10 oz.) seedless raspberry jam or jam of your choice
- 4 whole graham crackers, crushed

1. Preheat oven to 350°. In a large bowl, mix the first 5 ingredients. In a small bowl, mix melted butter and vanilla; add to oat mixture, stirring until crumbly. Reserve 1 cup mixture for topping.
2. Press the remaining mixture onto the bottom of a greased 9-in. square baking pan. Spread jam over top to within ½ in. of edges. Add crushed graham crackers to reserved topping; sprinkle over jam.
3. Bake 25-30 minutes or until edges are golden brown. Cool in pan on a wire rack. Cut into squares.
1 square: 220 cal., 9g fat (6g sat. fat), 23mg chol., 161mg sod., 33g carb. (18g sugars, 1g fiber), 2g pro.

Recipe Index

Equivalents & Substitutions

EQUIVALENT MEASURES

3 teaspoons = 1 tablespoon	**16 tablespoons** = 1 cup
4 tablespoons = ¼ cup	**2 cups** = 1 pint
5⅓ tablespoons = ⅓ cup	**4 cups** = 1 quart
8 tablespoons = ½ cup	**4 quarts** = 1 gallon

FOOD EQUIVALENTS

Macaroni	1 cup (3½ ounces) uncooked = 2½ cups cooked
Noodles Medium	3 cups (4 ounces) uncooked = 4 cups cooked
Popcorn	⅓-½ cup unpopped = 8 cups popped
Rice Long Grain	1 cup uncooked = 3 cups cooked
Rice Quick-Cooking	1 cup uncooked = 2 cups cooked
Spaghetti	8 ounces uncooked = 4 cups cooked

Bread	1 slice = ¾ cup soft crumbs or ¼ cup fine dry crumbs
Graham Crackers	7 squares = ½ cup finely crushed
Buttery Round Crackers	12 crackers = ½ cup finely crushed
Saltine Crackers	14 crackers = ½ cup finely crushed

Bananas	1 medium = ⅓ cup mashed
Lemons	1 medium = 3 tablespoons juice + 2 teaspoons grated zest
Limes	1 medium = 2 tablespoons juice + 1½ teaspoons grated zest
Oranges	1 medium = ¼-⅓ cup juice + 4 teaspoons grated zest

Cabbage	1 head = 5 cups shredded	**Green Pepper**	1 large = 1 cup chopped
Carrots	1 pound = 3 cups shredded	**Mushrooms**	½ pound = 3 cups sliced
Celery	1 rib = ½ cup chopped	**Onions**	1 medium = ½ cup chopped
Corn	1 ear fresh = ⅔ cup kernels	**Potatoes**	3 medium = 2 cups cubed

Almonds	1 pound = 3 cups chopped	**Pecan Halves**	1 pound = 4½ cups chopped
Ground Nuts	3¾ ounces = 1 cup	**Walnuts**	1 pound = 3¾ cups chopped

EASY SUBSTITUTIONS

WHEN YOU NEED...		USE...
Baking Powder	1 teaspoon	½ teaspoon cream of tartar + ¼ teaspoon baking soda
Buttermilk	1 cup	1 tablespoon lemon juice or vinegar + enough milk to measure 1 cup (let stand 5 minutes before using)
Cornstarch	1 tablespoon	2 tablespoons all-purpose flour
Honey	1 cup	1¼ cups sugar + ¼ cup water
Half-and-Half Cream	1 cup	1 tablespoon melted butter + enough whole milk to measure 1 cup
Onion	1 small chopped (⅓ cup)	1 teaspoon onion powder or 1 tablespoon dried minced onion
Tomato Juice	1 cup	½ cup tomato sauce + ½ cup water
Tomato Sauce	2 cups	¾ cup tomato paste + 1 cup water
Unsweetened Chocolate	1 square (1 ounce)	3 tablespoons baking cocoa + 1 tablespoon shortening or oil
Whole Milk	1 cup	½ cup evaporated milk + ½ cup water

Cutting Techniques

MINCING AND CHOPPING

Holding the handle of a chef's knife with one hand, rest the fingers of your other hand on the top of the blade near the tip. Using the handle to guide and apply pressure, move knife in an arc across the food with a rocking motion until pieces of food are the desired size. Mincing results in pieces no larger than ⅛ in. and chopping produces ¼- to ½-in. pieces.

DICING AND CUBING

Using a utility knife, trim each side of the frui, vegetable or other food, squaring it off. Cut lengthwise into evenly spaced strips. The narrower the strips, the smaller the pieces will be. Stack the strips and cut lengthwise into uniformly sized strips. Arrange the square-shaped strips into a pile and cut widthwise into uniform pieces.

MAKING BIAS OR DIAGONAL CUTS

Holding a chef's knife at an angle to the length of the food slice as thick or thin as desired. This technique is often used in stir-fry recipes.

MAKING JULIENNE STRIPS

Using a utility knife, cut a thin strip from one side of vegetable. Turn so flat side is down. Cut into 2-in. lengths, then cut each piece lengthwise into thin strips. Stack the strips and cut lengthwise into thinner strips.

CUTTING WEDGES

Using a chef's knife or serrated knife cut the produce in half from stem end to blossom end. Lay halves cut side down on a cutting board. Set knife at the center of one the halves and cut in half vertically, then cut each quarter in half vertically. Repeat with other half.

ZESTING

Pull a citrus zester across limes, lemons or oranges being careful not to remove the bitter white pith. The small holes in the zester will yield thin, narrow strips of zest. Use full strips to garnish or, if recipe instructs, chop into fine pieces and use as directed.

▲ **Mincing**
Pieces no larger than ⅛ in.

▼ **Chopping**
¼- to ½-in. pieces

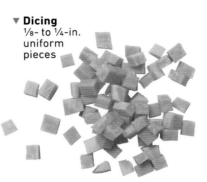

▼ **Dicing**
⅛- to ¼-in. uniform pieces

► **Cubing**
½- to 1-in. uniform pieces

▼ **Bias/Diagonal Cuts**
Size of pieces based on desired length and thickness

▲ **Julienne Strips**
Pieces roughly 2 in. long

▲ **Wedges**
Size of wedges based on desired thickness

▲ **Zesting**
Size of strips or chopped zest based on desired preference